The Early Years

This reader contains a series of specially commissioned articles which have been written by two groups of people:

- 'Experts' in the field of early childhood education such as Lilian Katz, Janet Moyles and Mary Jane Drummond and established teachers and practitioners.
- Students – including teachers, nursery nurses, playgroup workers, nannies, childminders – enrolled on an Early Childhood Studies Scheme.

They write in a range of styles and 'voices' to provide a unique range of perspectives on early childhood education. Theory is clearly translated into practice through the use of classroom examples and students' 'voices'. This fascinating and highly readable book will be of value to anyone interested in the education and care of our youngest children.

Sandra Smidt is a well-known early-years specialist who currently works in South Africa as part of a National Pilot Project on Early Childhood Development. She has recently written A Guide to Early Years Practice (Routledge, 1998).

The Early Years
A Reader

Sandra Smidt

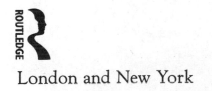

London and New York

First published 1998 by Routledge
11 New Fetter Lane, London EC4P 4EE

Typeset in Goudy by J&L Composition Ltd, Filey, North Yorkshire
Printed and bound in Great Britain by Page Bros (Norwich) Ltd.

British Library Cataloguing in Publication Data
A catalogue record for this book is available from the British Library

Library of Congress Cataloguing in Publication Data
The early years: a reader/ [edited by] Sandra Smidt.
    p. cm.
Includes bibliographical references and index.
ISBN 0–415–17282–9 (alk. paper)
1. Early childhood education. 2. Child development.
3. Education, Preschool. 4. Play. I. Smidt, Sandra, 1943–
LB1139.23.E276 1998
372.21–dc21
97-47650 CIP

ISBN 0–415–17282–9

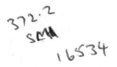

The material in this reader was originally published by the
University of North London Press in the course reader for the
Early Childhood Studies Scheme: *I Seed it and I Feeled it: Young
Children Learning* (1996). The editor and publisher are grateful for
the university's kind permission to reproduce it here.

Contents

List of contributors

Mary Jane Drummond is Tutor in the Education of Children 3–11 at the University of Cambridge Institute for Education and an external examiner for the Early Childhood Studies Scheme.

Bernadette Duffy is Head of the Dorothy Gardner Centre, London.

Hilary Faust is an Early Years consultant and worked previously at the University of North London.

Lilian G. Katz is Professor at the University of Illinois, USA.

Penny Kenway works at the Equality Learning Centre in North London.

Gillian Lathey is a Senior Lecturer at the Roehampton Institute, UK.

Janet Moyles is a Senior Lecturer and Co-ordinator for Early Years Education at the University of Leicester. She is the author of *Just Playing?* (1989) and editor of several other books on play and learning.

Fran Paffard is an Early Years specialist.

Betty Rosen writes widely on storytelling.

Carol Ross is an Early Years specialist who has written widely on gender issues.

Evelyn Slavid is a Tutor at Kingston University, Surrey, UK.

Sandra Smidt is a well-known early years specialist who currently lives and works in South Africa. Previously she worked as the co-ordinator for the Early Childhood Studies Scheme at the University of North London.

Birgit Voss is a Nursery Class Teacher at Pooles Park Infant School, London.

Margy Whalley is a well known Early Years specialist and Head of the Pen Green Centre, Corby.

At the time of writing, **Sue Allen, Gillian Allery, Lynne Bennett, Margaret Boyle, Susan Bragg, Beverley Cain, Beata Clarke, Sarah Cotter, Nancy Coyne, Lucie Dickens, Maria Figueiredo, Trish Franks, Duane Hernandez, Gerardine Lanigan, Jacqui Perry, Mary Smith, Pam Stannard, Josie Steed, Emma Stoddart, Angela Tacagni** and **Angela Tindall** were all students on the Early Childhood Studies Scheme at the University of North London.

Preface

Anyone who has watched a young child learn and develop is aware of how rapid learning is in the earliest years. You have only to think of how children acquire their first language and compare that with your own attempts to learn a new language as an adult to realise that there is something special about the learning that takes place in these years. This realisation is not something new. Those working with young children have been aware, for centuries, that the first few years of life are crucial. It is only in the last few decades that a neurophysiological explanation for this has been found, as researchers have been able to demonstrate that the connections between brain cells (the physiological basis of learning) are formed most rapidly during these years. But what is more exciting and more challenging is the realisation that these neural connections are most effectively and rapidly laid down with each new experience a child has.

For those working with young chilren, something they intuitively knew now has some basis in research findings. Those working with young children knew that children needed a rich and stimulating environment in which to grow and develop. That is why nurseries and playgroups offered children toys to play with, sand and water to explore, clothes to dress up in and songs to sing. And many children benefited from the stimulating environments in which they found themselves. More recently, however, awareness has been growing that the provision of many different activities *per se* is not enough. Attention has shifted to examining the role of the adults working with young children and looking to see how adults can best support and extend children's learning and development.

There are many workers within the settings and facilities available for the care and education of young children before they reach compulsory school age. Some of them are qualified teachers, others are qualified nursery nurses. Some have been trained as Montessori teachers and others have followed Pre-School Alliance training programmes. Some have trained as nurses or as social workers. Many have had no formal training to work with young children, but have found themselves doing this work because it fits in with domestic requirements, because they like the company of young children or merely because they have fallen into the job. So in the United Kingdom there is a huge body of workers – mainly women – with years of experience, highly developed skills of observation and a genuine and deep concern for the wellbeing of children – but often lacking any understanding of what is known about how young children learn best.

In 1992 the University of North London set up a graduate training programme aimed at these workers. The idea was to recognise the experience and skills of those with or without formal qualifications and to build a modular programme leading to a number of recognised qualifications, culminating in an honours degree. This book was first published as a Course Reader to support those students and the articles in it were commissioned from experts in the field of early childhood or were taken from the written work of students on the course. The book thus offers readers a range of voices and a range of styles. The 'experts' often write in a more formal style, although many of them have adapted the style to suit the audience they are addressing. The voices of students vary enormously too.

The book is divided up into seven Parts. These are not meant to represent, in any way, a complete 'curriculum' for the early years. Rather they represent some basic concerns and the underlying principle that practice based on theory is better than practice based on instinct.

The basic concerns of the book are to try and explore current thinking on how young children learn best and to offer some examples, drawn from the work of students, which show how an understanding of this can inform practice. Another basic concern is to ensure that opportunities and activities provided for young children are genuinely opportunities for all children – for boys and girls, for children speaking only English or speaking more than one language, for black children and white children. Building on the fact that all those working with young children are used to paying attention to the children as they play and learn, emphasis is placed on how the daily observations workers make can provide the evidence for children learning and the basis from which new learning can be planned. And attention is paid to the importance of language – both spoken and written language. Anyone skimming through the contents section will notice huge gaps in the curriculum. There is no section on mathematics nor one on investigation. The section on parents is small and there is no mention of music or dance or drama. This is not because these areas are regarded as unimportant, but because the focus of the book is linking theory with practice and because the book does not set out to cover the entire early years curriculum.

It is a book to dip into. We hope that you will enjoy dipping into it and will find the range of styles and voices as fascinating as the range of contributors.

Sandra Smidt

1   Introduction

What is basic for young children?

Lilian G. Katz

Professor Katz is an acknowledged expert on the education of young children and has spent many years considering what the adults working with these young children need to know in order that learning and development are enhanced. Based in the USA, but aware and up-to-date on developments in the field of early childhood throughout the world, Lilian Katz takes a principled stand on how adults, through their own values and ideas, can be desirable role models for young children. She argues that many settings for young children offer them trivialised versions of reality and that this does these children a disservice.

Her chapter is included as the opening piece of this collection since the underpinning philosophy of it is a recurring theme throughout the book. Katz argues that the well-being of each and every child is inextricably linked to the well-being of all children.

The article is a philosophical rather than a practical one. It offers ideas which may be new and sometimes difficult to absorb, but the closing line of the piece is something worth reading over and over again:

> 'But to care for and about others' children is not just practical; it is also right.'

A group of young students were discussing their reactions to their teaching practice experiences. One described her experience in deeply disappointed tones. Among her complaints was that the programme director refused to let the children have small animals in the nursery. I listened appreciatively for a while to the righteous indignation only the young and inexperienced can enjoy. I then asked her as gently as I could: 'What are the chances that a child can develop into a competent adult without having had animals to play with in the nursery?' 'In other words,' I said 'what do you believe is really basic for young children?' A lively discussion followed, leading all of us to search our own assumptions for answers to the question: What does each child have to have for optimum development? My answer to this question is outlined below by offering six interrelated propositions that I hope will be helpful to you as you inspect your own answers to the same question.

All six propositions below rest on the assumption that whatever is good for children is only good for them in the 'right' proportions. Just because something is good for children, more of it is not necessarily better for them. This generalisation applies to so many influences on children's development that I refer to it as the 'principle of optimum effects'. Among the many examples are attention, affection, stimulation, independence, novelty, choices of activities and so on. All of these can be thought to be good for children, but only in optimum amounts, frequencies or intensities. With this principle as backdrop, here is my list of what every child has to have for healthy development.

A SENSE OF SAFETY

The young child has to have a deep sense of safety. I am referring here to psychological safety, which we usually speak of in terms of feeling secure, that is the subjective feeling of being strongly connected and deeply attached to one or more others. Experiencing oneself as attached, connected – safe – comes not just from being loved, but from *feeling* loved, *feeling* wanted, *feeling* significant, to an optimum (not maximum) degree. Note that the emphasis is more on *feeling* loved and wanted than on *being* loved and wanted.

As I understand early development, feeling strongly attached comes not just from the warmth and kindness of parents and caregivers. The feelings are a consequence of children perceiving that what they do or do not do really matters to others – matters so much that others will pick them up, comfort them, get angry and even scold them. Safety, then, grows out of being able to trust people to respond not just warmly but authentically, intensely, and honestly.

OPTIMUM SELF-ESTEEM

This proposition applies to all children, whether they live in wealthy or poor environments, whether they are at home or at school, whether they have special needs or typical needs, whatever their age, gender, race, ethnic group or nationality. Every child has to have optimal – not excessive – self-esteem.

One does not acquire self-esteem at a certain moment in childhood and then have it forever. Self-esteem is nurtured by and responsive to significant others – adults, siblings and other children – throughout the growing years. Even more important to keep in mind here is that one cannot have self-esteem in a vacuum. Self-esteem is the product of our evaluations of ourselves against criteria we acquire very early in life. We acquire these criteria from our families, neighbourhoods, ethnic groups and later on from peer groups and the larger community. These criteria against which we come to evaluate ourselves as acceptable and worthwhile, and against which we evaluate and experience ourselves as lovable may vary from family to family. In some families beauty is a criterion; in others, neatness or athletic ability or toughness are criteria against which one's worth is evaluated or estimated. Consider for a moment that such personal attributes as being dainty, quiet, garrulous, pious, well-mannered or academically precocious, might constitute the criteria against which young children are evaluated as being estimable.

It is, of course, the right, if not the duty, of each family to establish what it considers to be the criteria against which each member is judged acceptable and upon which esteem is accorded. The processes and the patterns by which these judgements are implemented are not likely to occur at a conscious level in either formulation or expression.

One of our responsibilities as educators is to be sensitive to the criteria of self-esteem children bring with them to the early childhood setting. We may not agree with the family's definition of the 'good boy' or the 'good girl', but we would be very unwise to downgrade, undermine, or in other ways violate the self-esteem criteria that children bring with them to the early childhood setting. At the same time we must also help children acquire criteria in the setting that serves to protect the welfare of the whole group of children for whom we are responsible. I cannot think of any way in which it could be helpful to children to undermine their respect for their own families.

FEELING THAT LIFE IS WORTH LIVING

Every child has to feel that life is worth living, reasonably satisfying, interesting and authentic. This proposition suggests that we involve children in activities and interactions about activities which are real and significant to them, and which are intriguing and absorbing to them. I have in mind here the potential hazard inherent in modern industrialised societies of creating environments and experiences for young children which are superficial, phony, frivolous and trivial. I suggest also that we resist the temptation to settle for activities that merely amuse and titillate children. Thus, criteria for selecting activities might include that they (a) give children opportunities to operate on their own experiences and to reconstruct their own environments and that they (b) give adults opportunities to help children learn what meanings to assign to their own experiences.

Visits to early childhood programmes often provoke me to wonder whether we have taken our longstanding emphasis on warmth and kindness, acceptance and love to mean simply 'Let's be nice to children'. As I watch adults being nice and kind and gentle, I wonder also whether if I were a child in such pleasant environments I would look at the adults and ask myself something like 'Everybody is kind and sweet, but inside them is there anybody home?'

Children should be able to experience their lives throughout their growing years as real, authentic, worth living and satisfying, whether they are at home, in child care centres, in playgroups or in schools.

HELP WITH MAKING SENSE OF EXPERIENCE

Young children need adults and others who help them make sense of their own experiences. By the time we meet the young children in our care they have already constructed some understandings of their experiences. Many of their understandings or constructions are likely to be inaccurate or incorrect though developmentally appropriate. As I see it, our major responsibility is to help the young to improve, extend, refine, develop and deepen their own understandings or constructions of their own worlds. As they grow older and reach primary school age, it is our responsibility to help them develop understandings of other people's experiences, people who are distant in time and place. Indeed, increasing refinement and deepening of understandings is, ideally, a lifelong process.

We might ask: 'What do young children need or want to make sense of?' Certainly of people, of what they do, and why they do it, of what and how they feel; and of themselves and other living things around them, how they themselves and other living things grow; where people and things come from, and how things are made and how they work, and so forth.

If we are to help young children improve and develop their understandings of their experiences we must uncover what those understandings are. The uncovering that we do, and that occurs as children engage in the activities we provide, helps us to make good decisions about what to cover next and what follow-up activities to plan.

AUTHORITATIVE ADULTS

Young children have to have adults who accept the authority that is theirs by virtue of their greater experience, knowledge and wisdom. This proposition is based on the assumption that neither parents nor educators are caught between the extremes of authoritarianism or permissiveness (Baumrind, 1971). Authoritarianism may be defined as the exercise of power without warmth, encouragement or explanation. Permissiveness may be seen as the abdication of adult authority and power, though it may offer children warmth, encouragement and support as they seem to need it. I am suggesting that instead of the extremes of authoritarianism and permissiveness, young children have to have around them adults who are authoritative – adults who exercise their very considerable power over the lives of young children *with* warmth, support, encouragement and adequate explanations of the limits they impose on them. The concept of authoritativeness also includes treating children with respect – treating their opinions, feelings, wishes and ideas as valid even when we disagree with them. To respect people we agree with is no great problem; respecting those whose ideas, wishes and feelings are different from ours or troubling to us, may be a mark of wisdom in parents and of genuine professionalism in teachers and childcare workers.

DESIRABLE ROLE MODELS

Young children need optimum association with adults and older children who exemplify the personal qualities we want them to acquire. Make your own list of the qualities you want the young children for whom you are responsible to acquire. There may be some differences among us, but it is very likely that there are some qualities we all want all children to have: the capacity to care for and about others, the disposition to be honest, kind, accepting those who are different from ourselves, to love learning, and so forth.

This proposition suggests that we inspect children's environments and ask: 'To what extent do our children have contact with people who exhibit these qualities?' 'To what extent do our children observe people who are counter-examples of the qualities we want to foster, but who are also presented as glamorous and attractive?'

It seems to me that children need neighbourhoods and communities which take the steps necessary to protect them from excessive exposure to violence and crime during the early years while their characters are still in formation.

Children need relationships and experience with adults who are willing to take a stand on what is worth doing, worth having, worth knowing, and worth caring about. This proposition seems to belabour the obvious. But in an age of increasing emphasis on pluralism, multiculturalism and community participation, professionals are increasingly hesitant and apologetic about their own values. It seems to me that such hesitancy to take a stand on what is worthwhile may cause us to give children unclear signals about what is worth knowing and doing and what is expected.

Taking a stand on what we value does not guarantee that our children will accept or agree with us. Nor does it imply that we reject others' versions of the 'good life'. We must, in fact, cultivate our capacities to respect alternative definitions of the 'good life'. My point is that when we take a stand, with quiet conviction and courage, we help the young to see us as thinking and caring individuals who have enough self-respect to act on our own values and to give clear signals about what those values are.

In summary, these six propositions are related to our responsibilities for the quality of the daily lives of all our children – wherever they spend those days, throughout the years of growth and development. We must come to see that the wellbeing of our children, of each and every child, is intimately and inextricably linked to the wellbeing of all children. When one of our own children needs life-saving surgery, someone else's child will perform it. When one of our own children is struck down by violence, someone else's child will have inflicted it. The wellbeing of our own children can be secured only when the wellbeing of other people's children is also secure. But to care for and about others' children is not just practical; it is also right.

REFERENCE

Baumrind, D. (1971) *Current Patterns of Parental Authority.* Developmental Psychology Monographs, (4), 1–102.

Part I
How young children learn

Introduction to Part I

Sandra, at the age of two, was taken to the docks by her parents and saw one of the metal structures that the boats were tied up to. She was intrigued by this unfamiliar object and set about exploring it – touching it, smelling it and walking round it. Then she announced 'I seed it and I feeled it and it's not a dog!'

With this one simple sentence she described the processes that many small children go through as they try to make sense of a new or unfamiliar object or situation. She explored it using her movements and her senses: she then compared it to other objects to which it bore some resemblance (in her mind, at least) and with which she was familiar. On the basis of this she decided that it clearly did not fit into her chosen category 'dog'.

Vast tomes have been written about how young children learn. Piaget believed that young children learn through two processes which he called assimilation and accommodation. In the above example the child was assimilating new information and attempting to accommodate this into her existing knowledge. Young children, he believed, are not empty vessels waiting to be filled up with knowledge, but actively seek to understand the world in which they live. Through exploring their world using their movements and their senses, they begin to find patterns which allow them to categorise and classify things. Piaget believed that the role of adults in supporting learning was to provide children with a rich and stimulating environment, full of things they could explore. For him the interaction between child and adult was not essential. Vygotsky and Bruner, by contrast, believed that talk and interaction were essential for learning. For them the role of the adult was more complex and learning more social than for Piaget.

In recent years evidence regarding learning in the early years has shown just how complex the process is. The work of researchers like Colwyn Trevarthen (1988) has demonstrated that the connections between brain cells are laid down most rapidly in the early years and that the development of these connections – the very essence of learning and thinking – depends on stimulation. Margaret Donaldson (1978) has shown how hard children work to bring their previous experience to bear on new situations and how important it is for children to consolidate their new learning in situations which allow this. Donaldson and others have shown how young children, exposed at too early an age to formal decontextualised learning, learn failure. Donaldson argues powerfully that young children, in order to be able to build on what they already know and can do, need to be in situations which make 'human sense' to them.

Much work has been done on the importance of play as the primary way in which young children are able to bring together their existing skills and knowledge and try them out in new combinations. This work has involved a careful definition of play and an understanding of what makes play different from anything else. Much of the research has focused on play as a mode of learning – and highlighted the fact that, since play is self-chosen and carries no risk of failure – it is the mode through which young children learn best.

In Part I we consider just what it is about early learning that makes it special and also think not only about how young children learn, but about how young children learn best.

REFERENCES

Donaldson, M. (1978) *Children's Minds*, Fontana.
Trevanthen, C. (1988) 'Brain development', in R.L. Gregory (ed.) *The Oxford Companion to the Mind*, Oxford University Press.

2 A developmental approach to the curriculum in the early years

Lilian G. Katz

In this chapter, Professor Katz argues that what is learned and how it is best learned depends on the age of the child. She goes on to say that how something is learned depends on what the something is as well as on the particular developmental characteristics of the learner. In essence she poses three questions:

1 What do we think young children should be learning?
2 When should they be learning it?
3 How will it best be learned?

These questions are pivotal and are themes which are addressed throughout many of the pieces in this book.

Everyone responsible for planning a curriculum must address at least the following three questions:

1 What should be learned?
2 When should it be learned?
3 How is it best learned?

Responses to the first question provide the *goals* of the programme for which pedagogical practices are to be adopted. The second question is the *developmental* one in that it draws upon what is known about the development of the learner. In other words, child development helps to address the *when* questions of programme design. The third question turns specifically to matters of appropriate *pedagogy* itself; it includes consideration of all aspects of implementing a programme by which the programme's goals can be achieved, depending, of course, on what is to be learned, and when it is to be learned. In other words, responses to one of the three questions are inextricably linked to responses to the other two.

Thus *what* should be learned and *how* it is best learned depends on *when* the learning is to occur. Similarly, *how* something is learned depends upon *what* it is, as well as upon the developmental characteristics of the learner. For example, virtually all stakeholders in early childhood education would place literacy high on the list of answers to the question, 'What should be learned?' However, they are likely to diverge considerably upon the question of *when* as well as *how* it should be learned – the latter considerations being related to each other. Terms such as *emergent literacy* and *preliteracy* have recently appeared in the early childhood literature, partly in order to address the confounding of the when and how questions. Even though the three questions are clearly linked, for the sake of discussion, they are taken up separately below.

WHAT SHOULD BE LEARNED?

The values and preferences of the parents served by the programme would seem to have first claim among criteria for determining what should be learned. However, parents are rarely a homogeneous or monolithic group with a clear consensus about the goals of their children's education. While the community and parents' preferences contribute to determining the goals, the special expertise of professional educators should be brought to bear on addressing the questions of when and how the goals can be best implemented.

Four types of learning goals

Whatever specific learning goals and objectives are identified by clients and educators, they are all likely to fit into each of four types of learning goals:

1   knowledge
2   skills
3   dispositions, and
4   feelings.

defined as follows:

Knowledge

During the preschool period, this can be broadly defined as ideas, concepts, constructions, schemas, facts, information, stories, customs, myths, songs and other such contents of mind that come under the heading of what is to be learned. Three Piagetian categories of knowledge – social, physical and logico-mathematical – are often used in discussions of the knowledge goals in early childhood education.

Skills

These are defined as small, discrete and relatively brief units of behaviour that are easily observed or inferred from behaviour (for example, skills such as cutting, drawing, counting a group of objects, adding, subtracting, friendship-making, problem solving skills, and so on).

Dispositions

These are broadly defined as relatively enduring 'habits of mind', or character-istic ways of responding to experience across types of situations (including persistence at a task, curiosity, generosity, meanness, the disposition to read, to solve problems). Unlike an item of knowledge or a skill, a disposition is not an end state to be mastered once and for all. It is a trend or consistent pattern of behaviour and its possession is established only if its manifestation is observed repeatedly. Thus a person's disposition to be a reader, for example, can only be ascertained if he or she is observed to read spontaneously, frequently and without external coercion.

Feelings

These are subjective emotional or affective states, e.g. feelings of belonging, or self-esteem, confidence, adequacy and inadequacy, competence and incompetence, and so forth. Feelings about or towards significant phenomena may range from being transitory or enduring, intense or weak, or perhaps ambivalent. In early childhood education attitudes and values can also be included in this category; in education for older children they merit separate categories.[1]

In principle, pedagogical practices are developmentally and educationally appropriate if they address all four categories of learning goals equally and simultaneously. Pedagogical practices are not appropriate if they emphasise the acquisition of knowledge and the mastery of skills without ensuring that the dispositions to use the knowledge and skills so learned are also strengthened. Similarly, if the desired knowledge and skills are mastered in such a way that dislike of them or of the school environment itself develops throughout the learning process, then the pedagogy may be judged inappropriate. Similarly, if a pedagogical approach succeeds in generating feelings of joy, pleasure, amusement, or excitement, but fails to bring about the acquisition of desirable knowledge and skills, it cannot be judged appropriate.

Most stakeholders in early childhood education are likely to agree on broad goals in all four categories of learning. For example, most education authorities' curriculum guides list such goals as knowledge and skills related to literacy and numeracy and various items of cultural knowledge, plus such dispositions as the desire to learn, creativity, cooperativeness, and so forth; the list of goals related to feelings usually includes 'positive feelings about themselves', or 'self-confidence'.[2]

Once the knowledge, skills, dispositions and feelings to be learned have been agreed upon, the next question is *when* they should be learned.

WHEN SHOULD IT BE LEARNED?

Learning in the four categories of learning goals proposed above occurs constantly, whether intentional or incidental. However, a developmental approach to curriculum planning takes into account both dimensions of development: the *normative* and the *dynamic* dimensions. These two equally important dimensions of development are defined as follows:

1   The *normative* dimension of development addresses the characteristics and capabilities of children that are typical or normal for their age group (e.g. the typical size of vocabulary of four-year-olds, the average age of first walking or of understanding numerical concepts).

Age norms also provide useful starting points for curriculum planning. Knowledge of age-typical interests, activities and abilities can provide a basis for preliminary planning of a general programme of activities, and the selection of equipment and materials. For example norms of development provide a basis for assuming that most two-year-olds need daytime naps, most four-year-olds do not understand calendar concepts, or that, typically, most five-year-olds can begin to write their own names, etc.

Age norms are also useful for alerting teachers to individual children whose patterns of development depart noticeably from their age group and who warrant close observation by which to ascertain whether special curriculum and teaching strategies are required.

2   The *dynamic* dimension of development deals with an individual child's progress from immaturity to maturity. This dimension addresses changes over time *within* an individual and the *long-term* effects of early experience rather than the normality of typicality of behaviour and abilities of an age group. This dimension has three aspects:

(a)   *Sequence*, refers to the order or *stages* of development through which an individual passes, e.g. in achieving mastery of first language. The curriculum and teaching practices consider what learning and developmental tasks have to be completed before the next learning can occur. For example, it is reasonable to assume that introduction to a second language is most likely to be beneficial following mastery of one's first language.

(b)   *Delayed effects* refer to the potential positive and negative effects of early experience that are not manifested at the time of occurrence, but may influence later functioning (e.g. early infant–caregiver attachment may influence later parenting competence).

Some practices that are effective in the short term may have delayed or 'sleeper' effects that are deleterious in the long term (e.g. rewards and punishments, unsatisfactory early bonding and attachment, etc.). Some practices that may not seem important to development during the early years may have positive delayed effects later. Whether positive or negative, 'delayed effects' are those that do not show up until later in the course of development.

(c)   *Cumulative effects* refer to experiences that may have no effects (either positive or negative) if they are occasional or rare, but may have powerful effects if frequent (e.g. the cumulative positive effects of frequent block play or cumulative negative effects of frequent but mild criticism).

A developmental approach to curriculum and teaching practices takes into account both dimensions of development in that what young children *should* do and *should* learn is determined on the basis of what is best for their development in the long term (i.e. the dynamic consequences of early experience) rather than simply what works in the short term.

HOW IS IT BEST LEARNED?

This question takes us directly to matters of pedagogy, such as consideration of teaching methods, activities, materials and all other practical matters designed to achieve the learning goals, and to take into account what is known about learners' development.

Learning in the four categories of goals is facilitated in different ways. In the case of both knowledge and skills, learning can be aided by instruction as well as by other processes, but dispositions and feelings cannot be learned from direct instruction. Many important dispositions are inborn – e.g. the disposition to learn, to observe, to investigate, to be curious, etc. Many dispositions appear to be learned from models, are strengthened by being manifested and appreciated, and are weakened when unacknowledged or ineffective.

Feelings related to school experiences are learned as by-products of experiences rather than from instruction. Both dispositions and feelings can be thought of as incidental learning in that they are incidental to the processes by which knowledge and skills are acquired. To label feelings as incidental is not to belittle them, or to devalue the role of pedagogy in their development; rather, it is to emphasise that they cannot be taught didactically. Children cannot be instructed in what feelings to have.

Recent insights into children's development suggest that in principle, the younger the child, the more readily knowledge is acquired through active and interactive processes; conversely, with increasing age children become more able to profit from reactive, passive–receptive pedagogical approaches or instructional processes. In other words, pedagogical practices are developmentally appropriate when the knowledge to be acquired or constructed is related to the child's own first-hand, direct experiences and when it is accessible from primary sources. This is not to say that children do not acquire knowledge and information from such secondary sources as stories, books and films. The extent to which they do so is related to whether young children can connect the materials within the secondary sources to the images and knowledge they already possess. With increasing age and experience children become more able to profit from second-hand, indirect experiences and secondary sources.

Thus pedagogical practices are appropriate if they provide young children with ample opportunity to interact with adults and children who are like and unlike themselves, with materials, and directly with real objects and real environments.

However, interactions cannot occur in a vacuum; they have to have content. Interactions must be about something – ideally something that interests the interactors.

What criteria can be used to determine what knowledge or content is appropriate for young children? For example, should young children spend up to ten minutes per day in a calendar exercise? Should young children in southern Florida be making snowflake crystals out of Styrofoam at Christmas time? Should substantial amounts of time be allocated to observance of public holidays and festivals? Why? And why not? What factors, data or other matters should be taken into account in answering questions such as these? One way to approach these questions is to derive principles of practice from what is known about the nature of children's intellectual development.

In principle, a substantial proportion of the content of interaction should be related to matters of actual or potential interest to the children served by the programme. Since not all of children's interests are equally deserving of attention, some selection of which interests are the most worthy of promotion is required. Current views of children's learning and their active construction of knowledge suggest that those interests most likely to extend, deepen and improve their understanding of their own environments and experiences are most worth strengthening during the early years.

NOTES

1 In the case of young children, undesirable attitudes and values are assumed to be a function of faulty developmental progress rather than of general institutional socialisation. For example, dishonesty or greed in a five-year-old are more likely to be interpreted as symptoms of poor child-rearing or psychosocial environmental influences rather than as problems of attitudes and values *per se*.

2 See, for example, State of Iowa, *Kindergarten: A Year of Beginnings*, Des Moines, Iowa, 1983; State of Connecticut, *A Guide to Program Development for Kindergarten*, Part 1 (1988) Harford, CT: State Board of Education; Oklahoma State Department of Education, *Beginnings: Early Childhood Education in Oklahoma*, 3rd edn, Oklahoma City, OK: State Department of Education 1986; Patricia Morgan Roberts, ed. *Growing Together: Early Childhood Education in Pennsylvania* (Harrisburg) PA: Pennsylvania Department of Education, 1989.

3 Welcome to our nursery centre

Lucie Dickens

At the time of writing, the author was a student on the Early Childhood Studies Scheme. Lucie, as part of her assessed work, critically examined some of Lilian Katz's views. She presented her work in the form of a booklet written for parents and explaining why her nursery follows a developmental approach. In this extract she attempts to explain certain key issues to parents:

1   Why it is important to start from what the child already knows and can do and what the child is interested in;
2   Why young children need long periods of uninterrupted time in which to explore their interests;
3   Why it is important that young children are offered meaningful situations in which to play and learn;
4   Why children should be regarded as active learners and not passive recipients;
5   What adults can do to promote learning;
6   Why it is important for parents and workers to work in partnership for the benefit of the child;
7   How learning can best be planned for when it is based on close observations of what the children can do and are interested in.

Lucie examines the crucial question, initially posed by Lilian Katz: should we be thinking about what children *can* do or about what children *should* do in order to continue learning?

What is education for? Most people would agree that we educate and care for our children because we want them to become active learners, with a positive self-image and the capacity to become independent thinkers. We want our children to be able to communicate effectively with others and hold the fundamental values of caring and sharing, even within a society geared towards competition. The formative years of a child's life is where the foundations for these skills, attitudes, knowledge and concepts are laid.

(Siraj-Blatchford, 1994)

This information booklet has been designed especially for you, the parents and carers, to tell you about the developmentally appropriate curriculum and what it means for you and your child's learning. It will introduce some beliefs and values we use in our work with the children. I hope that by taking the time to read this booklet, you will understand some important points about the developmentally appropriate curriculum. As you progress through the booklet we will explain some theories and principles which contribute to it.

What and how your child learns in the early years of life will have a direct link to future learning and on the rest of life. At this Nursery Centre the emphasis is on quality learning through a developmentally appropriate curriculum. Children are naturally curious about their world or immediate environment, which enables them to come to understand the basic things about their environment. A developmentally appropriate curriculum encourages children's self-directed learning by providing them with an environment that is rich in materials to explore, manipulate and talk about.

Childhood is a very important part of life, when the child's mind is at its most receptive and absorbent. Research has shown that neural connections in the brain are developing most rapidly in the first five years of life and curiosity is essential to this development. Basic human brain structure is the same world-wide. What happens to us and around us as young children influences its development.

Childhood can be a very difficult part of life as the young child tries to make sense of all the many influences in her/his life – parents, siblings, extended family members, nursery, television, local community and more.

The influences the child encounters may not all be useful. Children in Britain today will be best equipped for life if they are exposed to positive ideas about living in a multicultural community, about race, gender roles and disability. In the nursery these issues of equal opportunity are very much part of the values we hope children will pick up, and anti-discriminatory practice is constantly going on.

Children are beings in their own right and need to be listened to and encouraged along in their development. Three things that will be helpful for young children learning are: first, to give a realistic view of life, involving giving accurate information about their immediate environment, the community in which they live and the wider world; second, children can be given manageable responsibilities, which enable them to feel that they are part of a group and their efforts are valued; third, children may need guidance regarding their behaviour as they try to make sense of what is acceptable where. They learn by watching people around them, as well as by how they themselves are treated. Giving consistent behaviour standards and boundaries to children in their early years allows them to develop a clear base from which they can function smoothly.

Now your child is stepping out into the wider world and broadening her/his experiences, we value your participation and partnership as we aim to build on what your child already knows. This method of working with children is called 'a child-centred approach'. This quote from Blenkin and Kelly (1986) explains further:

> . . . child-centredness in education . . . is to be taken as implying that the child and his or her development are the first consideration in educational planning and that all else is secondary to that.

The more we, the adults, communicate and share information about your child – what she/he is interested in at home, what has been happening at nursery – the more we will understand your child and expand her/his interests based on previous experience. Every parent or carer wants what is best for their child and we hope that you will want to become involved with the learning that your child is doing here, then you can continue these interests at home, just as we expect your child to develop interests she/he brings from outside the nursery. This way of working together is beneficial to your child as continuity helps to sustain her/his interests. We will have termly reviews together, as well as more informal talks on a more frequent basis, whenever we have something to share about your child. We would like you to join with us in recording an ongoing file of your child's achievements.

Planning what to provide for the children is an integral part of the developmentally appropriate curriculum. . . . We observe the children at play and from these observations we evaluate their interests, their current abilities and needs. The staff hold planning meetings monthly and daily to discuss the observations and what is going on in the classroom, which enables us to make decisions about our provision for learning – for instance, what challenges and opportunities could we provide to enable each child to further develop and extend what they are already doing.

> The developmental question is what is it that children should do that best serves their development in the long term.
>
> (Katz, 1988)

I have been impressed by Katz's points about the need for adults to thoroughly question what children 'should do' as opposed to what they 'can do' that will be most useful in the long run.

Ideas about the best way to bring up or educate children, like any area of interest in the world today, are constantly changing and developing, so our own experience of early childhood including our education, is probably rather different compared to what young children today may experience. Research has shown that some of the most valuable things a child can learn at nursery are invisible, because they are not paintings or pieces of writing or number work. These attributes that I will mention are supportive of Siraj-Blatchford's work quoted at the beginning of this document. They are things like being independent, being able to make their own decisions, take responsibility for things, being self-motivated, having a good feeling about their own abilities without an adult having to back them up. They are active rather than passive in the learning, being able to communicate well with others, being able to develop the idea of sharing and caring. Encouraging children to develop these attitudes is an important part of the developmentally appropriate curriculum.

One aspect of Katz's work of particular interest is about 'dispositions' in people and how we adults, working with children, should be constantly aware of this aspect of learning. She describes them as ' . . . habits of mind, tendencies to respond to situations in certain ways'. The responses adults encourage from children can strengthen certain dispositions. Therefore, in the nursery, we will be giving children examples of positive dispositions that will be an asset to them – like friendliness, curiosity, creativity, having interest, being cooperative, being hard-working, being helpful and caring.

Our nursery curriculum allows children the time and space to develop at their own pace. Individual children vary enormously in their level of development, although they are all of a similar chronological age. The nursery is a non-competitive environment, where there is no such thing as success or failure because we do not believe in testing. Our interest lies in the process of learning, rather than the end product.

We encourage the children to be active learners as a vital part of our curriculum. I will use a quote from Blenkin and Kelly (1986) to explain what is meant by this:

> the importance for development of the child's being actively and positively engaged with the content and process of his or her learning.

Here the children have considerable power over their environment and how they choose to use it. They have open access to the wide range of materials from which to choose what they want to work or play with and these are accessible on low shelves and cupboards. They are encouraged to be responsible for putting things away again on completion of their play. This freedom of choice is offered because we want children to be in control of their learning, to explore, experiment or experience within the nursery spontaneously, when they are motivated by or interested in something, rather than have adults impose things on them which may not be of interest to the child at that moment or may interrupt her/his concentration on something else.

David Elkind looked at the damage children can suffer if they receive formal education too young. Adults can actually interfere with a child's learning by inflicting their own ideas of what a child should be learning. This could work against the attitudes and dispositions which hope to encourage as children could become unnecessarily dependent on adults to direct them or give them ideas of what to do. As a result children could become less reliant on their own initiative. This does not mean that we never intervene with children's play and learning. We choose to intervene carefully, at times when a child may benefit from having his or her interest reinforced. We also intervene when children may need an adult to help them in negotiation or problem solving and to channel a positive approach to their experiences and learning if it is, or has become, unproductive developmentally or if behaviour is unacceptable.

REFERENCES

Blenkin, G.M. and Kelly, A.V. (eds) (1988) *Early Childhood Education: A Developmental Approach*, Barnes and Noble.

Elkind, D. (1986) 'Formal education and early childhood education: an essential difference,' *Phi Delta Kappa*, May.

Katz, L. (1988) 'What should young children be learning?' *American Educator*.

Siraj-Blatchford, I. (1994) *The Early Years: Laying the foundations for Racial Equality*, Trentham Books.

4   To play or not to play? That is the question!

Janet Moyles

This chapter argues simply, but passionately, that providing play opportunities for young children is not only important, but essential if they are
to grow up as balanced, independent, thoughtful people – able to
respond to change and to crisis. Janet Moyles highlights what is special
about play – that aspect she calls 'ownership' and she shows how
insensitive intervention in play can hijack the child's agenda and turn
the play situation, which is full of potential for learning, into something
sterile and driven by the adult's desire to 'teach' something. She goes
on to look at what adults can do to support learning through play.

INTRODUCTION

As I travel around the country talking to different groups of early years educators,
there are a number of questions which I am invariably asked and to which I
constantly seek answers. On the assumption that the reader will have similar
questions in mind about play, this chapter offers some very brief responses as
well as raising a few questions of its own for play practitioners to consider: what is
play and what value does it have?

This is probably the most difficult question because it all depends on the *values*
of the person asking the question. Play is not one single action or activity or a way
of doing something that is easily defined. It is a combination of all these and it has
direct relationships with learning as well as with people's potential and motivation
for learning. It is useful to formulate one's own working construct of play and, after
several attempts, the best I can offer at the present time is:

> Play appears to be the engagement of people in a variety of activities over
> which they have ownership and which motivates them to persist towards new
> learning.

Very broadly, we could say that play is a person's way of understanding the world
and its contents and contexts in order to gain an awareness of both one's place in
that world and one's control over it. As an example, adults nearly always need to
play with a new item of equipment – computers are the classic example – to find

out both about the object but also their control over it. What is important to remember is that the learning about the object and our mastery *could not really happen in any other way.*

This is what children are doing all the time when they are playing: they must play in order continually to build new concepts and understandings. Adults do this all the time, if they can only admit it! It is necessary to accept that many aspects of adult play have become deeply internalised: for example, we can only laugh at jokes if we understand the play on words. But to do this we have first to have had a myriad of opportunities for different kinds of play to act as a physical and mental framework for different concepts and ideas, eventually leading to an internalising of skills and thoughts; in other words symbolic thinking. Such thinking enables us to become readers, writers, mathematicians, artists, creators and scientists, without the constant need for external props. The important thing to remember is that we will only be able to do without external props when we have had sufficient play to be secure and confident in our knowledge and mastery.

Play is a natural *tool* for learning and for communication for all young animals, including the human animal. Play is a *fun* way of learning about yourself and your own skills and abilities. Play is a *motivator* for curiosity and a means to explore problems without that being a problem in itself.

WHAT ARE THE CONNECTIONS BETWEEN PLAY AND CHILDREN'S LEARNING?

Young children learn through all their senses – by touching, feeling, smelling, tasting, hearing, moving and exploring. From this they generate perceptions about the world and its events, from which, in turn, they create mental images which are the mainstay of their developing conceptions of the world. Concepts form the basis of knowledge and understandings about all aspects of their lives (Longford, 1987) and this is inexorably intertwined with the development of language. As language development progresses issues of fantasy/reality are explored, imagination and creativity develop, and general understandings of the world are evolved, tried out and re-evaluated until 'learning' has occurred.

Play has a major role in motivating children's curiosity and ensuring that they explore materials in a playful way in order to learn about properties, textures, shapes, smells, colours, feelings and so on which form the building blocks of all learning. Once children understand thoroughly what the material or context is, they are freed to be creative and imaginative with it and to gain control over it for their own purposes. Eventually they will then learn that everything has parameters beyond which you cannot force it to go further. This forms the basis of Corinne Hutt's theory (Hutt *et al.*, 1989).

This process is also seen in several modes of learning where the need to acquire and understand the basic elements precedes the wider applicational aspects which, in turn, are restructured and modified as learning proceeds (Norman, 1978, Bennett *et al.*, 1984). Significantly learning is, and should be, very diverse and we will each take on board through our play a unique persona as a learner. We can only learn for ourselves – no-one can do it for us – and, similarly, we can only play for ourselves. There is no short cut way whatever the politicians or the media would have parents believe! If children do not have these very necessary first-hand experiences through play, then their development will be impoverished. Colwyn Trevarthen (1992), in his brain studies work, has shown, at the level of our present knowledge, how the brain needs stimulation at an early age in order that the massive network of connections, which form the basis of our understanding, is formed and continues to develop.

Because we do not know what the future holds, these basic play and learning theories need steadfastly to be reinforced in people's minds, for what it offers is creative thinkers for the future rather than circus-type 'performers' who can simply jump through imposed hoops. It may be possible to teach all four-year-olds to read fluently, but one must question whether this is the most appropriate thing for them to do: it is my belief that, rather than expanding children's experience, at least in the short term it restricts them to a very narrow, and potentially sterile, range of opportunities. (See Geva Blenkin, 1984, for further discussion on this.)

There are many researchers who have shown the benefits children accrue through various types of play, particularly in the areas of social skills, language, creativity and problem solving. Smilansky and Shefataya (1990), for example, suggest that children who are 'good', imaginative players are better adjusted socially and emotionally, have heightened concentration, better self-knowledge and self-discipline, are more flexible and empathetic towards others, are more cooperative and sensitive, are better able to make generalisations and have increased capacity for the development of abstract thought and mental images. Gura's investigations of play led her to suggest that

> there appears to be a high correlation between play in childhood and the creativity associated with important scientific and technological developments.
>
> (Gura, 1994: 144)

Perhaps most importantly, play acts as a scaffold for all other basic learning in that it allows children to cope with not knowing long enough in order to know: it frees them from worrying about doing things wrong and gives them confidence to try out other experiences. All children learn to establish their own identity and their place in the order of things through play, particularly sociodramatic contexts. Play enables children to interrogate the world in which they find themselves without loss of self-esteem and, above all, play enables children to learn what learning is – and should be – fun and enjoyable. This is the vital feature if we are to have happy and well-balanced, flexible learners and citizens for the future.

WHAT IS THE RELATIONSHIP BETWEEN PLAY, CHILDREN'S CHOICE AND CONTROL?

One of the main things which separates play from non-play, is the concept of 'ownership' (Moyles, 1989, 1991). If a child is playing deeply with particular play materials, then taking that away with questions such as 'What colour is it? What shape is it? What does it feel like?' takes the ownership away from children and leaves them feeling that their personal agenda must be less important than that of the adult. Eventually the child will simply wait to be told what to do and cease to raise their own questions (Fisher, 1990: 30). It is easily recognised that this also takes away the children's choice as to what they need to learn and absorb from this activity and, perhaps even more importantly, it also takes away their control over the situation. They need to acquiesce immediately to the control and values of the adult and quite often the result is that the play goes 'off the boil' and children move on to something else.

Many parents will bear witness to play's beneficial effects in promoting concentration, especially when it comes to bedtime! If we want children to concentrate then we must leave the ownership and, therefore, a majority of choice and control with them as much as possible. This does not mean that we cannot intervene as adults – what it does mean is that we must do this in a way which values the children's own agendas and assess how far this 'fits' our agenda for curriculum experiences. When adults get really sensitive to this, it is easy to find out that the two agendas are often very similar!

In children's choices for play materials, adults need to think very carefully about both what they are offering to children through their provision and how they are offering it. What one provides in its own way will 'structure' children's play – if there is only dry sand to play with, then children and adults will run it through their fingers, watch it flow, see it pile into neat little mountains and so on. How we make provision relates to whether children have sensible choice or whether the situation is quite overwhelming. Can you imagine being around a 3 or 4 years of age and entering a preschool centre that must look like Aladdin's cave! How do you go about choosing what to do (Heaslip, 1994)? Most children will try to find the familiar so as to gain some comfort in the known within this kind of situation and then what do the adults say – 'No, don't do that. You played in the sand all day yesterday!'

Choosing effectively can only come about when one has learned how to choose and this is where adults come into the play situation in a big way. How do children learn to choose – by choosing, in the same way that they learn to read by reading and write by writing! Children may not necessarily understand how to use a particular play material and may avoid it if they feel at all insecure or play is not part of their normal cultural framework. The adults can play with the material themselves and, in so doing, will model for the children a few of its features and joys: even the most reluctant child will almost inevitably join in and explore the materials with an adult. Once this has happened, they may well then make it something they choose on another occasion.

WHAT GENDER DIFFERENCES SHOULD WE EXPECT IN BOYS' AND GIRLS' PLAY?

Many people will recognise that boys tend to be more collective by nature in the way they play, engaging in much more associative and parallel play than many girls (see Thorne, 1993). They also engage in much more rough and tumble type play and this is almost 'expected' by adults. Girls have been shown to be more cooperative and more empathetic in their play (Ross and Browne, 1993), engaging each other in both spoken and unspoken moments which nevertheless hold great meaning.

We need to remember, however, that this is the *interpretation of play*, the way adults perceive it, and children will not even recognise what they are doing, for this has been part of their development from birth. Many people say 'boys will be boys: we should not attempt to change this'. But what is it to be a boy? It is only our society's construction! If we want more caring males then male children should have opportunities to play caring roles. If we want more technological females, then female children should have opportunities for constructional play. In these ways, expectations placed on either sex should effectively, and in time, be modified.

There is a need to remember that many cultures have clear role delineation for their males and females and, in the context of schooling, we may well be confronting this with different families. Our conviction must be firmly based in the concept of equality of opportunity for all children enshrined in the United Nations Convention on the Rights of the Child (Newell, 1991) and in the entitlement of all children to the best possible experiences of care and education. Anyone who wants to undertake any role in society should have an equal chance of doing so, but one cannot be an engineer without understanding how materials work and how to put them together or work as a nurse unless one understands both the nature of being a caregiver and being in a service position to others.

This raises the question of which children are 'allowed' into certain kinds of play. Girls have been shown often to leave the construction materials when boys advance on the scene and boys can avoid the home corner which is often considered the domain of girls (Askew and Ross, 1988). These values have, whether we like it or not, been passed on by the adults and the sociocultural framework in which children find themselves. There is a need to show children that all materials and contexts have something to offer both sexes and all different cultures. Vivien Gussein Paley showed that when children suggested to others that 'you can't play', it was the role of a sensitive adult to ensure that children were confronted with this and offered opportunities for discussion (Paley, 1991). Like adults, children who are encouraged to struggle with ideas, concepts and aspects like fairness, will inevitably learn more in the kind of open, trial and error situation of play activity.

Adults must analyse what they observe in a determined, gender-free way: one of the best pieces of advice is to try to disregard whether the child is a boy or a girl. What is the play? What is its quality? What does it tell us about the child's learning? What information does it give us through which to support the next stage of learning?

We seem somehow afraid as adults to confront children with the 'issues' in life such as making choices, being assertive or talking through things that offend others. We need as adults to challenge damaging stereotypes and really learn to practise anti-bias education of all kinds. We hold the future in our hands very literally when we are dealing with young children and we must not be afraid, in a simple way to discuss with them these very basic issues. Instigated through play situations they pose no real threat to anyone, yet, because of the motivating nature of play, they can probably do more to change attitudes than anything else.

It is also vital that adults value what girls make, for example boys often construct tall structures and these are praised for their height, strength, form and stability. Girls often construct perimeters and things associated with homes and these are quite often dismissed either wittingly or unwittingly with a 'Yes, that's very nice' kind of attitude without the questioning which is often associated with boys' models. We need constantly to challenge our own values about gender and racial stereotypes: a good way is to video a session with adults and children and then explore in depth during the viewing what attitudes are being portrayed by both groups. Video certainly offers the opportunity to see ourselves as others see us!

HOW SHOULD ADULTS INVOLVE THEMSELVES IN CHILDREN'S PLAY?

When intervening in children's play and very practically speaking, an obvious thing to do is to 'count to ten' (in one's head) before interrupting a play episode – this gives the adult time to absorb what is happening in the play and, if it is all progressing well with learning apparent either from the children's actions or their words, then leave well alone or, better still, use the evidence in order to generate enhanced provision next time.

Adults need to recognise that what children bring to the play tells us a lot about where they are in their learning and their understanding about a range of different factors. Children play what they know (Schwartzman, 1978) and build on from what they know in their play. If what they know is stereotyped and biased, then this will be reflected in their play – think about the distorted images of adults children sometimes convey in their 'home' or 'school' play! Just as we would prevent children from sticking their fingers into the fire to know that it burns, we need to have the confidence to acknowledge that bias of all kinds is equally unacceptable and ensure that children are taught other views and other values. Stories played out in pretend or sociodramatic play can often bring these points home in a child-oriented way.

It is also not wise for adults to put too heavy an emphasis on the product of play by, perhaps, insisting that children make labels for their models or asking 'what is it?' type questions. This often attaches to the child's paintings and creations an adult interpretation of representation and makes children afraid to use their own initiative. I can always remember the teacher who was really cross with a child who had, up until a certain point, painted a wonderful picture of herself and her sister playing in bed, and then painted it black all over when the 'light went out'!

Without doubt the most important thing for adults to do is what I might call 'intervene by value'. If adults really value play – and everyone needs to search their own hearts for the depth of their personal commitment to play – then this will be apparent in many ways. If the way we speak, act, support play situations, care for the resources of play as much as books and paperwork, shows that we, too, play, do not talk about 'work' and 'play' as if work was the only worthwhile activity – 'You can play when you've finished your work'. 'Stop playing about and go and do something sensible!' – we, the adults, convey our values related to play.

Associated with this must be a plea to ensure provision of 'free flow play' (Bruce,

1991) for all children. This kind of play enables children to take 'safe' risks. When a child is engaged in sociodramatic play they can 'risk' being a harsh adult without actually suffering that harshness: they can 'risk' the tower falling down because it can be rebuilt. It seems that some youths in our present society are trying to indicate play deprivation as children and now need to experience excitement and risk taking and this manifests itself as joy riding, burglary and other socially unacceptable behaviours – a high price to pay for the denial of play?

CONCLUDING REMARKS

We may not be able to prove what children learn through their play (Smith, 1994) but we can see what evidence their play offers for expression of learning. Anyone who spends time observing children in play contexts and noting how, through actions and words, children are able to give clear indications of prior experiences and learning, will soon be convinced of play's merits for children.

REFERENCES

Askew, S. and Ross, C. (1988) Boys Don't Cry: Boys and Sexism in Education, Open University Press.

Bennett, N., Desforges, C., Cockburn, A. and Wilkinson, B. (1984) The Quality of Pupils' Learning Experiences, Lawrence Erlbaum.

Blenkin, G. and Kelly, A. (eds) (1994) The National Curriculum and Early Learning, PCP.

Bruce, T. (1991) Time to Play in Early Childhood Education, Hodder and Stoughton.

Fisher, R. (1990) Teaching Children to Think, Blackwell.

Gura, P. (1994) 'Scientific and technological development in the early years', in G. Blenkin and A. Kelly (eds) The National Curriculum and Early Learning, PCP.

Heaslip, P. (1994) 'Making play work in the classroom', in J.R. Moyles (ed.) The Excellence of Play, Open University Press.

Hutt, S.J., Tyler, S., Hutt, C. and Christopherson, H. (1989) Play, Exploration and Learning: A Natural History of the Pre-School, Routledge.

Longford, P. (1987) Concept Development in the Primary School, Croom Helm.

Moyles, J.R. (1988) Just Playing? The Role and Status of Play in Early Education, Open University Press.

Moyles, J.R. (1991) Play as a Learning Process in your Classroom, Collins Educational.

Newell, P. (1991) The UN Convention and Children's Rights in the UK, National Children's Bureau.

Norman, D.A. (1978) 'Notes towards a complex theory of learning', in A.M. Lesgold (ed.) Cognitive Psychology and Instruction, Plenum Press.

Paley, V.G. (1991) You Can't Say You Can't Play! Harvard University Press.

Ross, C. and Browne, N. (1993) Girls as Constructors in the Early Years, Trentham.

Schwartzman, H. (1978) Transformations, Plenum Press.

Smilansky, S. and Shefataya, S. (1990) Facilitating Play: A Medium for Promoting Cognitive, Socio-Emotional and Academic Development in Young Children, Psychosocial and Educational Publications.

Smith, P.K. (1994) 'Play and the Uses of Play', in J.R. Moyles (ed.) The Excellence of Play, Open University Press.

Thorne, B. (1993) Gender Play: Girls and Boys in School, Open University Press.

Trevarthen, C. (1992) Play for Tomorrow, BBC Television video text.

5 Observing symbolic play

Gillian Allery

The author of this chapter is one of the students on the Early Childhood Studies Scheme. Gillian, like many of the students, is skilled at observing children at play. As one of her assessed assignments she was invited to observe a child at play and look for evidence of symbolic representation – in other words, to find an example of a child using one thing to represent another. The ability to make one thing stand for another is crucial in early learning. We live in a highly symbolic world. The words we speak, the texts we read, the images we see, the logos we encounter, the numbers we use are all symbols. In order to be able to move away from the here and now and into the abstract world of letters, numbers and symbols, young children need to explore symbolic representation through their play.

As you read through Gillian's piece you find evidence of Colin, aged only 2 years, 7 months, using a ball to represent a baby and a bucket to represent a pram. You will also see how he is able to involve another child in his symbolic world. In this example the children are using external props – the bucket and the ball. Older children can create worlds in their heads and are no longer dependent on having physical props. As Janet Moyles said in the previous article:

> 'we have first to have had a myriad of opportunities for different kinds of play to act as a physical and mental framework for different concepts and ideas, eventually leading to an internalising of skills and thoughts: in other words, symbolic thinking. Such thinking enables us to become readers, writers, mathematicians, artists, creators and scientists, without the constant need for external props. The important thing to remember is that we will only be able to do without external props when we have had sufficient play to be secure and confident in our knowledge and mastery.'

I had decided to observe the children outside in the garden and, for a while, I thought it might be a fruitless task, as the children were using things just as they were intended to be used. That is until I saw Colin, aged 2 years, 7 months. Colin went over to the mop bucket outside the kitchen back door. It is a yellow bucket on four wheels. Colin pulled it by the handle away from the door. He pushed it around the garden, quite fast at first, but then slowing to a walk. He stopped, seeing a football on the ground. He picked it up and said 'In you go, baby'. He then pushed the football in the bucket around the garden.

Anabel, aged four and a half, came over to Colin.

'Can I have the ball, Colin?'

Colin looked at her. He seemed puzzled. She picked the ball up and kicked it away from her.

'Nooo!' Colin cried and ran after the ball. One of the workers, Debbie, spoke to Anabel, saying 'Colin is playing with that, Anabel. Come with me and I'll get you another.'

Colin picked up the ball 'Don't run away, baby. It's all right,' he said lovingly. He then put the ball under his arm and pulled the bucket over to a small chair. He sat down on the chair and put the ball in the bucket. 'Going shops in a minute, baby, shops and sweets, baby, yeah?' he said.

Anabel ran over to Colin. 'Is that a baby, Colin?'

Colin looked pleased. 'Yeah,' he replies.

'Can I play?' Anabel asked.

'No pram, you got,' Colin said, holding tightly to his bucket. 'I'll get one. Wait, wait there.' Anabel ran to Debbie. 'Debbie, I need a pram,' she said. Debbie looked around the garden and pointed to a wooden doll's pram standing unused.

'There you are, Anabel. There is a pram,' said Debbie.

'No,' said Anabel, 'a yellow one like Colin's please.'

'Oh, a bucket,' Debbie said, 'I don't know if we have another one.'

'No, it's a pram, Debbie, one like Colin's got I want,' Anabel said indignantly.

'Oh, all right. I'll have a look,' said Debbie and taking her by the hand they went inside.

Colin, meanwhile, was picking leaves from a bush in the corner of the garden. He carried them carefully back to the bucket/pram and threw them in. 'Dinner, baby,' he said.

Pat then called the children for lunch. Colin picked up the ball and went inside. Pat said, 'Leave that outside, please Colin, till after lunch.' Colin turned around and ran over to the bucket and put the ball/baby in the bucket and wheeled it into the shade. He patted it and went in for lunch.

COMMENTS ON THIS OBSERVATION

Colin, it seems to me here, is engaging in imaginative play. He uses the bucket as a pram and the ball as a baby. I don't know if Colin saw the ball as a baby or used it as a baby in the absence of a doll. Anabel at first seemed to think Colin's game was silly, but soon engaged in imitative play and decided she, too, wanted a bucket for a pram. The purpose-built pram was rejected as not good enough.

Colin uses imitative play when he says 'it's all right' lovingly to the baby after Anabel has kicked it. He also promises the baby a trip to the shops and sweets. It's obvious that he has had some experience of seeing a baby in a pram or indeed it may be the memory of his own pram that has caused him to push the pram out of the sun whilst he had his lunch. The bucket and ball and leaves are all symbolic representations of something else.

6 Louise drawing

Observation notes

Nancy Coyne

In this chapter, Nancy Coyne recorded what happened when she sat alongside four-year-old Louise as she was drawing a special picture for Nancy. Aware that adults can intervene inappropriately and impose their agenda on a child, Nancy struggled to leave ownership of the drawing with the child. She attempted to pay close attention to what it was that Louise was doing rather than focusing on the end product – the actual picture. Nancy, by trying to tune in to Louise's agenda, allowed Louise to be in control. Nancy's role as the adult was to help Louise reflect on what she was doing and to validate her explorations.

As you read through this short piece see if you can identify the sorts of phrases Nancy uses as prompts for maintaining a dialogue – things like 'That's interesting' or 'That's a good idea'. She is careful not to question the child too much and the questions she does ask are related to the process Louise is going through. So Nancy asks 'Are they playing a game?' when Louise says she is going to draw children holding hands. Many adults might have been tempted to grasp a possible teaching point when Louise said she was going to draw four people because she was four. Nancy resists the temptation to ask something like 'Can you count them?' or 'How many would there be if you drew another one?' You will notice that, at one point, Louise comments that she doesn't like the colour black and that it is a boy's colour. Nancy's response to this is particularly sensitive in that she challenges the child's judgement, but in a non-threatening way by saying 'I like black clothes'.

Louise picks up a green pen and starts to draw zig-zags on the paper.

Nancy: That looks interesting.
Louise: I'm drawing stairs.
Nancy: Oh, let me see how you draw stairs.
Louise: It's very easy. You just go up and down, up and down, like this.

She was nodding her head up and down at the same time.
She drew a circle and then began to scribble around it.

Louise: I'm doing long hair all the way round. Look at the person I did.
Nancy: Oh, that's lovely. Is it anybody I know?
Louise: Me, silly! Can't you tell by the hair?
Nancy: Oh, silly me!
Louise: I think I'll draw four people because I am four.
Nancy: That's a good idea.
Louise: I'll make them all hold hands.
Nancy: Are they playing a game?
Louise: Yes, Ring-a-Ring of Roses. I'll do black for a boy because black is a boy's colour. I don't like black. Do you?
Nancy: I like black clothes.
Louise: You should be a boy then. (Laughs)
Nancy: Cheeky girl!
Louise: Next is yellow for a girl.
Nancy: That's a nice bright colour.
Louise: Yes, that's why I like it. It's the same colour as the sun.
Nancy: That's right.
Louise: Do you like them all holding hands? They are at a birthday party, so I'll give the special one a crown so we'll know whose birthday it is.
Nancy: I think that's a very good idea.
Louise: Another boy and then a girl. I have to give them all a name now.

(She points to each one and names them – Roger, Sina, Bana, Keiren, Mark, Keiren again.)

Nancy: They are nice names.
Louise: Now I'm going to give them all a nose.

(She banged the pen hard at each face to give them each a nose.)

Louise: How do you spell Ring a Ring a Rosies?

I spelled out each letter and she wrote them down with her tongue between her teeth. Then she wrote her age and her name.

7 Playing with magnets

Gerardine Lanigan

In this chapter, Gerardine Lanigan describes in detail what happened when a group of three- and four-year-olds were playing with magnets. In her detailed observation notes we find support for Moyles' statement that 'Play has a major role in motivating children's curiosity and ensuring that they explore materials in a playful way in order to learn about properties, textures, shapes, smells, colours, feelings and so on which form these building blocks of learning.' Here, as in the last chapter, Gerardine tries very hard to follow the children's agenda and sees her role as being that of scaffolding their learning by helping them reflect on what they know and take the next step in learning and understanding.

Gerardine then analyses her observation notes in order to try and establish what the children already know, what they can do and what they are paying attention to. Those of us concerned with early learning know how important it is to identify what the child can do and use this as the basis for planning.

Finally Gerardine charts the play process she observed, noticing that:

- First, the children explored the objects, using every means available to them as they tried to answer the implicit questions 'What is this thing?', 'What does it do?' This is what Corinne Hutt called *epistemic play*.
- The children then moved on to discovering what they could do with the objects. This is Hutt's '*ludic play*'. As children do this they bring together all they have already learned and play becomes an integrating mechanism.

Willy (3 years, 11 months) picks up two magnets. He begins to push them together and pull them apart. 'Look what it can do!' He continues pulling them apart and watching as they come together again.

Damian (4 years, 3 months), who is standing watching picks up the magnets when Willy puts them down. He puts them together and puts them up to his eyes. 'I'm making swimming goggles.' He then stands them together on their poles. 'Look, a bridge!'

Damian now puts the magnets on the table. They attract. He then picks up one of the magnets and a wooden brick. Nothing happens. He tries with the glue pot. Again, nothing happens. 'It won't stick to the brick or the glass, but it sticks to the paper clip.'

I then asked, 'I wonder why?'

Damian tries the sponge and then the metal sharpener. As the sharpener moves across the table towards the magnet Damian begins to laugh. 'That shoots down, look!'

He picks up the spoon. 'Yeah, a spoon'll stick and a knife. Both do stick to the magnet. It's a bit of a funny trick.'

I then said, 'Some things did stick, but some didn't.'

Damian said, 'Let's put them in a pile.' He begins to put the metal things back on the tray. Ollie (3 years, 10 months), who has been watching from across the room comes over. He asks, 'Do hands stick?' He picks up one of the magnets and holds it against the palm of his hand.

Damian responds, 'No.'

'Why?' asks Ollie.

'Because it hasn't got the thing – the magnet thing.'

I repeat his response, 'The magnet thing?' Damian goes on, 'The bit that sticks.' Damian and Ollie begin to go around the classroom trying the magnets against the different surfaces – e.g. the wall, the wooden shelves, the books.

Damian says, excitedly, 'It sticks on the radiator.'

The boys return to the table and try the magnet on the surface of the table. Ollie says, 'Not on the table.'

Damian says, 'Magnet them all up.'

He holds the magnet over the table and watches the metal items rise up. He shouts to me, 'Gerardine, look!'

I say, 'Some things are still on the table.'

'They haven't got the right things in them, the right bits and bobs. Look, look!'

The metal sharpener attracts the paper clips. Willy, who has been watching Damian from the book corner, now returns to the table. He tries the wall nut, the glass pot and the knife. He then goes straight to the radiator. He returns to the table and waves the magnet over the paper clips and says, 'Every time I try to take them off they come back on again.'

Willy begins to sort all the things which are attracted to the magnet. He lines them up in a straight row and puts all the remaining objects back on the tray. He then stands one of the magnets on its pole. The metal items move towards the magnet. He says, 'It's a river going under a bridge.'

Meanwhile Emma (4 years, 7 months) picks up the other magnet and waves it over the table. She giggles as it collects the paper clips.

I say, 'I wonder why they stick.'

Emma points to the poles and says, 'This bit.'

I ask, 'What's so special about that bit?'

She replies, 'Well, it sticks and it's a magnet bit. I'm going to try something magic. I'm going to try to get these bits off if I can.'

All the clips have stuck together. Emma begins to draw the clips to the other magnet. She then removes all the clips and begins to push the magnets together. Because the poles are racing each other it doesn't work. She says, 'This doesn't work. Feels funny when I try to put them together.'

She now spreads her arms far apart and continues to try and force the magnets together. After several more attempts she looks closely at each magnet and begins to twist them around in her hands. She pushes the magnets together and they meet. She says, 'That did it! They have to be the right way. It looks a funny shape, like a butterfly.'

COMMENTS ON THIS OBSERVATION

Each child explores and manipulates the magnets trying to make sense of them, finding out what they are about, what they do.

Willy discovers that the magnets can attract each other: 'Look what it can do.' Following this, Damian also puts them together to make goggles and then a bridge.

Through their play the children are exploring the properties of the magnets. They are engaging in epistemic play, concerned with what magnets are and what they do. Damian then discovers that the magnets attract certain objects. Following from that discovery he investigates how the magnets react to aspects of his environment – e.g. the shelves, books and radiator. He is discovering for himself what else he can do with them, building on the discoveries he has already made. In this way Damian has moved on from epistemic play to ludic play.

Each child begins by observing the magnets, looking closely at them and moving from there they begin to question both verbally, as Ollie did when he asks, 'Do hands stick?' and non-verbally, as when Damian checks it and finds the brick, the glass and the sponge are not attracted to the magnet. As a result of this Damian predicts what will stick. 'Yeah, a spoon'll stick and a knife.'

None of the children arrived at the activity knowing that magnets attract metal, but through their play they are working out the rule. Their curiosity leads them to have a go, to experiment and investigate. Emma waves the magnet over the paper clips and they rise up from the table. She then discovers that she can remove them from one magnet by using the other. However, no matter how hard she tries, the magnets repel each other. After some investigation and experimentation she realises that turning one the other way works.

Damian's investigations lead him to the realisation that, in some cases, one object attracted another – as when the paper clips stick to the knife. Damian also puts his findings to the test by discovering what happens when he tries the magnet out around the room. He alters one of the variables – i.e. if the magnet doesn't stick to the wooden shelves, will it stick to a book or to the radiator?

The children also showed an ability to communicate their findings and to verbally draw conclusions. When Ollie asks why the magnet doesn't stick to his hands, Damian explains, 'Because it hasn't got the thing – the magnet thing.' When I wonder why some things are not attracted he explains that they don't have the right 'bits and bobs'. Willy, describing his findings, says that even when he moves them, the magnet continues to attract the paper clips. Emma is very specific about what part of the magnet attracts. She points to the poles: 'Well, it sticks and it's the magnet bit.' After her attempts to match the magnets she draws the conclusion, 'They have to be the right way.'

8 'Tricks'

Maria Figueiredo

It is largely through play that young children begin to notice some of the patterns in their world. They may begin to realise that apples and oranges and pears can be grouped together as fruit, but that hard-boiled eggs, for example, although still edible, do not fit into this category. They may begin to realise that anything dropped – however heavy or light – will fall to the ground. The dawning realisation of the rule-governed nature of the physical world and of the social world is a fundamental part of early learning.

In this chapter, the author observes how six-year-old Louis played with 'mathematical tricks' in his search for pattern and rules. His previous experience and his very mature understanding of both language and mathematics are impressive, as is his perseverance. So although Louis's interest came from a formal learning situation where he was required to learn the 'times tables', this sparked an interest in him which – since it was self-chosen – he pursued with enormous enthusiasm and over a prolonged period of time.

Louis is learning the times table and his teacher taught him the 'trick' to work out when the 9 times table is correct. He found it very interesting and, as a result, was convinced that he could find other 'tricks' to work out the other tables.

All throughout the following week, holding paper, pencil and a calculator, Louis was determined to find a similar 'trick' for the other tables. From time to time he would come up to me, very excited, saying that he had found the trick, but when he started to explain it to me he began to realise that it did not work. I observed him adding, subtracting, making up new rules, checking the results in order to get his trick right. By the end of the week his enthusiasm had begun to fail.

Despite his obvious disappointment his will power helped him carry on trying. In the following week he came up to me, extremely excited, because he had finally found a 'trick' to the 5 times table. His explanation of his newly found 'trick' was accurate and clear, which showed he had worked on it a great deal.

This is how he explained it:

Louis: Imagine you are doing 5 × 4. Now 4 is an even number, so for even numbers you break them into half and then add a zero to the number. See?

He held up the paper to me so I could see his work:

$$5 \times 4 = ?$$
$$4 / 2 = 2$$
$$= 20$$

Me: (Amazed!): Well done!

Louis: Now listen carefully because the odd numbers are harder. Imagine we are doing 5 × 3: 3 is the number you are going to work on, so this time you go for the number before 3 which is 2. Then break it into half, which is 1 and add a 5 to it, which makes it 15!

In Part I we looked at children learning through play. We have seen how children, led by their insatiable curiosity about the world, use every means at their disposal to explore it, trying to discover the rules which govern it and to gain control over these. You have only to think of Louis and his mathematical tricks or of Damian and his explorations to find evidence of this.

We have touched on how important it is that children are able to build on what they already know and can do – the starting point for all development. In the activity with the magnets none of the children knew beforehand that magnets attract metal objects but they did know how to discuss, how to question, how to try things out and how to predict. The content of their learning was 'magnetism' but what they learned about problem solving, sharing ideas, listening to one another and investigation went much further than that.

We have considered what is developmentally appropriate for young children and touched on some extremely important questions, like what should young children be doing that will best ensure that they continue to be curious and active learners. We have read some examples of how adults, who are prepared to let go of their own agendas and follow those of the children, are able to help children consolidate their learning and take the next step. This involves adults paying close attention to what it is that the children are paying attention to and shifts the adult focus from any end product to the process the child is following.

We have seen in some of the observation notes how children are able to learn from each other as well as from the adults around them. Interaction is at the heart of learning, but, as Katz reminds us, interactions must be about something and ideally about something that is of interest to those involved. In all the observation notes included here you find evidence of this.

Part II
All our children

Introduction to Part II

Lilian Katz, in the opening piece of this collection, says:

> the wellbeing of our children, of each and every child, is intimately and
> inextricably linked to the wellbeing of all children.

In our nurseries and playgroups, in our crèches and daycare centres, are
children who come from a wide range of backgrounds, having a set of
diverse experiences and often speaking languages other than English. We
will encounter boys and girls, black and white children, Muslim and Jewish
children, children who may have visual impairment or speech delay, advantaged and disadvantaged children. Every setting for young children offers to
some extent this rich diversity of culture, language, class, gender and
experience.

Those working with young children are accustomed to seeing each child as
an individual. Workers in the early-years sector are used to starting from what
children already know and can do. These are fundamental principles of high
quality learning situations for young children. More than that, however, they
offer workers the very real possibility of ensuring that each child – each
individual – in the group has equal access to all the activities on offer and
to the time of the adults. If, for example, three-year-old Soraya is to be seen
as an individual, some essential things must be known about her: what
languages does she speak and understand?; what sorts of things does she
like to do at home?; what have her early experiences been like?; what objects
and activities will be familiar to her and allow her to build on what she has
already experienced? Any worker planning for Soraya's learning and development will take all this into account when planning activities that might
attract Soraya and will observe what Soraya does. In short, then, a learning
environment constructed around the perceived needs and interests of individual children is most likely to ensure that all children have equality of both
access and opportunity.

It is important, however, to remember that there are groups in society who are disadvantaged and discriminated against. Girls, children from working-class families, children speaking languages other than English; children from ethnic minority groups; children with disabilities, and so on. An awareness of how society impacts on children is important and it is important that those working with young children know that it is possible to create within the crèche or the classroom or the church hall an environment which does not promote some of the values of the wider society. Children, in the early years, learn about fairness and justice. Children who are fortunate enough to encounter a rich diversity of languages and cultures in the early years, together with adults who are prepared to address issues of fairness and justice, will find living in our linguistically and culturally diverse society easy. They will know that people are different and will respect and value difference. They will not mock the sounds of other languages nor laugh at names which are unfamiliar. They will know that it is as acceptable to eat with your fingers as with a knife and fork and will appreciate the diversity of music and images and stories. They will know that it is possible to challenge stereotypes and to insist on fairness.

Many of those working with young children have already made consider-able strides in providing what might be termed a 'multicultural' curriculum – and this is something to be applauded. Workers have gone to considerable lengths to ensure that the dressing up clothes and the artefacts and the images and the books reflect a diversity of cultures. Many workers will have considered how to ensure that they cook foods related to those eaten at home by many of the children. These aspects are important, but there is more that can – and needs to – be done if we are to create an environment which is genuinely anti-racist and anti-sexist. If three-year-old Soraya is continually mocked for not speaking English or is called names or bullied, the fact that there is an Iranian coffee-pot in the home corner will do little to help her know that she and her family and her culture are respected and valued.

In this section you will find pieces which consider how genuine equality for all children involves not only a consideration of resources and materials, but, more profoundly, a consideration of attitudes and values.

9 Supporting young children

Birgit Voss

Birgit is a nursery school teacher, working in a nursery class in inner London. She herself is bilingual and she has spent most of her working life considering the particular needs of young bilingual children and of their parents. Anyone visiting her classroom is immediately aware that this is a very mixed group of children in terms of language, culture, gender, ability and class. The resources, the activities and the images all reflect this.

In her chapter Birgit explains how she sets about planning for a new term and how, in doing this, she draws on her in-depth knowledge of the children already in the group and her developing knowledge of the children about to join the group. Her knowledge of the new children comes through a careful programme of home visits.

The writing is intensely personal and the reader gets a clear sense of the values underpinning the work of Birgit Voss and her team. The chapter highlights how a genuine celebration of linguistic and cultural diversity, together with an awareness of the knowledge, interests and needs of all children, ensure that no child is denied access to any of the activities on offer in the nursery or to the time and attention of the adults. Where planning is based on what you know and observe about the children, the learning and development of each child are promoted.

So here we are, Autumn 1994. A new term has begun and I have just finished the first week. What have we got in my class for the next four months? Who are these children that I am supposed to teach according to their needs and interests, taking into account the individual experience they bring to school? When I say 'I', of course, I don't mean 'I'. Actually, there are quite a few bodies involved in the 'delivery of the curriculum, providing a safe, happy and stimulating environment for all our pupils' (OFSTED). There is Jean, the Nursery Nurse, two Primary Helpers, who cover for our breaks. There is the lunchtime helper, our Section 11 teacher. (Unfortunately we only enjoy her company for one term. Next term she will take our transferring children up to the summer reception class which now starts after Christmas.) There is also my co-teacher who takes the class one day a week – I only work four days. The headteacher comes to read a story once a week and we always have a number of students/visitors. Therefore 'I' am the leading member of quite a large team which is trying to deliver our Early Years Curriculum.

We all have different viewpoints, different strengths and values, different levels of awareness, different educational backgrounds (and different salaries!). Our teaching staff is entirely female, which most certainly has a limiting effect on some of our pupils, since we are able to offer no male role models. In 1982 in inner London there were twelve male nursery teachers out of a total of 600. We may express our aims differently. I might say, 'I try to ensure that each child has equal access to all areas of the curriculum. I know the forces and pressures of racism, sexism, class bias, able bodyism, ageism – and possibly other oppressive systems based on prejudice – might have a negative effect on our pupils' learning and well-being and may hold them back from fulfilling their whole potential.'

Jean, on hearing this would probably look to the heavens and, with a sigh of exasperation, say, 'Oh, Be, what does that mean? Such jargon! How can our parents understand that? Can't we talk proper English with one another?' She has a point, of course, but Germans like me simply like to make long sentences! And the whole team would certainly agree that we all want our pupils to be happy.

So what have we got then, this term, and how can we ensure that they are all happily learning?

For the first two weeks of term we have only the eighteen children who were part-time last term. Twelve stay for lunch, six go home and return afterwards. We have facilities to ensure a high quality lunchtime for twelve children only. Six children sit with a member of the team at each of the two tables and lunch is, of course, not simply about food intake. All areas of the curriculum can be covered in that one hour. It is often the right time for 'intimate' conversations and children have shared many family secrets and things that troubled them during lunch.

We already know these eighteen children quite well. Four girls and fourteen boys. Why do I get a slight sinking feeling looking at this distribution? Help! So many boys, such imbalance! Is this my sexism speaking? My fear of the many Batmans and Captain Scarletts trying to kill each other constantly, brandishing swords and pointing guns made from anything at all – sticklebricks, pencils, blocks, straws – noisy behaviour, looking so much more competitive and combative? Looking more closely I reassure myself that some of these fourteen boys actually don't like rough and tumble noisy play. It is more natural to them to do things quietly and gently. So there is some hope. And one of the girls has to be watched; she can be quite spiteful and vicious to others. Still, there is a better class dynamic when the boy/girl ratio is more even. It will get slightly better when our part-timers join us. Then we will have thirty-three children in all, more boys than girls, sixteen bilinguals (five at the beginning stages of English), one boy with speech problems, another with behaviour that borders on autism. I wonder if we should get the Educational Psychologist in to observe him?

Even though we know some of these children very well already, it is always surprising how one's expectations have to be adapted. Young children change at a fantastic rate and they often behave very differently when they start coming full-time. I consider it one of the beauties of our work: it's always full of surprises! The long summer holiday emphasises the changes. Some of our pupils have changed in appearance – different hair, grown taller, use words with greater sophistication, grown more confident. Some have become more attached to their parents and a previously happily settled boy is showing unexpected depths of rage, anger and upset at his mother's leaving. He is also using English now as though it was his first language (which is, in fact, Urdu). Yet another little girl who simply couldn't settle last term and whose piercing howls disrupted school life for weeks now smiles sweetly at her dad and with excited chatter in Bengali takes her leave from him. She takes Jean's hand, looks at her with big, trusting eyes, smiles again, gets a little cuddle and I am amazed once again. No tears at all? Yes, it's possible. Even the children we think we know very well we have to observe carefully again, make our mental notes about their progress and changes and, at the end of the day, when the last child has finally gone (usually picked up late), Jean and I swop our notes. At this stage we only record our observations verbally. Later on, when we have collected more data we will commit something to paper. Each child has a record where we enter relevant changes and collect samples of work.

This record is usually started at the home visit. It is an adapted version of the Primary Learning Record (used by the other classes in our school) and parents help me to fill in the first page. It is our policy that each child gets this opportunity to meet me in the safety of her/his home environment. Last term, because of our continuous cuts in funding, the headteacher had to cover for my visits – an indication of how important we think this first home school link is. This term the Section 11 teacher will cover for my visits.

I usually take a puzzle, a book, some drawing material and a photo book with pictures of the team, the school, our class and the children at work. We look through this book together, often with grandparents, aunts and uncles, as well as parents and the child and siblings. I chat a bit about the kind of things children can do in our class. The pictures speak for themselves when I am unable to communicate in the family's language. That, and a great deal of body language, smiles, gestures usually get the message across.

During the visit, I also take some photographs of the child. They are used later when the child comes to school to mark her/his space on the coat hooks, the towel hook and the third, whole body one, for the magnet board. The home visit is a good opportunity to ask the parents to write their child's name in the family's language. I usually let them write it into the record. From there I can enlarge it on the photocopier at school and use it in our graphics area and anywhere else where the child's name appears in English. A very easy way to get dual language writing samples!

When these children join us (we admit one per session for about two weeks, starting during the third week of term) the often painful process of separation is facilitated by having met me and having talked about the visit with the parents.

Naturally we do encourage parents to stay with their child as long as we think necessary.

From my home visits I know that some of the bilingual children joining us are very much at the beginning stages of learning English. I make a note of the different languages our little community will be using for the next four months: Gujerati, Bengali, Turkish, Urdu, Cantonese, Persian, Arabic, German and, of course, English. I check these against our present resources. We have cassette and video story tapes in all the languages but Cantonese. We have plenty of writing samples, newspapers and magazines in Chinese as we had some Chinese-speaking children earlier. When we celebrated Chinese New Year – the Year of the Dog – we stocked up during a visit to the local Chinese supermarket. We also have appropriate clothes, fabrics and homebase equipment – and lots of pictures. The parents seemed very open, friendly and cooperative during the home visit. I am sure they would love to make some story tapes, maybe some songs for us – something to organise.

For the other bilingual children we probably, at this stage, do not need to prepare anything different from what we normally offer. The way children learn in our class by firsthand experience, building on and extending what they already know, is ideally suited to acquiring another language. Children are encouraged to collaborate with each other and research has shown that bilingual children working and learning with their English-speaking peers get to know English very fast. We provide many opportunities for rehearsal and repetition of natural language patterns and, of course, we have many stories with additional visual support (things like story props, either two- or three-dimensional). The team is aware that often children in the beginning stages of learning English go through the 'silent period'. This is a time when data is collected and processed. They need to listen, observe and feel confident before they dare to utter the first English word. Bombarding them with direct questions, insisting on a response can be very intimidating during this time. How often do we teach by asking questions? Even I, who through my own experiences am very aware of this silent period phenomenon (I didn't dare speak an English word for nearly a whole year when I first came to this country!), catch myself asking silly questions, but having done so also provide the answer and do not expect it from the child. There are many opportunities in a busy nursery classroom in which spoken English is not a requirement for participation in an activity.

For example, there is the use of the magnet board. This is used for story props but also the photo cutouts and names. The photo cutouts consist of a full-length portrait of the child, cut out and covered in clear, self-adhesive film. A bit of magnetic tape is stuck to the back which then sticks the picture onto anything metal. Often children, in groups or alone, arrange and re-arrange these figures, inventing their own stories or re-enacting familiar ones. They also get arranged according to friendship patterns. Occasionally one 'disappears' under the carpet or attempts are made to bite somebody's head off. I much prefer this aggression to be played out on the symbolic level than on the real person. A photo can be replaced!

The photo cutouts have the potential to reflect the whole class community, big and small, staff and pupils, all have their miniature reflections there. Like the mirrors we also have in our classroom, they confirm immediately that everybody has their place in our class – everybody belongs. One's image is present, reflected and valued. This is part of our ethos. We try to represent in the classroom, through pictures, fabric, imaginative play materials, puzzles, dolls and books, all our children's and staff's different cultures. We have a number of small saris, Chinese jackets, chopsticks. We have photos of daddies changing nappies and bottle-feeding babies. There are pictures of women car mechanics, a woman 'milkman', Indian women washing their clothes in the river. (Our reception classes and our class have chosen the topic 'water' to work through until half-term. In our school we plan together in year groups.) There are pictures of African women carrying babies on their backs and water/food on their heads. We have photos of male and female fire fighters on the wall, etc. The most important resource is, however, the children and their work. They provide endless opportunities for extension and reflection. I use photography a great deal, despite the lack of money. School cannot pay for this expense any more, so now the cost is covered by the class fund – i.e. parental support. Each child has three places, as a rule, where their photo is displayed (as explained earlier). Additionally I have illustrated many daily routines and sequenced activities. (E.g. We put put out our toothbrush, go to the loo, wash our hands and sit down. This also has a little song.) Things like fingerpainting, cooking, being outside, working in the garden, playing with water, looking after babies – anything at all can be extended further by making a little book, keeping it as a record. This is a valuable way of introducing literacy in a relevant, meaningful context.

The needs of bilingual children and beginner readers are similar, when it comes to book making. Both groups benefit from repetitive language patterns, easy and clear texts in different contexts with obvious clues to meaning. We have many, many photo books with very simple texts or captions. With some help from the parents these can easily become dual-text books.

A further check through my records on newcomers reveals another gap in our resources. A little boy will join us whose family consists of two mothers and a brother. We have nothing at all to reflect homosexual relationships in our class.

How can I validate his experience? And will I break some sort of law if I do so? Well, if I do then good teaching is probably illegal. And I do think that homophobia is one of 'the other oppressive systems based on prejudices which might have a negative influence on our pupils' learning and wellbeing and hold them back from fulfilling their whole potential'. Luckily I noticed that Letterbox Library have a book among their stock list which depicts a lesbian relationship. It's called *Ash's Mums* for £3.99. I am sure we can afford that and I will order it, although I do not know what it will be like. I do, however, trust Letterbox Library's judgement. Their books are carefully selected and screened. When this little boy and his mums come to our school they will find this book prominently displayed on the shelves and they can feel accepted and at home. I am looking forward to this term. It feels like it might be very stimulating and exciting. I just hope that I can stand the pace. Luckily we will be able to do a great deal more, thanks to the input of our Section 11 teacher. She has already made us a number frieze in Urdu, Bengali, Cantonese and English, using photographs of the children. And we are planning little outings with small groups and turn-taking games. We will be able to give more individual attention when listening to story tapes, and, having additional staff, we might try exciting recipes (maybe something Chinese or Indian) for our cooking session. We will be able to shop for the ingredients with the children beforehand – very good!

If we are even more lucky, perhaps the Turkish/Bengali mother–tongue teachers (appointed by our Education authority) will be allocated to our school and work with us for a few sessions. Grateful for little crumbs we have to be nowadays. In Sweden it is a child's statutory right to be taught in her/his mother tongue. Would that be too expensive? My guess is that it would cost half of what the Government has recently spent in all, introducing and changing the National Curriculum.

It is useful to learn a few words – maybe greetings – in all the languages of the children. We have these written up in the book corner and send the children home with a greeting in their home language. The Language Census of 1986 revealed that, in London schools, 172 different languages were spoken. That means that one quarter of all pupils have a home language other than English. The most frequently spoken language in 1987 was Bengali, followed by Turkish, Chinese, Gujerati, Urdu, Spanish, Punjabi, Arabic, Greek, French, Yoruba, Portuguese, Italian and Vietnamese. Under the Inner London Education authority this diversity was recognised and provision was made for it. For two years I worked for a team which specialised in making people working with young children aware of the needs of bilingual pupils. Many new resources were created by this team and we worked out a set of beliefs that guided our work. These beliefs, quoted by Liz Finkelstein in an article called 'Some Children in my Nursery Don't Speak English' (1990) still hold true today:

1   Language issues must be tackled in the context of equality of opportunity and with particular reference to issues of race, gender and class.
2   Bilingualism is a positive asset, an important resource that nursery staff should recognise, value and build on in the classroom.
3   It is essential for nursery staff to create an environment where children's diverse cultural experiences are recognised and shared in a positive way.
4   Parents have a vital role to play in their children's education both at home and at school. Their understanding of issues such as bilingualism, cultural diversity and racism can help to broaden the experience of everyone in the nursery.
5   The learning of English as a second language can be supported by:

   • bilingual children working and learning with their English-speaking peers;
   • providing additional visual support;
   • providing opportunities for rehearsal/repetition of natural language patterns;
   • encouraging continued development of the home language;

- creating opportunities for informal interaction between adults and children and making maximum use of any opportunities that arise, and;
- creating opportunities in which spoken English is not a requirement for participation in an activity.

6   Children should not be withdrawn from the usual nursery activities for ESL work as this can:

- deprive the children of a familiar supportive learning context where there are natural models of English, and;
- create divisions and resentment between children and pass on negative messages about the place of bilingualism in this society.

7   The cognitive development and linguistic development of children are closely linked and this needs to be considered when organising resources and activities both in children's home language(s) and in English.

(*Primary Teaching Studies*, volume 5, no 2, February 1990)

The kind of teaching which benefits bilingual children is good teaching which actually benefits *all* children.

10 Towards anti-racism

Food for thought

Angela Tacagni

Angela Tacagni is a nursery nurse working in the reception class of a multi-ethnic, multicultural inner city school. In her writing, as a student on the Early Childhood Studies Scheme, Angela explains a small piece of research she carried out in her classroom where she introduced a topic on food and tried to ensure that the way in which she introduced and supported the topic moved away from previous monocultural approaches. You will see that she is influenced by the work of Iram Siraj-Blatchford (1994) and of Stuart Hall (1985) and that she understands that providing a learning environment which genuinely allows all children the same opportunities means more than offering some token resources.

As you read through her work pay attention to what she says about why she selected 'food' as a topic and how she used parents as a resource. Consider how she came to understand that racism, in many societies, is deeply embedded and profoundly institutionalised.

My research was carried out in a reception class in a multi-ethnic inner London school. There are nine different cultural groups represented in my classroom. The languages spoken include Lingala, Tigrinian, Somali, Vietnamese, Cantonese, Bengali, Tamil and English. The curriculum is planned around half-termly set topics. During my research the children are in their first term in mainstream school and the topic is food. Having taught this topic before from a largely monocultural perspective, my aim was to redress this balance and provide the children with a more representative curriculum. Due to inequalities deeply embedded in our education system and society as a whole, I felt it was necessary to take an anti-racist approach and to consciously work to ensure that the topic was relevant to and representative of all the children in my class. When planning my topic I used a check list devised by Iram Siraj-Blatchford (1994) which suggested features of an anti-racist curriculum.

My first concern was to find appropriate resources and examples from a range of cultures over and above the everyday multicultural toys, posters, etc.

> In order to promote anti-racist values children need to be surrounded by the beauty from a variety of cultural contexts and everyday artefacts which encourage and promote cultural diversity and challenge stereotypes.
>
> (Siraj-Blatchford, 1994)

Children need to see their own lives reflected in order to develop a positive image of themselves and of other cultures. As Stuart Hall explains:

> We have to know who we are before we can know who other people are.
>
> (Hall, 1985)

Resources are needed to promote self-awareness and identity. Children will gain messages about cultural superiority and take on negative stereotypes if there is no opportunity to see how all children and families live their everyday lives.

Multicultural books and artefacts ordered from our Local Authority Library Service proved to be an important part of the topic. The various cooking and eating implements were unpacked as a class activity and we shared our knowledge and ideas about their uses. This put the children from minority ethnic groups in an unusual position of power as they were able to share their knowledge with us. They were also able to see their home culture reflected in the curriculum. For example, two Chinese children were able to identify the small noodle steamer. George (aged 4) explained, 'My granny has that. I ate from it.' Steven (also aged 4) continued, 'It's for cooking food. You put meat and things in it.'

The books and artefacts were used throughout the topic and were readily available to the children. This gave them the opportunity to explore their own cultural identity and to share their experiences with the rest of the class. At the end of one morning session, Shukri, a four-year-old Somali girl, put the wooden bowl on her head and walked around the room. I questioned her and she explained that her mother had told her that this was how you carried water. From that moment, the wooden bowl became one of the most popular resources in the classroom and children could often be seen carrying it on their heads. I was able to use the children's interests in planning and to extend their learning. Shukri's example prompted me to find books and posters giving further illustrations of the various ways in which people carry water and food. Both fact and fiction books are very important learning resources and have a vital role to play in an anti-racist cur-riculum. It is essential that they are checked to make sure that they show positive images and relate to the cultural identity of the children. Using the school library and staff room, the local libraries and our Local Authority Library Service, I was able to find a wide range of books which were an invaluable resource during our topic.

Learning experiences must be meaningful to the children and must be drawn from a diversity of cultural experiences.

> If the classroom resources and curriculum reflect the children's lives they will
> be more likely to want to engage in and learn from the activities we provide.
>
> (Siraj-Blatchford, 1994)

When learning about milk we came across a drawing in a Somali book showing a
man milking a camel. Ahmed Wali, a Somali refugee child, wanted to share a
Somali rhyme that he knew about a camel and later he spoke to me about leaving
Somalia and coming to live in this country. Ahmed Wali and the other Somali
children in the class taught us all the rhyme about the camel and we shared it with
other classes. He also corrected some of the children's ideas about the colour of
camels. He insisted that a camel was brown, like my watch strap. This was important in promoting his self-identity and that of the other Somali children.

One of the values of a topic on food is in its universality and deep cultural
significance. However, lunchtime at school presented a largely Western perspective
on food and on eating. This made it more important to draw on the children's
experiences and to represent their cultural traditions.

> Racism is as much a structured absence, a not speaking about things, an
> incapacity to see black experience.
>
> (Hall, 1985)

One of my aims was to cook and eat food from a variety of cultural traditions.
Concrete knowledge about each child's experience was essential as a starting point
in order to avoid making false assumptions. I asked parents about their traditional
foods and whether they cooked and ate traditionally at home. I explained about
our topic and invited parents in to cook. Involving parents and community groups
in visiting, talking and working with the children is an important feature of an anti-
racist curriculum.

The cooking and eating experiences proved to be very valuable in a number of
ways. First, the minority ethnic children felt proud to model for us and show us
how to eat. This had a positive effect on their self-esteem as they realised that
everyone approved of and valued their way of eating. For example, the Chinese
children in my class were not happy about the idea of using chopsticks and did not
use them at home, although their parents did. When we came to eat together, the
majority of the children were keen to use chopsticks. Seeing that their home
culture was accepted by their peers, the Chinese children became enthusiastic to
join in and to show everyone how to use chopsticks properly. They felt a great
sense of achievement when they were successful.

A similar example can be seen with Shewitom, a five-year-old Ethiopian girl. Her
mother explained that she did not like the traditional food that was cooked at
home, but wanted to eat food like that she had at school. Her mother came in to
cook and we all shared traditional Ethiopian food. Shewitom was very proud to
show us how to use the pancake to pick up the vegetables. The majority of the
children enjoyed the food and the Somali children explained that it was like the
food they ate at home and that they, too, ate using their hands. Shewitom experi-

enced a sense of acceptance of her traditional food and its way of eating. This acceptance is very important to children.

An anti-racist curriculum should offer opportunities for children to explore that no culture, language or religion is superior to any other. This meant that it was important to create a multilingual environment where children felt confident to use their home language. If children receive negative messages about their home language this will lead to a poor self-image and negative feelings towards their family background. When looking at different foods and during cooking and eating, I encouraged the children to use their home languages. At first some children were not confident to share their home language, but, as this became part of everyday practice, it became a natural and enjoyable experience. As well as encouraging the use of spoken language I wanted to create a language-rich environment with bilingual signs and scripts. The Cantonese and Bengali Community Language Teachers, parents and brothers and sisters proved to be a valuable resource. For example, I asked Shewitom's mother to write down the name of the food that she had cooked for us. She explained that Tigrinian script was different from English and she wrote the word phonetically. The next day she brought in a magazine and a scroll depicting the Tigrinian alphabet and she explained that Shewitom was able to write her name in Tigrinian. Shewitom and her mother were happy to share a part of their background when an atmosphere valuing multilingualism was created. Although this action research was only undertaken for half a term, positive results could be seen. A teaching colleague commented on how confident and happy my class were to use their home language and how difficult he found it to encourage this. A teaching student commented on the children's confidence in using their home languages when looking at cookery books during a paired reading session.

An important part of the work involved being prepared to tackle racist incidents. It was not until the end of term that I overheard a racist remark in the creative play area involving a five-year-old child and a black doll. The child said 'Black people go in the trash,' and she tried to stuff the doll behind the cot. Failing to do this she threw it on the floor. I dealt with this incident, but was disappointed that the ethos that had been created during the topic had not had the effect of combating racism. This incident raised my awareness of the need for a whole school commitment to an anti-racist approach, with clear policies and procedures for dealing with racist incidents. We live in a racist society and, as Stuart Hall says:

> School is a formative institution. It forms black and white children. We must take this crucial opportunity to get into schools, to tackle the formation of racist attitudes and relationships, before they set in adult ways in outside society.
>
> (Hall, 1985)

REFERENCES

Hall, S. (1985) *Anti-Racism in Practice*, video, ILEA (for ACER).
Siraj-Blatchford, I. (1994) *Laying the Foundations for Racial Equality*, Trentham.

11 Raising the status of talk in the classroom

Beverley Cain

In this chapter, Beverley Cain, also a nursery nurse and a student on the Early Childhood Studies Scheme, describes the arrival of six-year-old Aykut in her class. He arrived speaking very little English and Beverley found herself having to deal with a single bilingual pupil; the attitudes of the monolingual English children, and with finding ways to help Aykut reveal all that he already knew and could do.

Beverley's approach was to try and raise the status of 'talk' in her classroom. It became a vital part of the curriculum and, thus Beverley was able to challenge the views held by the monolingual children and offer Aykut meaningful situations in which he could play and talk in his first language, Turkish, and in his emerging English.

Beverley's situation was clearly different from that of either of the previous two authors, both of whom had a rich diversity of languages and cultures in their classrooms. But she was sufficiently sensitive to believe that all the children in her class deserved equal access to the curriculum and to her time. The fact that Aykut was the only bilingual child spurred her on to find ways of building on what he already knew and could do. The end result must surely have been beneficial for all the children.

Aykut was very reluctant to speak because he knew very little English and also because he was the only bilingual child in the class. The children thought that he could not speak. He said almost nothing in their reception class which he joined in the latter half-term of the summer term, arriving in England from Turkey only a few days before. He had to spend time to listen and learn to speak the language. Mills and Mills (1993) indicate that: 'this apparent silence is a strategy which bilinguals develop to watch their peers intently and follow their behaviour'. I explained to the children that this child could speak very well in Turkish, but that he needed some help with his English. He could use some English phrases before he came into our class. He said things like 'toilet, please', 'drink water' and 'draw cat'. I had to raise the status of talk within the classroom. The children were made to view talk as valid work in all areas of the curriculum. For example, they would explain how a three-dimensional model was built using polyhedrons, identify features on a map of the playgroup and make predictions for a science experiment on heating and cooling.

A listening area was provided for meaningful talk. Sometimes the home corner was transformed into a shop, a post office, a garage or a hospital. Aykut was involved in all these activities. A quotation book was put up with pictures of people and speech bubbles. So, in the post office, for example, the post office clerk and the customer were shown; in the hospital, the doctor and patient. Sometimes the children were asked to continue conversations within the speech bubbles.

I told Aykut that if he wanted to speak in Turkish he was free to do so. The raised status of talk did help Aykut to express himself through speech. He began to show his drawings to the other children in the group. One excited child in his group ran up to me and said 'Miss, Aykut showed me his drawing and said "This is my mum".' He also wrote these letters under his picture:

ITEtcio.

Aykut used Turkish and English words when trying to talk about his work or about a book. We praised him. Adlington (1988) states that we should not wait until a bilingual child is fluent in English and can use the language skilfully before allowing them to get involved with the written form of the language. Aykut made definite progress in writing. Sometimes he would ask 'Paper, please' and point to the listening area. On receiving plain paper he would go to the listening area and copy the writing from the speech bubbles. He would ask me or the other children to read it for him. He wrote on speech bubbles which he made for himself. For example he wrote:

'I AyuT t yEGCku'

I talked to him about his pictures and bubbles. He touched the letters and said 'Aykut buy sweets.' I asked him if I could tell the children and he said yes, so I did. I learned from this piece of writing that this child's name was spelled with two dots over the 'u' which was different from how it had been written in the register. Savva (1988) states that many children, including bilingual children, use letters in their own names when they begin to explore writing.

REFERENCES

Mills, J. and Mills, R. (1993) *Bilingualism in the Primary School*, Routledge.

12 Developing an anti-racist policy

Pam Stannard

Pam Stannard, a student on the Early Childhood Studies Scheme, was working at a centre for young children in inner London when she wrote this chapter. In it she describes some of the features of the equal opportunities policy that staff at the centre wrote, as part of a process of examining their provision, their resources and, most importantly, their own attitudes. The writing of such policies have become common practices in schools and other settings. Sadly, the truth is often that the policy is written by one or two people and remains a statement on paper rather than a change in attitudes and practice.

Pam was working with young children under the age of 3 and she explains why the staff decided to choose the unusual name 'Yin Yang' for their group room. Part of her explanation relates to some of the themes already explored in this section: that all children and adults have different needs, skills and experiences and that one way of respecting this is to regard differences as being complementary and variety as offering richness.

As you read through this very brief extract, pay particular attention to the emphasis on attempting to eliminate discrimination.

On choosing a group room name, the staff wanted a name that reflected equality and independence, with the recognition that we all have different needs and skills and that sometimes we need to complement each other and enhance our chosen tasks and lifestyles. We felt that the meaning of Yin Yang reflects these ideals.

● Many Chinese believe the universe is made up of two forces:

  YIN is feminine

  YANG is masculine

● Yin and Yang are opposites that work together to create a balance. The well-being of the world, body and soul are believed to depend on this balance.

- Yang: the male cosmic element. Yang qualities are hard, left, warm. In Mandarin Chinese, Yang is the sun. Yin and Yang contain the seeds of each other.
- Yin: the female cosmic element that is opposite but complementary to Yang in Chinese dualistic philosophy. Yin characteristics are soft, right, cold, shade. In Mandarin Chinese, Yin is the moon.
- The birthday chart consists of sun shapes for boys and moon shapes for girls.

ANTI-DISCRIMINATION POLICY

The Centre is committed to the elimination of harassment, discrimination and prejudice experiences by individuals and groups within the centre on the grounds that they are women, black, Jewish, Irish or members of any other ethnic minority group, lesbian, gay or disabled. We also oppose discrimination on the basis of religious belief, class and age.

It is the responsibility of all users, centre employees and management to enforce this policy at all times and to challenge and confront discrimination.

FESTIVALS AND HISTORICAL EVENTS

Festivals are celebrated as learning activities for the whole centre. We aim to convey an awareness of, rather than a belief in, a festival whether religious, cultural or secular. Every year we review what, how and why we celebrate. This year, as well as celebrating different festivals we have decided to observe historical events i.e. the death of Martin Luther King and Nelson Mandela's release. Also, as part of our all-round awareness, we are having an International Women's Week and a Disability Awareness week.

EQUAL OPPORTUNITIES POLICY

The Centre works with an equal opportunities policy that enables all children to have equal access to activities and resources.

13 'I Know Lots Languages'

Young bilingual children and their peers

Hilary Faust and Sandra Smidt

In this chapter you will find a strong argument for good nursery practice. In other words, by starting from where children are, allowing them to pursue their own interests through play, finding out about the languages, cultures, expectations and values of their homes those working with all children – monolingual, bilingual and multilingual – will ensure that the curriculum on offer genuinely supports individual development.

Both authors were senior lecturers at the University of North London at the time of writing and both were involved in the Early Childhood Studies Scheme: Sandra Smidt as Coordinator and Hilary Faust as leader of what was known as the Nursery Certificate Course – a programme for qualified teachers wanting to specialise in working with young children. The chapter was initially conceived as a handbook for teachers and as such it is very practical in tone, offering a range of suggestions and 'tips' for those working with young bilingual or multilingual children. But it is important to realise, as you read through this, that all the tips are based on what is known about how young children learn best; about what it feels like to be the speaker of a language other than the host language and about how a second (or additional) language is most successfully achieved.

Much of the emphasis of the chapter is on ways of helping young learners acquire English. This is clearly essential for children going to school and growing up in Britain. What the chapter stresses, however, is that a second language is best acquired when a child is encouraged to use all that he or she knows in his or her first language. Giving explicit recognition and respect to all the languages of the group is vital. Moreover, acquiring a second language – like any learning – is likely to be most successful where children can build on what they already know. A child like Aykut, whom we encountered in Chapter 11, arrives at school or nursery already knowing a great deal. If he is given the message that, because he has not yet acquired English, he knows nothing, his self-esteem and his learning will be damaged.

Minh Duc is the only Vietnamese child in his crèche. All the other children were born and brought up in England.

Suzie is aware that there are fourteen languages spoken by the children in her nursery class. These include Punjabi, Gujerati, Greek, Cantonese, Russian, Tamil and Spanish.

In Rehana's playgroup, all the children, except for Michael and Kwan, come from Bangladesh and speak Sylheti.

All of these children are some of the fortunate ones in this country to benefit from nursery education. For Minh Duc, Rehana and her friends and many of the children in Suzie's class, it is vital that they learn to speak English so that they can communicate with their peers, succeed in the educational system and become equal and participant members of this community.

There is much research evidence to show that the best way for these young children to learn English is for them to maintain their first language, or mother tongue, so that they retain their own self-respect and respect for their language and culture and so that they continue to be able to communicate with their families and communities.

All of our children will grow up in a world which is increasingly multicultural and multilingual. For the monolingual English children, the experiences, in the early years, of other languages and cultures will not only better equip them to become broad and balanced people, but will provide them with experiences which will enrich and enhance their learning and development. We have only to think of how we, as adults, dream of going on holiday to faraway places, not only to enjoy a different climate and food, but also to experience something of the art, culture, history, traditions and customs of other societies. Knowledge and experience of these are an enriching experience.

In the early years young children are busily engaged in trying to make sense of the world and are acquiring skills, knowledge, feelings and dispositions which will last throughout their lives. The richer the provision, the greater the skills and sensitivity of the staff in nurseries, the greater the chance that all the children, through their play, will become effective communicators and problem solvers, able to form and maintain relationships and develop respect for other languages and cultures.

CULTURES AND CUSTOMS – WHAT WE NEED TO KNOW

There are as many variations within cultures as there are between them. It would be both simplistic and insulting to try and sum up the various cultures in our communities in a few words. We have only to ask ourselves 'What represents English culture?' to know that any simple answer like 'fish and chips' or 'the changing of the Guard' is no more than a crude stereotype. English culture, like all cultures, is complex and varied.

There are some questions we need to ask ourselves, however, which will avoid us causing offence to deeply held beliefs and centuries-long practices. The more knowledge we have about the languages and cultures of our children and their families, the greater the sensitivity to these we will show.

Artefacts

All cultures have objects and artefacts that are particular to them. These are the easiest things to find and the simplest way of demonstrating to our children and their parents that we are aware of and celebrate at least some visible and tangible aspects of their culture. Home corners can easily be equipped to reflect this by introducing things like Turkish coffee pots, Indian rugs, chapatti pans, magazines and newspapers in other languages, Chinese bowls and chopsticks, wall hangings and fabrics, and so on.

Languages

It is essential to know what languages the children and their families speak and to ensure that these languages are evident in the books, notices, labels in the class-room. In addition to this we need to know what the scripts of these languages look like and what the graphic conventions are. English is read from left to right, but Hebrew is read from right to left. Knowledge of this will enable us to better understand children's early attempts at writing.

Festivals

Christmas and Easter are not the only festivals to be celebrated in a multi-faith society. We need to know what the major festivals of our children are, when they occur and what they celebrate. Many schools now celebrate Diwali and it is important that, in celebrating festivals, we take care not to be tokenist and celebrate only the colourful and exotic aspects of the festival, but that we understand what it is that the festival represents. Local community leaders can offer advice on this to those working in nurseries.

Food

We are used to ensuring that the dietary requirements of many of our children are met by providing vegetarian meals for vegetarian children. We need to know, from parents, exactly what foods children may and may not eat. We also need to take care that we do this in a respectful manner and don't refer to 'ethnic' food.

Names

We need to learn to write and pronounce names correctly. A name is a very personal symbol of our existence and it is important that we take the trouble to learn names and not abbreviate or Anglicise them. We also need to learn about first names and surnames and ensure that we don't assume that the name written or spoken first is the first name.

Sacred/profane objects or animals

Many cultures hold certain objects or animals as sacred and these may not be used in a way which causes offence. For many Muslims, for example, the use of pigs in a story may cause offence.

Dress

Styles of dress and attitudes to things like covering the head, legs and arms need to be respected. Find out, for example, whether or not children may take off their clothes to go in the paddling pool.

WHAT PEOPLE SAY ABOUT BILINGUALISM

We often hear people say things which indicate that there are, in our society, some widely held beliefs about multilingualism which may need challenging.

'Try and speak English to her at home'

This implies that speaking the mother tongue will impair the learning of English. In fact, the opposite is true. There is now much research evidence to show that competence in one language is likely to enhance competence in another. Children who are encouraged to become fluent and/or literate in their first language develop what are called 'metalinguistic skills' – that is, they understand about language itself. They begin to understand that marks on paper are symbols, that writing may be speech written down. They begin to learn that you can decode these marks. This enables them to transfer these skills to second or subsequent languages. So young children who develop linguistic concepts in their mother tongue will easily transfer these concepts to the second language.

Research in Bradford showed that where Punjabi-speaking children in a reception class were taught half the time in English and half the time in Punjabi, not only did their Punjabi improve but so did their English. In fact the improvements were greater than in a similar group taught all the time in English.

So the message is clear. Supporting young children in speaking their mother tongue will not only allow them to feel respected and valued, but also help them acquire English. Another point worth noting is that asking parents to speak English at home where English is a second language puts parents in the position of not being able to use language as powerfully as they would if they used their first language. The quality of the communication is important and likely to be damaged if communication takes place in an unfamiliar and often stilted and limited form.

'Being bilingual means being disadvantaged'

Recent research shows that bilingual children become aware at a much earlier age of language as an abstract system. As we explained in the previous section, bilingual children begin to think about language itself and this awareness helps these children when learning other abstract and symbolic systems – for example, learning to read. Bilingual children have been shown to have greater cognitive flexibility, greater sensitivity to others and greater adeptness at creative thinking. A word of warning, however. There is still, in our society, a clear hierarchy of languages. Often we regard children who are bilingual in European languages like French or Russian as being 'clever' or 'advantaged', whereas the Sylheti bilingual child, for example, is still seen as 'needing extra help'.

'To teach bilingual children English means teaching them to know lots of words and to label things'

Many traditional approaches to teaching young children English focus on getting them to label or name objects, to recite numbers and colours or to repeat set patterns of response – for example, 'This is a green dress. This is a blue dress'. Research shows that successful learning of a second language depends largely on motivation and the need to communicate. Young bilingual children are highly motivated to learn English and they need to communicate in many different situations and with many different groups of people – teachers, nursery workers, their friends, and so on. So bilingual children need to develop a wide range of language use in order to survive in the informal contexts of the peer-group world and the more formal contexts of schooling. Evidence also shows that children learn best when they can make sense of what is on offer and don't, in fact, have it broken down into small and seemingly meaningless parts. Children learn a second language best when the focus is not on the simplified aspects of the language itself but rather when language is part of a meaningful situation. Returning to the earlier example of traditional language teaching, in everyday usage the formal full-sentence response of the type 'This is a blue dress' is rare. More often, in normal conversation, we use abbreviated colloquial forms – 'It's a blue one' or just 'Blue'. The formal structure is inferred from the context and the meaning. Teaching children to learn, parrot-fashion, certain forms of the language does not help them use the language for communication.

'Teachers and adults provide children with the only valid language models'

Peer group talk is vital to language acquisition and development. Children who have many opportunities to talk with one another in pairs or groups learn from one another and support one another. Young children are sensitive to the needs of their peers and are able to offer bilingual peers both support in acquiring and using a second language and models of how to speak everyday English. In other words, children are able to play the role of teacher through their play and interaction with their bilingual friends.

'In order to help bilingual children learn English they should be taken as a small and separate group on regular occasions, so that the teacher can give them the appropriate input and activities'

Research actually indicates that this model of teaching hinders rather than helps children learn a second language. Children are removed from peers who can provide them with models of English language use; they are placed in sometimes stressful situations where the input is likely to be about teaching simple words or phrases and they are made to feel different from their peers.

In this brief section we have referred to some common misconceptions about bilingualism and pointed to the results of some recent research. To sum up:

- All children learn best when they feel respected, confident and equal to their peers;
- All children learn best when they are interested and involved in their learning;
- All children learn from one another as well as from the adults they encounter;
- All children learn best when the learning situation makes sense to them;
- Bilingualism can help children's intellectual and cognitive progress;
- Supporting the development of the first language enhances the learning of second and subsequent languages;
- All children should be seen as individuals with individual needs;
- Good nursery practice, based on these principles, should allow bilingual children to flourish.

Some of the research evidence can be found in the references (see p. 76).

FIRST IMPRESSIONS

Welcome to our centre

For most children and their parents the nursery class will be their introduction to formal schooling. For all children and their parents the first impressions they gain and the ways in which they are welcomed, respected and consulted will form the basis of their expectations of what education will be like for them and for their children. Coming into an environment which looks cared for and attractive will immediately make people feel less anxious and, if within that environment there are objects that are recognisable, labels and explanations that are understandable, evidence that 'your' culture and language are respected and given prominence, the initial impression will be a positive one.

It helps all parents, but particularly those for whom English is not the first language, if the centre makes as explicit and understandable as possible the whole confusing world of the English education system. Simple things, like clear signs and labels for finding the way into the building: photographs to show who is who; welcome signs in parents' own languages. For many parents the first contact with the centre will be to register the child for a place. Form filling is necessary but tedious and, for many people, sometimes threatening. Centres have found some ways of making this process less difficult.

Example

One nursery school makes it known to parents in the local area through the health visitor and local clinic that each Friday, for example, is a day when prospective parents may call at the school, meet other parents, talk with the head and/or nursery teacher, be helped to fill in the registration forms and be taken round the school to get a feeling of the school in action.

Once the child has been registered and a place offered, centres can ensure that parents and children are eased into moving away from home in a number of ways. Some facilities offer parents the option of a home visit prior to the child starting. The emphasis is on meeting the child and parents and not on assessing the child's home. Some have a special social gathering where prospective parents and children are invited to meet one another and the staff and to be told something about how the centre operates, what the children do, how parents can be involved, and so on. Where there are bilingual parents, care needs to be taken to provide translators at such gatherings or to use clear visual materials like specially-made books or videos to illustrate the points being made.

Welcome to our group

In order to ease parents and children into your group you will want to:

- Ensure that the room and equipment are attractive and well cared for;
- Display a welcome sign in the languages of the children in your community;
- Display photographs of the staff with their names;
- Try and have evident some sort of easily understandable explanation of how your group works, what the children do and learn, how they learn.

Example

In one nursery class the staff have made a book of photographs illustrating what the children do – imaginative play, block play, outdoor play, and so on. The photographs are of the children in the class and next to each is a simple explanation of what the children are doing and what they are learning:

> Children playing in the home corner pretend to be different people, act out difficult situations, learn about counting and matching and use what they have already learnt at home to help them learn more at school.

- Make sure that you have a wide selection of books which reflect the languages and the cultures in the group. Display these so that it is not only the English books which are prominent.
- Try and have interpreters on hand – another parent, an older child, a member of staff;
- Try and make sure any information that goes home is available in the main languages of your class;
- Avoid tokenism and exotica. Having welcome signs and books in other languages displayed will do little unless you understand why you have them.

SETTING UP A PARTNERSHIP WITH PARENTS

It is vital that you, the adults, learn as much as possible about the children in your room and about their languages, their cultures, the expectations of their parents, and about what is acceptable in each child's home and culture. In this way you will avoid doing or saying things which may cause offence to certain people, or mis-understand things that are said or done.

- Would you read the story of the three little pigs to a group of mainly Muslim children?
- Would you ask all the children to tell about when they were christened?
- Would you offer all the children pork sausages at a party?
- Would you insist that all children took off their clothes to go in the paddling pool?

Of course, as a good early-years practitioner you will want to know as much as possible about each child in your gruop and you will find this out – most often – from the parents or carers. Take time about this information gathering. Try and do it in a quiet and private place and help the parent feel relaxed in what could be a difficult situation. Indicate to the parent that he or she is the expert about the child and invite information that only parents will have – what the child was like as a baby, what she or he likes to do at home, about siblings and grandparents, and so on. This information, recorded, provides an excellent basis on which to start building from what the child already knows (a first principle in early-years educa-tion) and to assess progress against this starting point.

Example

There are a number of 'records' devised by local authorities or individual schools which encourage this type of parent 'conference' based on the work of those who developed the Primary Language/Learning Record.

You will want to ask the parent about any special dietary requirements the child has and should try to find out as much as possible about the child's linguistic environment.

There is much research evidence to show how important a partnership with parents is in children's progress at school. Parents need to be kept informed of all that happens to their children, how they settle down, make relationships, develop and learn. You, the practitioner, need the parents to tell you about the child and her/his progress and development at home. Where school and home share a genuine concern about the child and her/his progress, this dialogue is essential.

You may also want to invite parents to come into the nursery to share their skills with you. They may be able to tell or read stories in the languages of the community or offer aspects of their own culture to be shared with all the children. Language and culture are inextricably linked and a celebration of cultures will also be a celebration of languages. If you are a monolingual teacher you will need the parents to help you promote multilingualism.

SETTLING THE CHILD IN

Starting school or nursery is a huge step in a young child's life and one that needs to be handled sensitively. How much more traumatic if no-one speaks your language, understands your needs or takes time to make you feel special.

- Don't have too many children starting at the same time. If you only have to handle one or two children you are able to devote the time to them and to their parents.
- If possible, have some older children or other adults around who speak the same languages as the child being admitted. If this is not possible, you can – through gesture, body language, physical closeness – convey to the child that you are there for her or him, to try and understand.
- If possible, have another parent, familiar with the nursery, to help the parent feel at ease – ideally someone who speaks the same language as the parent of the new child.
- Offer some soothing activities – dry sand, dough – things that are not too 'messy', which may be threatening for some children;
- Try and learn some simple words in the languages of the new children – things like 'hello', 'toilet', etc.;
- Try and think of simple things which might make the nursery feel less alien to the child;

> *Example:* A nursery class played a tape of Chinese music for a new Chinese child who was finding it difficult to settle.

- Encourage parents to stay with the child if they can. Explain to them how important this is for their child, but don't make parents feel guilty if it is impossible for them to stay.

- Do try and pronounce the child's name – however unfamiliar – properly and don't try and Anglicise or simplify the name.

PROVISION

The environment we create for our children is crucial. We have the power to provide a world which reflects only English culture and language, or one which draws on other cultures and languages, particularly those which the children bring with them. Music, books, images, artefacts, utensils and toys which reflect our multicultural society are available if we wish to provide them. A chapatti board and roller on the dough table, Chinese dishes and chopsticks in the home corner, sieves from different cultures in the sand, drums from different cultures on the music table and spoons from different cultures on the display table ensure a rich, challenging environment.

Not only are we helping children to see the similarities and differences between cultural items, as well as allowing them to explore these, we provide important links between home and school. To hear Turkish music in the nursery will help Turkish children and parents feel accepted and respected. As we have said earlier, starting school can be a very traumatic experience, especially if the sights, sounds and even the smells are new and strange. How reassuring to find a Turkish coffee pot and newspapers in the home corner.

EXPLAINING IT TO PARENTS

Some monolingual parents may feel anxious about taking their child into a nursery class which looks unfamiliar to them. They may have picked up all sorts of misinformation about how their child's culture will be 'diluted'. It is very important that the reasons for providing multicultural and multilingual classrooms are explained to parents and that they are helped to understand that the provision itself will be a learning and enriching experience for all the children. Many of their fears are not grounded in reality and most parents will respond positively if their fears are treated seriously and if they are given carefully thought-out reasons for providing nurseries that reflect the languages and cultures of our communities.

LEARNING THROUGH PLAY

As all nursery practitioners know, play is the child's best way of making sense of the world and learning about it. When the child is playing she makes the decisions, directs the proceedings and formulates the rules, alone or in cooperation with other players. Because she is in control and knows the situation isn't 'for real', there is no risk of failure or getting it wrong. She can organise the home corner, write a shopping list or tend to patients in the hospital, freed from pressure and thus often operating at a high level of competence. Because beginning to speak in a second language feels like a risky business, where children must be prepared to 'have a go', play situations are ideal since they embody this special pressure-free quality.

Children will not, however, begin to play unless they feel secure and settled. If they are anxious about Mummy coming back or frightened by alien sights, sounds or smells, they cannot relax enough to play. So the settling in process is vital for emotional, social, intellectual and linguistic development. Learning how to say 'Mummy's coming back soon', in Gujerati or Greek may make a lot of difference. When a child feels secure enough he or she will usually begin to play, either alone or in a group.

If, for example, the child is playing in the sand she will have definite intentions about what she is exploring or enacting. She may be trying to find out if dry sand can be made into sandpies like damp sand, or burying everything to pursue an interest in covering things up. She may be using the play people to re-enact a favourite story. The adult can support the child's English by observing her play, trying to ascertain what her focus is, and talking with her about it.

> 'Oh, you've buried all the people in the sand'.
> 'I can't see them.'
> 'Where are they?'
> 'Can you see them?
> 'Oh, there they are!'

The fact that language is linked to an activity on which both people are focusing, but which the child has initiated, helps her to understand the meaning of the accompanying words. Sometimes this can become naturally repetitious, which also helps.

> 'I'll pour it in.'
> 'Now you pour it in'.

If the adult sensitively tunes in to the child's purposes and intentions and the talk reflects these, it will help her to understand and even to make her own contribution to the conversation.

Of course, children playing together is an ideal way of developing English. As holidaymakers know, young children with no common language will play happily together for hours on the beach, and appear to have no difficulty communicating. The important factors are that they want to communicate, to be friends and playmates, and that they understand the situation.

Teachers should feel confident that they are not the only language models available, and that for some children it may be easier to risk a new language in play with another four-year-old than with an adult. Indeed, it seems to be the case the children can help each other very effectively.

Having strong intentions (to build a bridge, make a robot, take the telephone to pieces or dress up to go to a party) will help children to speak in English, as they need to ask for a screwdriver, or the glue or want to explain to others why they are all dressed up. And it is primarily in play that children formulate and act out their intentions.

Non-play methods of teaching are not so successful. Many of us experienced the model of teaching languages as a separate subject, when we were at school. Most of us can testify that it doesn't work very well! Had we been supported in our learning of French or German by using it as a medium to learn other things, we may have been more successful.

Withdrawing bilingual children to do language exercise (labelling pictures, etc.) may be well-intentioned, but is counter-productive. Learning language and learning in general must go together and bilingual children need to learn with their English-speaking peers. The nursery, with its range of practical activities and its opportunity for play, provides the ideal setting for children to begin gaining meanings in English and trying out a few words in their new language. And, of course, they can use their home language comfortably with other children who share it to develop concepts and extend their learning.

PLANNING TO MEET THE NEEDS OF INDIVIDUAL CHILDREN

As with all good nursery practice, it is important to plan for individual children as well as for the group as a whole. In terms of bilingual learners this might include:

- Spending time with Amit who seems very isolated.
- Encouraging Bilaal and Amit to play together since they both speak Gujerati. Both seem interested in cars, so this might be the 'breakthrough'.
- Finding out the Turkish word for 'rabbit' since Gulsun seems very interested.
- Arrange for an older Urdu-speaking child to spend time with Haresh as he seems very unsettled and anxious.
- Arrange for Andrea's mother to come in to read a story in Greek. Andrea refuses to speak Greek in the nursery, even though we have a Greek-speaking nursery nurse student. We must try to convey that it's OK.
- Abdul loves *Where the Wild Things Are* – must arrange for Shahana's dad to tape it in Bengali, also make story props.
- Amy and Sonay have become good friends and often listen to the taped stories together. See if I can get *Titch* – their favourite – in English and Turkish.
- For the first time Halina joined in 'Heads, Shoulders, Knees and Toes' – beamed! Must include it regularly.
- Hussein can't cope with group time yet. Must make sure that we read stories with him outside that situation.
- Paul and Melissa were making disparaging remarks about other languages. Will try starting group sessions with 'Hello' in different languages. Need to involve parents.
- Mohammed is doing some interesting play writing. Is this like Arabic? Must check up.
- Despite being in the nursery for two terms Halina will only whisper, and that's

not often. Must talk to mum when she comes in. I wonder how she speaks Turkish at home.

- David doesn't seem to respond when we call his name. I wonder if they call him David at home. Perhaps they use his Cantonese name. Must ask dad. Perhaps get his hearing checked.
- Bimal played with the zoo animals for ages today. Tomorrow will supply Plasticine and match sticks to extend activity, and zoo books. Maybe make English/Bengali zoo book with mum's help.

These observations of children at play can be used to help identify what the child is particularly interested in, what this reveals about the child's learning and to plan activities directly related to the child's observed interests and needs.

LEARNING ENGLISH

All our children need to become proficient speakers, readers, writers and thinkers in English if they are to succeed in our education system.

What you can do to help children learn English

1   Set up your room with activities where the meanings and intentions are clear.

Example
Cooking is a good example. Children work in a group, all of whom are familiar with the process of cooking. The language used often offers repetition by the very nature of the task – 'Pass me the spoon, please.' 'It's your turn to use the spoon.' 'Please pass me the sugar.' 'Can I use the spoon to stir in the sugar?'

Other situations that are found in real life like washing the dolls' clothes, going shopping, planting seeds, and so on offer children opportunities to be involved and hear or use English in meaningful contexts.

2   In any good nursery class there will automatically be situations where children can play and where success is not dependent on either speaking or understanding English. Of course, situations like block play and water play are rich opportunities for language development but a child who has not yet acquired English is not excluded from such activities by her inability to speak or understand the language.

3   Offer children opportunities to play turn-taking games:

> *Example*
> Any number of simple board games or card games in which children take turns, often using a simple formula like responding to a question 'Who's got the green parrot?'

4   Encourage the children to speak and sing in their first language. Remember that proficiency in this language will help them acquire English and that, by inviting them to use their home language, you are showing them respect.

5 Encourage all children to sing and chant nursery rhymes. Recent research by Bradley and Bryant has shown that both the strong rhythmic pattern and rhyme and alliteration in these traditional songs and rhymes help children to become readers. Remember that nursery rhymes occur in all languages and ensure that you provide tapes of rhymes in other languages.

6 Use photographs of the children themselves for a host of activities.

- Photographs of the children, together with their names to label their coat pegs, milk bottles, etc.
- Photographs of the children cut out and laminated, with a strip of magnetic tape or velcro on the back allow children to use these figures on the magnet of felt board to make and recreate stories about themselves and their friends.
- Photographs of the children used in books about individual children.
- Photographs of the children involved in classroom activities to make books about these activities. You can make books about 'Shobhana loves to read in the book corner'; 'The day Bilal made a fantastic tower'; 'We turned our sandpit into a building site'; 'Kostas's mum brought in the new baby'; 'We made chapattis'; 'We went to see the animals at the City Farm' and so on. These simple books, with captions, ideally in English and one of the home languages of the children, give children meaningful reading materials, provide a record of classroom activites and allow all children to see themselves and their peers reflected in a valued format.
- Simple booklets, using photographs of the routines of the day, illustrated step by step help new children settle in an adjust to the life of the nursery. You can make booklets about lunch time, washing your hands, going to the toilet, tidying up and so on.
- A lotto game made up from pictures of known adults in the school.
- Pictures of areas in the nursery, with children's cut out photos to 'place' in different areas.
- Children's photos used in nursery made versions of their favorite stories (*Where's Spot?* for example, with children under the flaps or *Mr Gumpy's Outing* with children rather than animals in the boat).
- Use photographs to support the simple themes you are involved with – photograph the children back and front to show hairstyles, photograph all the different types of bread you bake with the children, etc. Children love these games and books and enjoy talking about them.

7 Use the names of the children for a host of activities.

> *Example*
> Ensure that children's names are clearly displayed and available in different places – on the wall, on little name cards, and so on.

- Make up stories using the names of children;
- Use well-known stories and change them to incorporate the children's

names – use the children instead of the animals in *Mr Gumpy's Outing*;
change *Peace at Last* so that each child makes a noise or does something
naughty to cause the parent/teacher to cry out 'Oh no! I can't stand this!'
- Put the children's names into songs like 'Down by the river where the
  green grass grows, there sits . . . washing her clothes' or '. . . hammers
  with one hammer, one hammer . . .'

8 Tell stories and read to the children. There are so many excellent picture
   books which take the children into the meaning of the story. Use books which
   have good quality pictures, repeating sequences and rhymes in the text.
9 Encourage children to re-tell stories they have heard and to use props to help
   them.
10 Invite parents to read to their children and tell them stories at home – in their
    home language or in English or in both.
11 Ensure that, amongst the books that children can borrow from the nursery to
    take home, you have a selection of books in dual text (i.e. in English and
    another language) and in the languages spoken by the children and their
    families.
12 Use every prop you can think of to help children make meaning:

- Story props:

> *Example*
> Cut out figures of characters in the story, colour them in, laminate them
> and use them on felt boards or magnet boards. Keep the props together
> with the relevant book, in a plastic wallet or large envelope. In one
> nursery there are sometimes two packs of story props to go with each
> book – one of recognisable figures drawn by adults and the other of
> children's delightful and idiosyncratic versions.

- Puppets – glove puppets, finger puppets, puppets made by the children;
- Cut out photographs of the children themselves on magnet boards;
- Soft toys like 'Spot' or teddy bears;
- Real things like fruit and vegetables, baby things – related to the story (e.g.
  an avocado pear for *Avocado Baby*, real food for *The Elephant and the Bad
  Baby*);
- Miniature cars and animals for, for example, *Mr Gumpy's Outing*.

13 Use gesture, inflection, different voices, sound effects to bring the story alive.
14 Have a tape recorder and headphones and a selection of stories in English and
    other languages. Encourage the children to listen to these with one another.
    You can buy these packs or ask parents to read stories in their mother tongue
    into a tape recorder. Young children love to hear familiar voices on tape.
15 Make books for and with the children, about them or about the stories they
    have heard or told. Try and get someone to write these in other languages.

Make them look attractive by using a laminator and a ring binder. Use photographs of the children or their drawings.

16 Involve parents in making books for their children.

> *Example*
> In one nursery school book-making classes for parents are a regular event. Parents come in and draw pictures or use photographs and make little books about when their children were babies, about family events, special sayings, etc. But go carefully – not all parents will want to or are able to join in such classes.

17 Invite parents in to tell stories in their home languages.

18 Invite the children to act out stories, providing props to support.

> *Example*
> One nursery made a large papier mâché egg, which children were invited to stamp on when acting out 'Ah! Said Stork'.

19 Set up a graphics area. In it you would have all the writing tools and types of paper and card you can think of to encourage children to play at writing. So you would include pens and pencils, crayons, rubbers, staplers, hole punches, paper clips, envelopes, writing paper, scrap paper, little blank booklets you have made, cards, old diaries, strips of paper for lists and so on. You might even include a typewriter.

20 In your graphics area – and elsewhere – ensure that you display scripts and alphabets in other languages.

21 Try and analyse the marks children make on paper in light of what you have

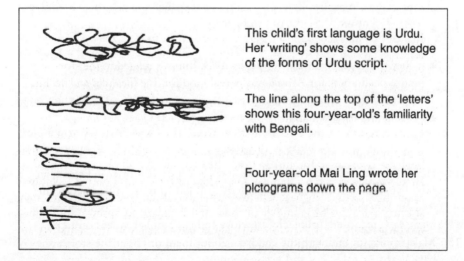

This child's first language is Urdu. Her 'writing' shows some knowledge of the forms of Urdu script.

The line along the top of the 'letters' shows this four-year-old's familiarity with Bengali.

Four-year-old Mai Ling wrote her pictograms down the page.

Figure 13.1 Early writing

learned about the language they use at home, so that you can interpret whether or not these marks are intended to be 'writing'.

Example
In the examples of writing in Figure 13.1, by nursery children, you can see how much children reflect their home languages in their early writing.

---

22   Allow children to be on the fringes of groups, watching and listening. It takes time to master a new language and comprehension comes before the willingness to expose yourself by using the language. Children need time to absorb, listen and consider before they risk speaking.

23   Think carefully about story times and how you will cater for the needs of bilingual children. Consider splitting the class up into smaller groups, but ensure that these are mixed groups of bilingual and monolingual children. Perhaps offer children a choice, telling them which books you will be reading.

24   Talk to children about language itself. Remember that metalinguistic understanding helps all children become more fluent and eventually literate, as well as helping them develop intellectually.

Example
Teacher to Kahir, age 4:

'What languages can you speak, Kahir?'
'I speak Bengali at home to my mum and my dad 'cos they speak it – and sometimes to Shahanara (sister). When I go Saturday school. I learn . . . what is it again? . . . I speak with my friends in English . . . [giggles], of course . . . except some friends like Abdul. Soraya told me numbers in Spanish. I know lots languages.'

---

25   Use and make Big Books (enlarged versions) so that you can help the children learn the conventions of print in English.

26   Remember that language learning does not take place separate from other learning. Young children do not learn in 'subjects'. Consider the language potential in every situation and activity on offer in your nursery.

27   Observe your bilingual children just as you do your monolingual children. Note what they already know and what they can do, in light of your knowledge of them and their language. Build on this.

28   Listen carefully to the errors children make. They will often tell you a great deal about how the child is progressing. Just as children, acquiring a first language, over-generalise and do things like assume that all plurals end in 's' or all past tenses in 'ed' (so they say things like 'sheeps' and 'I putted'), children acquiring a second language will over-generalise about language itself but may also use the rules of grammar of their first language to apply – sometimes inappropriately – to their second. These errors tell you that children are working incredibly hard to make sense of language.

PROVIDING MODELS

Children will develop both their first and second language if they are offered correct models in meaningful situations. Both the adults and the children in the child's life will provide these models – sometimes instinctively, but sometimes in more formal modelling situations.

In 'shared reading' or 'shared writing' situations, for example, the teacher provides a model and draws the child's attention to print as part of a meaningful situation and one which is non-threatening. A small group of children share a large format book with an adult. These books were devised to allow teachers to mimic, with a group of children, the close interaction with a book that mothers are able to provide for a child on the knee. The adult, by drawing her finger along the text, indicates to the children directionally. By drawing attention to particular words like 'Splash!' written in different script, or script that gets bigger and bigger to indicate words getting louder and louder, the adult invites children to focus more closely on the words on the page. Similarly, when an adult, with a group of children, writes out a song or story, she is showing the children how written English works.

It is important for young children to see the adults around them reading and writing for real purposes. When they see an adult writing a letter, for example, they are interested in this and play at letter writing themselves. When they see an adult silently engaged with a book with no pictures, they begin to understand that something mysterious takes place between the marks on the page and what goes on inside the adult's head. When the adult is prepared also to talk to the child about what she or he is doing, the child begins to appreciate that reading aloud and reading silently are parts of the same process.

REFERENCES

Dulay, H., Burt, M. and Krashen, S. *Language Two*, OUP, New York.
McLaughlin, B. *Second Language Acquisition in Childhood*, LEA, New Jersey.
Saunders, G. 'Bilingual Children – Guidance for the Family', *Multilingual Matters*.

14 Towards equality

Issues of gender for the early years

Penny Kenway

In this chapter Penny Kenway takes the issue of equality further as she looks at what the reality is for boys and for girls in many centres, playgroups and nurseries. She examines current research on issues of gender equality and offers practical suggestions to help workers develop an awareness of why addressing gender inequalities is important, how to question their own attitudes and how to provide an environment which 'broadens all children's horizons'. She points to the importance of continuing training and self-development and reminds us that it is our commitment, as early childhood workers, to liberating children, that is most likely to effect change.

Two small girls push their prams up the garden, chatting to one another about whether they should go to the park or the shops. Their stroll is interrupted by a small boy, who has been racing around the garden on a tractor. He now takes great delight in riding his tractor backwards and forwards across the path of the two girls. With an air of resignation, the girls ignore his behaviour, change course and carry on.

Many people who work with young children will recognise this scenario: girls choose to involve themselves in domestic role-play; boys choose bikes or something with wheels and before long start to take over the available space for play. The scenario would seem highly improbable if the sexes of the children involved were changed round.

THE PICTURE SO FAR

Yet, for almost two decades there have been workers in many early-years provisions and schools aware of and committed to counteracting sexism and the effects of traditional gender roles on children's behaviour and subsequent achievements.

Equal opportunities legislation has been in place since 1975, at least ensuring in law that males and females are not denied access to a range of services, including education and employment and that men and women should be paid equal pay for work of equal value.[1]

Since 1989 early-years groups which register under the Children Act have to show an understanding of the issues of gender, 'race', religion, and class. They must treat each child as an individual, break down stereotypes and encourage children to develop positive rather than negative attitudes to difference and diversity.

There is a large body of research which has tried to determine whether differences in aptitude, ability and behaviour between girls and boys are innate or learned.[2, 3] In other words, whether they are a result of biological differences or of sociocultural influences such as the toys children play with, what they see on television and what we say to them.

Girls' and boys' academic achievements have until recently shown consistent differences in performance. Boys' better spatial reasoning skills and mathematical ability were reflected in Maths and Science exam results at 15 and 18. But GCSE results now show girls to be equal with boys in these subjects – a result, perhaps, of the anti-sexist strategies to develop girls' confidence in these subjects, to offer positive role models and to give girls greater experience of the activities which develop mathematical and scientific skills.

Girls appear to have an early advantage in language and literacy skills, recognising more letters and numbers on average than boys on entry to formal schooling at five years. This advantage is maintained and they outperform boys in English, Languages, History and Geography at GCSE. However, while some girls are undoubtedly doing better, there are still many with low self-esteem and limited horizons. Some 86 per cent of all engineering and technology students are men, and women's average earning power is still less than two-thirds that of men. While more women combine full- or part-time work with having a family and men share some of the domestic chores, the main childcare responsibility remains with women. And meanwhile, there is now a growing proportion of disillusioned boys who underachieve academically.

THE IMPORTANCE OF GENDER EQUALITY IN THE EARLY YEARS

First, the early years are important for the development of a child's self-esteem and attitudes. Children need to be able to pursue their interests and develop their skills, secure in the knowledge that those who care for them support them in their endeavours. Traditional, stereotyped attitudes which restrict children's activities because they are considered inappropriate to the child's sex limit opportunities. (For example, by discouraging girls from physical activity such as running and climbing, we may limit their physical development.) Children learn at a young age what are appropriate activities and behaviours for girls and boys. Awareness that certain activities are not appropriate can be inhibiting and damaging to the child's self-esteem. So opportunities for them as individuals are lost. But second, they also go on to perpetuate stereotyped attitudes which restrict others around them. The strong influence of peer pressure throughout childhood can have a very limiting effect on children's actions and development. We need to help children find ways of challenging sexist attitudes and behaviour.

Third, traditional male and female roles are changing both at home and within the workplace. To meet the needs of the twenty-first century, we need to make sure we give children an opportunity to develop a broad range of skills, abilities and attitudes – those seen as essentially female as well as those seen as essentially male. Boys and girls need to have the chance to develop good communication skills, to learn to work as part of a team, to develop nurturing and caring attitudes as well as to be confident and assertive, to learn to question and take decisions.

WHAT RESEARCH TELLS US

Research studies have been inconclusive in proving that the behavioural and personality characteristics of being male or female, known as the gender roles, are innate. Although there are biological differences in anatomy, brought about by the male/female difference in chromosomes and hormones, it seems gender roles are largely influenced by cultural, societal and environmental factors. Further, just as we now understand that children are active participants in learning, so it seems reasonable to accept that children learn about gender roles through an interaction between themselves and the influences around them.[4] Parents would appear to be a major influence and research has shown that parents treat their girl and boy children differently in some ways. For example, girls are spoken to more than boys, but boys are encouraged to be independent at an earlier age.

Once children start to attend playgroup or school, they begin to influence each other. Young boys, in particular, can be quickly discouraged from playing with 'girls' toys'.

Television and advertising are potent influences, purveying strong traditional messages about appropriate behaviour and roles for girls and boys, men and women. Young children watch a lot of television and research has shown that for those children who already have traditional views of women and men, the more they watch, the more stereotyped their concepts of female and male roles become.[5]

GENDER DEVELOPMENT THEORIES

It is helpful to recognise that young children between the ages of 2 and 7 are in the process of learning about gender, in particular, about gender identity: who is female and who is male, and about gender roles: what is deemed suitable and appropriate behaviour for females and males in their society. There are several theories which attempt to explain the process.[6]

Lawrence Kohlberg's theory of cognitive development is a useful one, suggesting children learn about gender by engaging with the information around them. Kohlberg identified three distinct stages of learning about gender. Children's behaviour and attitudes are closely linked to the stage of gender development they have reached. Although the original stages have been modified, cross-cultural studies have borne out Kohlberg's findings. Children work towards the first stage of 'gender identity' between the ages of 2 and 3. They learn to label themselves and others as girl or boy, man or woman. They may frequently get this wrong or label themselves correctly one day, but change their minds the next.

During the second stage of 'gender stability', children begin to understand about the appropriate roles and behaviours of the sexes in their culture. Children are rarely told that sex is biologically determined and depends on anatomy, nor are they told that their sex cannot change although they see aspects of themselves and others which do change (for example, height or hair). They therefore often assume that clothes, hairstyle and behaviour are crucial. It is not until children are 6 or 7 and reach the stage of 'gender constancy' that their understanding of gender becomes more mature and sophisticated and they realise that sex cannot change. Some studies with children of this age show them to be least stereotyped in their attitudes. It is as if they have been freed from the concern that what they actually do may change their sex and they become more open to diversity. However, even for this age group, their beliefs are fragile and they can easily be persuaded back into traditional thinking about the roles of males and females.

As early-years workers, we can help children negotiate their way through all these stages, intervening where possible to offer children a wider range of experiences and models. And we can also help them to feel more comfortable with themselves by explaining what makes them a girl or a boy.

EQUALITY IN PRACTICE

It is important to recognise that our own attitudes and beliefs influence how easily we can accommodate children's choices and expand their opportunities in practice. Gender appropriate behaviour is deeply engrained and we may, with colleagues, need to talk about our experiences and our understanding of equality in order to be clear about how we can support and encourage children in non-stereotyped behaviour. Our own experience can also cloud our perception of what is really happening and because the children appear to be doing what is seen to be 'natural', we may fail to see that some children are not benefiting from some of the experiences we offer them.

Most practitioners genuinely believe they are providing equal opportunities. This is often interpreted as making sure all children have equal access to activities and resources. However, treating all children the same is not the same as treating all children with equal concern, nor is it meeting individual children's needs. We must take account of children's different experiences and plan appropriately for them as individuals according to their own developmental need. We must also be aware of the enormous pressures on children to conform to gender stereotyped behaviour. By the time they are 2 or 3 years old children's ability to choose freely has already been restricted by what is considered gender appropriate.

Before you can decide how to intervene to extend children's opportunities you need to be clear about what actually happens within your group. Monitoring for gender means asking questions about the different aspects which make up the early-years group.

The following are examples of the types of questions you might ask. Your answers will enable you to decide on what interventions you need to make to extend opportunities for girls and boys.

The children

- Watch individual children and note the activities they choose, those they avoid and the content of their play.
- Look also at groups of children and the ways they interact with each other. What influence do they have over one another's play choices and content? There may be some children who are allowed to cross gender boundaries and choose non-stereotyped activities. There may be others who continually limit other children, overtly making sexist remarks, 'You can't play football. You're a girl!'

Areas and activities

- Which activities appeal to girls, to boys or to both? You may find girls are reluctant to choose science or technology-based activities. You may find boys rarely play in the home corner or choose quiet table-top activities.

Materials and toys

- Do toys, books, and games include an appropriate balance of images of women and men, girls and boys, people with disabilities, minority ethnic communities, lone parents and gay and lesbian parents?
- Do books have a balance between female and male central characters? Are there both active and caring female and male characters? Do they express a full range of emotions?
- Are there differences in the way girls and boys use the toys? For example, do girls use construction materials to build houses, complete with furniture, while boys construct a wider range of models with wheels and moving parts?

The staff

- Are there both men and women, early-years workers? Do the men take responsibility for outdoor activities or the computer while the women help the children with puzzles or cooking activities?

Language

- Language is a powerful tool. Do you describe, and therefore value, similar characteristics in girls and boys differently? Are girls sensitive while boys are cry-babies? Are girls bossy while boys are born leaders? These types of remarks give children clear messages about what we think is desirable behaviour from boys and girls.

- Do you use terms like 'postman' or 'fireman'? Young children think that women are excluded from these jobs because using terms like these makes women invisible.

The environment

- Ask yourself key questions about the layout and appearance of the room. It is common to find that boys dominate the physical space, effectively limiting girls' play to small enclosed areas. What messages about male and female roles are conveyed to children through pictures and posters?

Some good practice guidelines

Be a good role model for children

You can encourage children to get involved in an area or activity by taking part yourself. Playing alongside children with clay, wet sand or mud will attract those children – usually girls – who may be reluctant to take part in messy play. Equally, your hesitation or lack of interest in particular activities will convey itself to the children. Because of their own experience, many women early-years workers lack confidence in science activities. Work towards feeling comfortable with the whole range of activities you offer to children.

Be clear about the learning outcomes from particular activities and then identify those which girls and boys miss out on

Find ways of developing new skills and concepts through familiar contexts. Some boys fail to develop early reading skills because they do not have enough experience of books and reading: by gathering together a collection of books on dinosaurs or transport, for example, you may draw boys to the book corner, encouraging an interest in books as well as the development of early reading skills. See *Girls as Constructors in the Early Years*[7] for a description of how girls were encouraged to make moving models by working from the familiar to the unfamiliar.

Reinforce non-stereotyped play and activities

If you praise a boy who plays gently with a doll or a girl who wants to kick a football, you enable them to choose more freely next time. You also send a strong message to other children that they, too, can choose beyond what is traditionally seen as appropriate for girls or boys.

Make sure you counteract sexism and intervene when children say they or someone else cannot do something because of their gender

'Girls only' or 'boys only' times are a useful strategy when one group is particularly dominant. This is often the only workable solution to ensure that girls have their turn on the bikes and wheeled vehicles or that boys have an opportunity to play in the home corner.

Expect similar standards of behaviour from girls and boys

For example, boys are often expected to be noisier. Girls are often praised as a group for their quiet behaviour. Children quickly fulfil our expectations of them so treat them as individuals.

Working with parents

It is important to work with parents on issues of equality. Work done in the nursery or school can very easily be undone by outside influences. Together, parents and practitioners make a strong team and the child's early years are crucial years for the formation of attitudes and values.

Example
A three-year-old boy is dressing up in colourful scarves and strings of beads. He puts on a hat, picks up a handbag and announces he is going to a wedding. Another father, just arrived to pick up his son, laughs and comments 'Boys don't wear those things but I must admit you make a very pretty girl.'

It is not easy to challenge parents but comments such as these are harmful. They limit children's activities and close off opportunities.

Parents need to be aware of your group's commitment to equal opportunities from the beginning when they first register their child. This can be achieved by making sure all parents receive a spoken explanation as well as a copy of the equal opportunities policy. Alongside guidelines on curriculum and how the group is run, the policy should contain practical examples of what equal opportunities in terms of gender means in practice for the children.

You need to have a good relationship with parents to talk about issues which might be contentious. Make sure parents feel welcome and supported; listen to parents' views; acknowledge their importance as their child's first educators. Most parents want the best for their child. If you are clear about learning outcomes and the reasons for gender equality in early-years groups, you will find it easier to persuade those parents who seem doubtful. For example, play helps young children to make sense of their experiences and the world around them. In the example described above the child's imaginative play helps social and emotional development.

There will always be one or two parents who perhaps hold traditional beliefs and do not share your values. It is important to respect the diversity of cultural and religious beliefs and you may find you have to compromise over certain activities. Equally though, it is important to maintain the integrity of your overall principle.

OUR COMMITMENT

The benefits of working towards gender equality with young children may take some time to be apparent. Young children can be very rigid about what girls and boys, men and women can do. But over the past twenty years, practitioners have found that interventionist strategies can work and children's attitudes do change with time.

Research in the USA has revealed the most important element which brings about change in children's attitudes is the degree of commitment and enthusiasm to gender equality from individual practitioners.[8] Our commitment to broadening all children's horizons should lead us to continually question our practice and how our own attitudes and the messages we transmit to children can have either a liberating or limiting effect on them. Our ability to develop depends too on the support we receive through staff development and training. Finally, our aim of expanding opportunities for both girls and boys fits comfortably with the theory of 'psychological androgyny', based on the work of an American psychologist, Barbara Bem.[9] Psychological androgyny is about creating a third gender role: about enabling girls and boys to develop and integrate the positive aspects of both male and female behaviour and aptitudes. The advantages for children would be their flexibility and adaptability – qualities we are told will be greatly needed in the twenty-first century – unfettered by the traditional gender roles and stereotyping which influence and inhibit us all.

Penny Kenway works for the Equality Learning Centre which is a resource, information and development centre for those working with children under the age of 8. The centre focuses on equality in practice and examines issues of culture, language, race, gender, sexual orientation, disability and children's rights. For more information on the work of the centre you can contact them at:

Equality Learning Centre
356 Holloway Road
London N7 6PA
tel: 0171 700 8127
fax: 0171 700 0099

You may also wish to join the centre and benefit from attending their seminar and lecture programmes or using their extensive library.

NOTES

1 The Sex Discrimination Act and the Equal Pay Act both originally came into effect in December 1975. The Equal Pay Act was amended in 1984.
2 For a brief overview of the research and the external influences on children, see 'Becoming who we are' in Hyder and Kenway (eds) *An Equal Future: A Guide to Anti-Sexist Practice in the Early Years*, National Early Years Network/Save the Children, 1995.
3 For a detailed discussion of the research into prenatal influences, see 'Prenatal influences', in Golombok and Fivush (eds) *Gender Development*, Cambridge University Press, 1994.
4 Ibid.
5 Durkin, Kevin, *Television Sex Roles and Children*, Open University Press, 1985.
6 Hargreaves and Colley (eds) *The Psychology of Sex Roles*, Harper and Row, 1986.
7 Ross, C. and Browne, N. *Girls as Constructors in the Early Years*, Trentham, 1993.
8 Guttentag, M. 'The social psychology of sex-role intervention', in B. Sprung (ed.) *Perspectives in Non-Sexist Early Childhood Education*, Teachers College Press, 1978.
9 Benn, J.P. 'The development of psychological androgyny: early childhood socialisation' in Sprung, op. cit.

15 Keys to the home corner

Sarah Cotter

This chapter was written by Sarah Cotter, a student on the Early Childhood Studies Scheme. She chose to observe what actually happened in the home corner and then analysed what she observed and related this to her reading. What she found will not surprise you. The home corner was used primarily by girls and only during certain times of the day.

Understanding the importance of the play that takes place in the home corner, she considered what she might do to entice the boys in and to make the home corner more generally available and inviting.

My findings showed that the time of the day the home corner was used were mid-morning and for about an hour in the afternoon. The rest of the time children were mainly involved in small world and creative activities. Very few boys played in the home corner. It was mainly girls, either playing on their own or in small groups playing 'mummies and babies'. When boys did venture into the home corner it was as individuals who might get involved in the girls' games or, more often than not, a group of three or four boys who would go in to throw things around or take things off the children who were already playing constructively.

From my observation I felt the opportunities were being offered to the girls for free flow play. As Tina Bruce (1987) says:

> Free flow play is about the way we apply and use what we have experienced and know as it becomes integrated and whole. It is the way children make sense of their learning.

What I wanted was to be able to offer the boys the chance to benefit from free flow play in this area to the same extent as the girls. While doing this I also wanted to offer girls other routes which their free flow play could lead them towards.

The resources in the home corner were the usual things – cots, cooker, sink, table, washing machine, cooking utensils, and dolls. To start with I wanted to make the home corner larger to allow the children to play independently without space restrictions. Another reason for doing this was to be able to bring in more resources which the children could relate to and give them broader opportunities to work through play. I agree with Sandip Hazareesingh (1989) who says:

> Meaningful learning can only occur if what the child brings in terms of concrete experience is seen by the teacher as the essential component of his/her planning of the curriculum and in the (resource based) organisation of the classroom environment.

My understanding of this is that the teacher must ensure that he or she represents the race, religion, language, culture and gender of all the children in the class.

To conclude this observation I would like to bring the following resources into my room: more multicultural cooking utensils; newspapers/magazines in assorted languages together with positive pictures of black families and no stereotypical images. To encourage the boys I would offer a box with assorted keys, as most children have something similar at home. My thinking behind this is it might interest the boys enough to enter the home corner and they then might find there are other things that they can relate to. It is essential to put posters up depicting equality in the areas mentioned earlier. Both boys and girls would benefit from having real food in the home corner (like cereal and raisins).

REFERENCES

Bruce, T. (1987) *Early Childhood Education*, Hodder and Stoughton.
Hazareesingh, S. (1989) *Speaking About the Past: Oral History for Key Stage One*, Trentham.

16 Sand for boys and girls

Emma Stoddart

Emma Stoddart, also a student on the Early Childhood Studies Scheme, was asked to choose an area of her room to monitor in terms of gender equality. Whereas Sarah Cotter had chosen the home corner, Emma chose the sand tray. Her findings are as unsurprising as those of Sarah Cotter. She found that boys used the sand tray more often than girls and that although all the boys played in the sand, 40 per cent of the girls in her small sample never played there. Her conclusion was that these girls were excluded and that she needed to consider what she could do to ensure that sand was accessible and inviting to all the children.

Her proposals for what she would do are interesting and involve not only considering what resources to offer, but also thinking about her role in terms of raising the status of sand play in the classroom. She also considers how to involve the parents in what she plans to do. Finally she highlights the importance of monitoring areas of provision in order to ensure that equality of access is operating throughout the learning site.

The tick list I made showed me that all of the boys used the sand tray compared with only three out of a total of five girls. It also showed that the boys used it more often than the three girls who did. Amelie and Heidi, the two girls who did not use it at all, would seem to be excluded. Therefore a gender difference showed in the children's behaviour patterns (bearing in mind the limitations of this one source of data).

Making the tick list raised my awareness of who used the sand tray, how and when and brought to my attention the fact that differences between children exist. I would like to encourage the girls to use the sand area more in their play and will try to do this by:

- Spending more time at the sand tray myself to show them that it is an area of the room I value and find interesting.

- Finding ways of involving sand in their current interests – for example, Caitlin is interested in making marks and I could offer her both wet and dry sand in which to make marks with sticks, spoons, forks and other implements. Amelie is interested in lifting objects up and watching them come down. I could show her how to use the dumper truck to lift up and put down sand.

I intend to make regular observations for the sand and other areas of the room to further my awareness of any differences occurring in children's choices of how and when they play. I'll involve the parents by letting them know what I am doing, keeping my findings in a file available for them to see, discussing the results with them and asking them for feedback and ideas.

Having just read *Untying the Apron Strings* (Browne and France 1986) I would also be interested to know whether I spend more contact time with girls/boys/younger children/older children.

This task has made me realise how important observation is as a tool to be used when working towards equal opportunities.

17 Girls as constructors

Carol Ross

In this chapter Carol Ross looks at why girls use construction toys less often and less creatively than boys. She makes some suggestions as to what those working with young children can do to redress the balance.

Carol has been working in the field of equal opportunities in education since 1982. She has been involved in research, curriculum initiatives and a range of special projects and has written a number of publications. At the time of writing, Carol was working as an Advisory Teacher for Equal Opportunities for Islington Education.

Here, she describes some research she carried out with her colleague Naima Browne into why it is that girls are often reluctant 'builders'. They examine just what it is about the process of construction that might be seen as threatening to girls and describe what they did in order to encourage the girls to take risks, to engage in open-ended activities and be prepared to both construct and dismantle.

Construction play in the early years makes a valuable contribution to the foundations of design, scientific and mathematical skills. But, observing that boys often dominate these activities, many teachers have expressed concern about the implication of girls' reluctance to engage in construction. Why do girls so often avoid this area – and how does this affect their confidence and ability? With boys still dominating higher-level courses in design and technology, mathematics and science (and with women filling a disproportionately low number of jobs related to these fields), it is important to encourage girls to become 'constructors' right from the start of their education.

With my colleague Naima Browne, I have been involved in a three-year action research project focusing on girls and construction play in early-years classrooms. We aimed to analyse the nature and level of girls' construction play and to use this analysis to develop practical classroom strategies and in-service training ideas promoting equal opportunities.

GIRL PLAY V. BOY PLAY

It is well documented that, from an early age, children identify social roles and behaviours in terms of gender (for example, when asked to draw a picture of a scientist, most children will draw a white man in a white coat). Our research strongly suggests that they also identify play activities in a gender-related way, affecting their attitudes and performance.

Our observations of early-years classrooms clearly showed girls and boys making different play choices and dominating different activities. We decided we needed to explore their perceptions. We photographed different areas and equipment in nursery and infant classrooms when not in use and used these photos to interview children about what they played with; what they believed other children played with; how they played; and what their preferences were. We were careful not to talk in terms of gender, but the children consistently identified most activities as 'belonging' to either girls or boys.

From our interviews it appeared that, when an activity was preferred by girls or by boys, over time it became the domain of one or the other. It seemed to affect the children's sense of entitlement to the activity – depending on whether it 'belonged' to girls or boys – and their willingness to play. We also noted that although children identified a lot of 'girl play' (such as making cardboard dolls' houses and sewing dolls' clothes), the confidence and skill the girls felt in these areas did not seem to transfer into construction activities.

It also emerged that much of 'girls play' is dominated by rules (such as jigsaw puzzles, skipping, domestic role-play), while many 'boys' games are open-ended (such as laying a train track, cars, bricks). We wondered if this contributes in some way to girls' reluctance to engage in construction (an open-ended activity). When children identified an activity as being played by both girls and boys, they described using it in different ways. For example, girls said that they used the Home Corner to play 'families' while boys said they used it to play 'dogs', 'cars' and action-hero games (again, showing differences in rule-bound versus open-ended play).

LEARNING FROM LEGO

To explore issues raised in interviews with the children we decided to focus on one construction activity, using a popular toy. We chose the Lego table, with teachers assigning equal numbers of girls and boys to play on it.

We noted some consistent outcomes: girls were often very reluctant to play with Lego, but would agree if an adult was present. Boys often used Lego in quite sophisticated ways, exploiting its three-dimensional properties. They worked individually, making and remaking their models.

Girls mainly used Lego for social play, making very rudimentary constructions as props for playing house. As soon as they sat down, boys would begin to separate the 'girls bits' of the Lego (windows, doors, the green base) from the 'boys bits' (joints and moveable parts). When women teachers joined the children at the Lego table, they often commented on their own lack of competence with the construction materials.

QUESTIONS TO ASK

We ended up with some very large questions which are central to the quality of children's learning experiences.

- Are girls getting fewer opportunities to develop mechanical, manipulative and spatial skills than boys, because social play influences their choice of activity and the strategies they used in those activities?
- Does feeling less entitled than boys to certain activities hold girls back in their development of skills and interest?
- To what extent is the teacher a role model in terms of gender?
- What are the educational implications of the ways girls and boys appear to use construction materials differently?
- How can girls be helped to participate and learn in construction activities which develop mechanical, manipulative and spatial skills?
- Could it be that, at some level, girls and boys are concerned with quite different learning processes – boys with doing and making and girls with social interaction?
- Does a focus on social interaction mean that girls may be more aware of how others react to them? Do they, therefore, feel a greater need to please the teacher? Does this mean they are less free to explore doing and making and more bound to produce finished products?
- Are there differences in the ways boys and girls make a task 'their own'?
- If boys are willing to take more risks in their play, what are the learning implications?
- Why might girls be worried about experimenting with new materials?
- If an activity is viewed as the girls' domain, are boys willing to experiment in that domain?
- How much does the question of 'entitlement' enter into the issue for both boys and girls?
- How transferable are skills relating to the three-dimensional activities? Does the fact that many boys may have more experience with other types of three-dimensional materials help them in these tasks?
- How do girls/boys experiment with materials? What are the apparent differences in approach? What would be the effect of extra practice for the girls?
- How do girls/boys view construction materials in terms of what can be made? Does perceiving Lego as being for making cars and so on mean that girls see these types of materials as not for them?

These questions became the basis for the next phase of our research, which was to develop ways to help improve girls' access to construction activities.

WHAT YOU CAN DO

Because construction materials are often dominated by boys, and girls may have had very little experience playing with these toys, it's essential to find ways of giving girls time and space for experimentation. We found that giving girls time on their own with construction toys gave them the message that it was an appropriate female activity. We reinforced this message by setting aside times when all activities on offer in the classroom were technology-related. We learned to remove the 'girls bits' (for example, parts that suggest making houses) and provided triggers for alternative models – such as animals, playgrounds and trolleys – that usually appealed to both girls and boys. Even given time for uninterrupted play, we realised that many girls simply didn't know how to use construction toys. We tried giving them a picture or a model to copy and found this provided an effective 'way in'. It allowed the security of a definite goal and, of course, copying itself is a familiar girls' activity. But we found that this needed to be followed up with strategies which took them further into exploring the properties and potential of the materials. To help the girls begin to 'own' and exploit construction materials, we developed an approach which began with 'safe' and familiar materials and moved gradually into situations which were less familiar and in which they had less confidence. By starting with activities where the girls were confident, competent and interested, we could introduce new concepts and materials, if we did so in small stages. For example, with one group of girls identified by their teacher as being extremely unwilling to use construction materials of any kind, we worked around invest-igating 'forces' and 'movement'. As the girls spent a lot of time in the Book Corner, we decided to start there. We read pop-up books as a way of introdu-cing the idea of three dimensions, forces and movement. Using familiar mater-ials (paper, scissors, paint, glue) we asked the girls to make their own pop-up books and cards. From there we moved on to making pop-up puppets, using junk modelling materials.

To help girls understand the principles involved and how the pop-up cards and puppets were put together, we provided samples for them to take apart. The girls were very worried about 'ruining' these things (unlike boys we have worked with, who, uninvited, will dismantle things) and we had to assure them that they would be put back together afterwards. Dismantling and reassembling created the oppor-tunity to encourage the girls to discuss how the things worked and the function of each component.

When we eventually introduced Mobilo and Rio Click, we allowed plenty of exploration time and then focused their play around looking at how the pieces could fit together and move. Again, we provided models to take apart and put back together. By the end of the sessions, the girls were making models where pieces acted upon each other to create movement and were taking apart and reassembling each other's models.

PLEASING TEACHER

Our research suggests that girls may be more concerned than boys with 'getting it right' and pleasing the teacher – and this can mean they are uncomfortable taking risks in approaching unfamiliar activities. But learning involves trial and error, and we found that the presence of an adult was often necessary to encourage girls to go further in their exploration and ease them over opting out when they lost confidence. At the same time we noted that adults would often take over when girls got stuck and that this discouraged initiative, undermined confidence and encouraged dependency.

Although girls are believed to be more fluent in their verbal ability, we found that they use language associated with technology less often and with less precision than many boys. Teachers should make a deliberate policy of using this language with girls while they play. Talking about rotation, revolving or hinging, for example, can help to clarify the processes they are using and empower girls in construction activities.

NOTE

This chapter was first published in *The Big Paper*, April 1994.

18 If I can't ask for it, I can't use it

Margaret Boyle

In this chapter Margaret Boyle, a student on the Early Childhood Studies Scheme, describes how she made a critical analysis of how the resources at her centre were stored and looked to see how this helped or hindered children's developing independence.

High quality early-years provision, based on the needs and interests of children as individuals, is – by definition – high quality provision for all children. One of the key factors underpinning high quality provision is the way in which resources are stored. In many facilities they are out of the reach of the children who are then dependent on adults to supply their every need. This makes the role of those adults that of 'organisers' and limits the time they have to interact with children more profitably. Where access to what you want or need depends on your ability to ask an adult, those children who are shy and withdrawn or those for whom English is not a first language are at a considerable disadvantage.

The majority of our toys are kept in a separate room in cupboards that are adult-oriented, with shelves at adult-height. The tiny space available in our room is space we have attempted to organise so that children can make sensible choices.

The bookshelf holder was entirely inappropriate. It was a rectangular metal frame rack, hung on the wall by twine. It stood approximately four feet (1.2 metres) from the floor. This presented many difficulties – inaccessibility, difficult for children to use independently, impossible to care for and keep tidy. It didn't encourage the children to browse, nor to respect and care for books. Happily we have since found a double-sided, freestanding wooden bookcase (which was being discarded by the roadside) and snatched it up.

The organisation of resources and their storage have wide-ranging implications. Where children cannot get the resources for themselves they are not able to make choices and, more importantly, to act on their choices. They are dependent on adults every step of the way. They even must have an adult open the door to allow them to leave the room to go to where the resources are stored! This lack of accessible resources in my centre required a lot of attention from the adults, as when they were involved in supervising children between rooms and down long corridors. Just think of how they might be making better use of time and energy elsewhere (i.e. with the children!).

Another factor involved in this poor organisation was that children were not able to follow up their choices from start to finish. Toys 'magically' appeared on tables. There was no opportunity for children to plan what to do, nor to carry out their plans. Then there was a complete lack of interest in tidy-up time, because there was no sense of continuity. The children may have believed that tidying up did not concern them as they didn't get the resources out to play with to begin with.

In analysing how our centre is organised there are some changes I would like to make:

1   I would like to change the values and priorities of staff and parents, both in the ways in which resources are used and how they are organised.
2   I would encourage changes that would allow access to resources, to encourage independence and personal choice. Children need to be able to plan, implement and evaluate their own personal agendas, not someone else's! First and foremost, I would encourage the acquisition of appropriate furniture before any more money is spent on additional toys. Second, I would add a sink to the room for messy activities and ensure that this would be at child height.
3   I would like to create defined areas. At present children don't know where to go and what to do since we are constantly changing the areas around (as in our here again/gone again home corner which children have use of only half-time, since it is shared betwen two separate rooms).
4   I would like to see a consistent flow of natural materials. It is not necessarily what resources you have, but how they are used. When the sand becomes dirty it is vital for it to be replaced. Yet because we are always worried about waste, we tend not to do this consistently. It is important to 'waste' in order for children to be able to explore properly.

The title of Part II, 'All our children', was chosen to indicate the importance of all children being genuinely offered equal access to the resources, the activities and the time and attention of the adults. Only by monitoring what is actually happening in our classes and centres and playgroups can we ensure that what we offer is evidently and always for 'all our children'.

We have looked at how important it is to monitor the resources and activities, the ways in which they are organised, who uses them and how. We have also looked at how important it is to know as much as possible about all the children in your group in order to offer activities which allow them to build on what they already know and can do. There are omissions in this section. You will have realised that there is no mention of children who have special educational needs. But, although we have paid particular attention to issues of gender, language and culture, the message we are putting across holds for all children. The best early-years practice starts with the individual child and with the practitioner developing an in-depth knowledge of that child. Knowing about each child – about his or her prior experiences, interests, the languages spoken at home, the difficulties the child has, the values and beliefs of the family – coupled with an understanding of how groups in our society are systematically disprivileged, are essential for all early-years practitioners.

Birgit Voss's overriding message (Chapter 9) still prevails:

> The kind of teaching which benefits bilingual children is good teaching which actually benefits ALL children.

Part III
Understanding children

Introduction to Part III

Everyone who works with young children spends a great deal of time observing them as they play. Often this observation is fairly casual and merely provides the observer with some amusing anecdotes about what children have said and done.

Yet the observation of children is probably the most vital tool in any practitioner's repertoire. In a programme that respects what is best about early-years education and care it is essential to start from where the child is and to plan a programme which will take each child forward in his or her learning and development. And you can only know where a child is by careful observation. noting what the child is paying attention to, what he or she is interested in and listening carefully to what the child says.

It is important to add that not recording what you see and hear carries the obvious danger that potentially significant observations will be lost. Practitioners need to devise ways of recording their observations and using these as the evidence of what children know and can do. This evidence also allows practitioners to plan what to offer next in order to meet the needs and interests which have emerged during the observation.

In Part III we turn our attention to observation and offer you both theoretical articles, like the opening piece, and observation notes made by students.

19 Observing children

Mary Jane Drummond

Part III opens with an article specially written by Mary Jane Drummond, who has written widely on aspects of early childhood education and is passionate in her belief that it is only through observation that one can know and understand what children can do and are interested in. She is an external examiner for the Early Childhood Studies Scheme and has a particular sympathy for and understanding of the learning needs of those working with young children.

Under the microscope

A four-year-old girl is looking at a collection of shells, rocks and pebbles, untidily arranged on a table with an assortment of magnifiers of different shapes and sizes. She selects one large spiral shell and examines it closely, first with the naked eye and then with some of the magnifiers. She uses the hand lenses, large and small, moving them to and fro to get the best magnification. She bends down and puts her face right up against the lens, as if she is trying to work out the best distance between her eyes, the lens and the shell. Then she puts the shell down on the table, placing it under a magnifying glass mounted on a tripod; she leans over the tripod, and looks intently at the shell, moving her head up and down, until she seems to be satisfied she has seen all there is to see. She picks up the shell again and holds it to each ear in turn. Then she puts the shell back on the table, under the tripod, and bends over it once more, laying her ear close to the lens, as if she were listening to the shell, through the magnifying glass.

This child was not alone with the shells and the lenses. Over in another part of the room, her teacher was working with a small group of her four-year-old classmates; at a table nearby the teaching assistant was reading a book with two more children. And there was an observer in the room – myself, watching her every move and making copious notes. When I saw her put the shell under the tripod and then lean down to listen to it, I nearly dropped my pen in the excitement of the moment.

Whatever was she doing? Was she ignorant? or stupid? No, neither of these. As I watched, I realised she was asking a question, not out loud, but privately, to herself. She had established that the magnifying glass made the shell look bigger; now she wanted to know 'will it make it louder?'

Isn't that an interesting question for an interested four-year-old to ask? Doesn't it show us something of how children think? Of course, four-year-olds don't know as much about the world they live in as we adults do, but look how they actively explore that world, trying to make sense of it, determined to work out how and why things happen. This young girl was, for those moments, an authentic scientist – generalising, hypothesising and experimenting. And I was lucky enough to be there to see her doing it.

This little incident took place nearly two years ago, but the memory of it is still fresh in my mind – not just because of the girl's original and spontaneous enquiry – but also because of the way in which it so beautifully illustrates everything that's important about observing children.

WATCHING CHILDREN – WHAT'S IN IT FOR US?

All adults who spend time with young children inevitably spend much of that time just watching them. We do so, in part, in the interests of their physical safety; most of us can remember hair-raising incidents when we 'only took our eyes off them for a moment' and when we looked round . . . disaster! But there's more to watching children than this.

First and foremost, when we watch young children, we can see them learning. And young children's learning is so rich, fascinating, varied, surprising, enthusiastic and energetic, that to see it taking place before one's very eyes, every day of the week, is one of the great rewards of being with young children, as educator, carer or parent. In a sense, watching children is its own justification. It opens our eyes to the astonishing capacity of young children to learn and to the crucial importance of these first few years of our children's lives. But when we watch children we do more than simply marvel at their intellectual and emotional energy; we can also learn, by watching carefully and thinking things over, to understand what we see.

Our own observations can help us understand what the great pioneers of early childhood care and education have taught us about children's learning. Our own observations can illuminate the work of psychologists, researchers and educators. As we watch and listen, their work seems less remote, academic or theoretical: the children bring it to life. As we listen to young children talking, for example, we can understand more clearly the work of Gordon Wells and the Bristol Study 'Language at Home and at School'. His important book *The Meaning Makers* (1987) describes how young children work hard, day after day, at 'making meaning', slowly piecing together their understanding of the puzzling people and things and ideas that make up the exciting world around them. Gordon Wells used expensive radio microphones, a large sample of children and a sizeable research team to collect his data; but we can learn about children's talk, about children making meaning, in a more straightforward way, simply by watching and listening

attentively. And we can learn for ourselves what Chris Athey (1990) calls children's 'schematic behaviour', and about what Margaret Donaldson (1978) calls
'disembedded thinking'. And about what John Matthews (1994) calls children's
'early mark-making' – we can learn all this, and more, simply by observing
children.

AN AUTUMN STORY

One day I was talking to a teacher who seemed to be very agitated and frustrated.
She told me about a boy of five she was working with, on a part-time basis, giving
individual support in the classroom, because the educational psychologist had
diagnosed him as having special learning difficulties. That diagnosis may or may
not have been accurate – but the teacher was certainly having teaching difficulties,
and, understandably perhaps, she was blaming the child. 'He's so ignorant', she
told me, 'so deprived and inexperienced. He doesn't know *anything*.' Thinking this
unlikely, I asked her to explain a little – what was the evidence for these alarming
charges? 'I'll give you an example,' she said. 'He doesn't even know what a conker
is!' Since this conversation took place in October, when all over the country
children's pockets were full of conkers, I found this story hard to believe and I
wanted to know how she knew her pupil didn't know what a conker was. The
teacher explained she had shown the boy a conker and asked him what it was. He
replied: 'It's an acorn.'

Now, with some genuine, first-hand evidence in front of us, we can start to
interpret and judge for ourselves. Do you agree with the teacher's verdict? Ignorant? Deprived? Inexperienced? Or do you see something else? Do you see an active
learner, an interested enquirer, a meaning-maker? Do you see a child who recognises the object the teacher shows him as the autumnal fruit of a deciduous tree,
but who has, in a moment of inattention perhaps, given it the wrong lexical label?
Just as we sometimes, inadvertently, say right when we mean left (a mistake which
can make quite a difference to a car driver in a busy city centre!)

To say 'acorn', when your teacher expects you to say conker, is evidence, as I see
it, of both knowledge and experience, combined (unluckily for the child) with
nothing more serious than a momentary lapse of memory. Had the child answered
at random, uttering words from a totally different area of his experience ('lollipop',
say, or 'fire-engine', or 'Mrs Thatcher'), we might have cause for concern. But he
didn't. In his search for the name of the object being shown to him, he went, so to
speak, to the correct filing cabinet in his mind, opened the right drawer, pulled out
the appropriate file – but handed his teacher the wrong sheet of paper.

This small incident too, like the child listening to the shell, made quite an
impression on me. It shows how easy it is, unless we guard against it, to look at
what children cannot do, instead of what they can do, at what they do not know,
instead of what they know, at what they have not learned, instead of what they are
learning at this very minute.

WHAT'S IN IT FOR THE CHILDREN?

We have seen how observing children, if we do it carefully, attentively, thoughtfully, generously, can give us insights into the richness of their learning. There are other important reasons for observing, trying to make sense of what we see: these are to do with the responsibilities of the adults who care for and educate young children. Young children's awesome capacity for learning imposes a massive responsibility on early-years educators to support, enrich and extend that learning. Everything we know about children's learning imposes on us an obligation to do whatever we can to foster and develop it: the extent to which we succeed in providing environments in which young children's learning can flourish. We cannot know if the environments we set up and the activities we provide for young children are doing what they should, unless we watch carefully, to keep track of the learning as and when it takes place.

Observing learning, getting close to children's minds and children's feelings, is part of our daily work in striving for quality. What we see, when we look closely, helps us to shape the present, the daily experiences of young children in all forms of early-years provision. The act of observation is central to the continuous process of evaluation, as we look at what we provide and ask: is it good enough?

Our careful observation of children's learning can help us make this provision better. We can use what we see to identify the strengths and weaknesses, gaps and inconsistencies, in what we provide. We can use our observations to move closer to quality provision for all children, and for individuals. We can identify significant moments in a child's learning, and we can build on what we see. If *you* had observed the child with the shell, how would you take her learning further? What would you bring in for her to explore? A stethoscope? A hearing trumpet? A megaphone? Or other kinds of magnifiers – binoculars or a telescope? Perhaps you would invite her to experiment with the enlarging button on the photocopier; or she might be intrigued by the images of shells thrown on a wall by an overhead projector – she would soon discover how to control the size of the image. Your observation would have helped you to help her – to take her one step further in her exploration of the world and how it works.

And the boy with the conker? What's the next step for him? Further observation, I think, and, preferably out of doors to start with, closer to oaks and chestnuts – and ash trees, sycamores, spindle bushes, sweet chestnuts and privet hedges. Back indoors, he may be intrigued by what's inside these fruits of the hedgerows. You can find out what interests him by watching, trying to understand what he is trying to understand. You can look back, to see what he has already learned; and then look ahead, and see the learning that is just about to take place, in the immediate future. With this understanding, you can be ready to support him and his learning: you can recognise his past achievements, and you can plan for the achievements still to come.

GETTING CLOSE TO LEARNING

The more closely we watch children, the closer we can come to their learning, their thinking, their questions, their pressing intellectual and emotional concerns.

There is a wonderful example of an educator doing just this in Tina Bruce's book, *Time for Play* (1991). A teacher notices an excited group of four-year-olds causing chaos just outside the home-corner. The noise level is unacceptably high; all the dressing up clothes are on the floor, and the children are crawling under them, over them and through them. At a moment like this, does a teacher trust children's intellectual strengths? Or call for a return to order? Can an adult believe that children are searching for meaning and understanding, when the careful order of the classroom environment has been so violently disrupted? This teacher did. In a sudden rush of faith and confidence, remembering the 'Peter Rabbit' story she had read them the day before, she realises they are burrowing. When the children confirm her insight, she finds some old sheets, bedspreads and four old clothes-horses, and, with her support, the children soon make a wonderful burrow. They are not in dreadful trouble for infringing classroom regulations: they are free to continue their imaginative play, based on the enclosing/enveloping schema that is the present centre of their interest.

A friend of mine, an infant teacher, whose classroom is a place of genuine intellectual search and discovery, talks about watching out for 'the grain of children's thinking'. All too often she says, teachers teach *across* the grain, failing to recognise the children's concerns, pressing on with their lesson plans, their aims and objectives, or the next section of their topic webs. All too rarely, she argues, do educators take the time to observe, time that will be well spent if it shows them the way that children are going; educators who get close to children's thinking in this way will be well placed to cherish and nourish that thinking. Getting close to learning, then, is a worthwhile goal for every educator; but getting close, we must never forget, does not mean taking over. If we set about doing children's thinking for them, pointing out their errors and misjudgements, showing them the proper way to do things, and telling them all the right answers to the problems they set themselves, there will be precious little left for them to do.

For example, a group of young children spent twenty-five minutes absorbed in water play. The nursery nurse had, at their request, added some blue dye to the water, and the children were intrigued by the different shades of blue they could see: paler at the shallow margin and darker at the deepest, central part of the water-tray. One child was even more interested in another, related phenomenon. He spent nearly ten minutes of this period of water play observing his own shoes and how their colour appeared to change when he looked at them, through the water and the transparent water-tray. The child seemed to be fascinated by what happened when he placed his feet in different positions; he leaned intently over the tray to see what colour his shoes appeared to be at each stage. He did not, of course, use the words 'experiment' or 'observation', but that was what he was engaged in, none the less. After each trial, he withdrew his feet into the natural light of day, as if to check that they retained their proper colour. Had the dye stayed in the water, where he'd seen it put? Or had some of it seeped out, into his shoes?

At the end of the morning session, the teacher and nursery nurse announced that it was time to tidy up. The children worked together to empty the water-tray of the sieves, funnels and beakers they had been using. They took out the jugs, the teaspoons and the ladles, emptied them and put them away. When they had nearly finished, the boy stopped and asked aloud of no-one in particular, 'How do we get the blue out?'

There is, of course, more than one way that an educator could respond to this question. But the one way that will do nothing for the child's learning, or for his understanding, is to tell him that it can't be done, or that he is wrong to even speculate about the possibility. The 'grain' of this child's thinking was running another way. Now the educator's task is not to take over, redirect his thinking, or solve his problem for him. The respectful educator, who is close to his chain of thought (following the grain of his thinking) will, rather, help him plan his next experiments, and the observations that will, finally, satisfy him, that not all changes in colour are reversible (shoes, yes, sometimes; water, sometimes, no).

CONCLUSION

Glenda Bissex is an American author and educator who, while studying for her master's degree in education, was trying to read one afternoon when her five-year-old son Paul wanted to play with her. Frustrated in his attempts to make her put down her book, Paul disappeared for a few minutes. When he returned, it was with a piece of paper on which he had printed, with rubber stamps from his printing set, the letters R U D F ('Are you deaf?') His mother was dumbstruck and, in her own words: 'Of course, I put down my book' (Bissex, 1980: 3). From that moment on she added to her academic study of the early acquisition of literacy the daily practice of observing her own son learning to read and write. Her account of what she saw is fascinating reading – not just for its entertaining title 'GNYS AT WRK' (taken from a note Paul pinned on his bedroom door at the age of five-and-a-half) – but also because of the way she uses her own, personal, first-hand observations, of her own first-born child, to throw light on young children's learning in general.

But she also takes every opportunity to raise difficult and challenging questions about the relationship between teaching and learning. There are passages in her book which make uncomfortable reading for all of us involved with young children's learning; Bissex suggests, gently, but firmly, that all too often children learn *in spite of* our attempts to educate. She emphasises, as I have tried to do throughout this chapter, the vital importance of listening, watching and waiting, if we are to have any hope of supporting and extending children's learning. In her unforgettable words:

> We speak of starting with a child 'where he is', which in one sense is not to assert an educational desideratum but an inescapable fact: there is no other

place the child can start from. There are only other places the teacher can start from.

(Bissex, 1980: 111)

Observing children is simply the very best way there is of knowing where they are, where they have been and where they will go next.

REFERENCES

Athey, C. (1990) *Extending Thought in Young Children*, Paul Chapman Publishing.
Bissex, G. (1980) *GNYS AT WRK: A Child Learns to Write and Read*, Harvard University Press.
Bruce, T. (1991) *Time for Play*, Hodder and Stoughton.
Donaldson, M. (1978) *Children's Minds*, Fontana.
Matthews, J. (1994) *Helping Children to Draw and Paint in Early Childhood*, Hodder and Stoughton.
Wells, G. (1987) *The Meaning Makers*, Hodder and Stoughton.

Mary Jane Drummond tells us that it is only by observing children that we know where they are, where they have been and where they are going. In this she builds on the work of the great pioneers of early childhood education. She reiterates what has been known, but not always acted on, for three-quarters of a century. Susan Isaacs, in the 1920s, working with children in the Maltings House School, studied children's intellectual development through her very detailed observations of young children at play. Her work has been influential on many people and set the tone for considering 'observation' as the essential tool for nursery workers.

20 Child study: Kizzy

Trish Franks

The second chapter in Part III was written by Trish Franks, a student on the Early Childhood Studies Scheme and working at the time in a centre for children under the age of 5 in inner London. As one of her assessed assignments Trish wrote a Child Study and, in the following extract, you can see how she has used her experience of observation and developed her skills of analysing her observations to allow her to arrive at some conclusion about a child. Although many childcare workers are experienced and skilled at observing children, they often find it difficult to know what to do with the information they have gained from the observation. In her analysis of Kizzy's learning Trish focuses most closely on her physical and social development. She carefully details just what conclusions she can draw from the evidence she has gained through her observations.

As you read about four-year-old Kizzy try your skills at analysing what you discover about her play and learning.

Russell and Kizzy have their own rules and each has their own individual agenda which is important if their play is to carry on. Kizzy is more prepared to give in to him and shows more sensitivity so that their play does not break down. At one point Russell moved away from Kizzy when she suggested that they do a puzzle again. 'Come on. Let's do it again,' she said. Russell moved over to the sand tray, ignoring her. She followed and quietly started to play in the sand tray alongside him. She found a conker in the sand and, taking responsibility for her own actions, placed it in the conker tray where she knew it belonged. 'Let's look for lumps,' she said. Another child, Jamie, joined them. Both Kizzy and Russell sensed that he wanted to join in, but he said nothing to indicate this. Kizzy showed sensitivity and support for Jamie when Russell told him 'You can't play' and Kizzy replied, 'Yes he can!'

Later Russell and Kizzy were placing the conkers in the sand tray. Kizzy turned to Jamie, who had now joined in. 'Good boy, Jamie. That's right. Put them there. Let's hide them.'

Here she was able to manage potential conflict between them appropriately by asserting herself. She believed she had the power to control the situation, showing respect for Jamie.

On another occasion Kizzy was returning a dinner trolley to the kitchen. She told a member of staff, 'Margaret says I've got to take the trolley back to the kitchen to get the dinner.' This tells me she can take responsibility for her actions and that her language is well developed. She is able to follow and recall instructions and communicate effectively with adults. She was able to demonstrate her physical development by opening the door to the group room using her fine motor skills. By gripping the door handle firmly she was able to manipulate it into the downward position. She then used her gross motor skills to push the door open with the weight of her body and her arm outstretched. Once the door was open she then released her grip on the handle, and began to guide the trolley through the doorway. Using her vision and mathematical judgement, she was able to negotiate the width and length of the doorway and trolley.

21 The importance of observation

Gillian Allery

You may remember having read a piece by Gillian Allery in Part I (Chapter 5) about Colin playing with a ball which represented 'his baby' and a mop bucket, which represented his pram. Through detailed and sensitive observation Gillian was able to analyse his learning and development and use this to plan his future learning.

In the third piece in this section Gillian Allery writes her thoughts about the importance of observation for her in her work.

> The key to the early childhood curriculum is to observe, support and extend.
>
> (Bruce, 1987)

Up until now I was not fully aware of the importance of observation and record keeping. Observation is the best possible way to gain knowledge about an individual child and to make this information available to staff and parents, and to enable staff to plan, support, improve and extend future learning.

> The early years educator can, through observation, identify a child's schematic interest and nourish it with worthwhile curriculum content. Matching curriculum to child can promote a child's motivation and development.
>
> (Nutbrown, 1994)

I chose Tyneesha, who was 3 years, 5 months old when I began observing her. Tyneesha was new to the nursery, so I thought it would be interesting to see how she settled in to her new environment.

When I talked to Tyneesha's mother she made it clear to me that she had realistic expectations of Tyneesha, encouraging her independence and giving her responsibility at home. Tyneesha had, at times, seemed preoccupied with dolls and the younger children in the nursery. Before going out to play she would arrange the dolls in the home corner, either in bed or sitting on the chairs. She would also frequently ask smaller children in the nursery if they were 'all right' or 'comfortable': and then make a point of telling a worker if a child needed the toilet or a nappy change. On speaking to Tyneesha's mother I was told that Tyneesha had a baby brother, who was with a childminder. Tyneesha, at home, would do everthing she could for her brother. She was encouraged to feed him and help at changing time and when Tyneesha and her mum dropped the baby off at the childminder in the morning, mum said they always made sure he was comfortable, either in his pram or in his high chair before leaving him. Tyneesha was obviously acting out the mother's role at nursery with the dolls and the younger children. This scenario made me think of **Piaget**'s theory that play is a rehearsal of skills-assimilation.

I felt that I knew Tyneesha more thoroughly as a result of my interview with the parent.

When I started my observations of Tyneesha I had the preconceived idea that she was a quiet, rather introverted child, without a great deal of confidence. A child who would follow but not lead. How wrong I was! When observing her closely I found her to be a quietly confident child. In one observation she initiated a conversation with the boys in the home corner, taking each opportunity to join in as it arose. When one of the boys dropped the cabbage on the floor she said 'You've dropped it. Shall I pick it up for you?' From there she went on to play a leading role in the organisation of dinner and ended up by telling the child to hold the baby and eat his dinner.

Tyneesha, I have learnt from observation, is extremely interested in mark making. She prefers to write words than to draw pictures. When I first noticed this I thought she was doing this perhaps as an adult-directed activity to please her mother with no purpose or meaning for herself. However, after observing her a few times, I realised it was a self-directed activity. She loves to hold a pen or pencil and make marks. She recognises words as symbols that can be shared with others.

In one observation I had intended to observe her in the book corner where she had some books on their sides, standing like tents, with Duplo people inside them. When she saw me with pen and paper, she completely changed her play. She decided writing was more interesting. She asked me to 'Show me Tyneesha.' I asked her if she wanted me to draw a picture of her. 'No, do my name,' she said. I did this for her and she took the pen and paper and, after carefully adjusting the paper, wrote it herself perfectly. She then wrote what she called the new name, which was actually 'mummy'. She was very proud of her possession and creation of the 'names'.

At one time I thought Tyneesha was showing evidence of Horizontal and Vertical Schema. She was writing marks on paper vertically and horizontally. Whilst playing with dough she rolled out two long sausages equal in length and laid one above the other in a T shape. Also I noticed that she lined the milk crates up in a long line whilst playing outdoors. However, after close observation, I realised she wasn't so much exhibiting a schema as re-creating the first letter of her name in lots of different ways. When I realised the importance of the letter T to Tyneesha, this theory was reinforced. In another piece of work she shows a number of Ts and when asked to explain this, she said it was her family and friends. She saw the letter T as a symbol and each T represented a member of her family and friends.

Observing Tyneesha closely and keeping records on her progress has allowed us to see what she can achieve unaided, what motivates her and what she enjoys doing best. From this information we can make appropriate provision with our curriculum.

REFERENCES

Ponue, T. (1987) *Early Childhood Education*, Hodder and Stoughton.
Nutbrown, C. (1994) *Threads of Thinking*, Paul Chapman Publishing.

22 Child study: John

Sue Allen

Chapter 22 was written by Sue Allen, also a student on the Early Childhood Studies Scheme. Sue studied a child with special educational needs, John, and used her skills of observation, combined with her developing theoretical knowledge, to write a Child Study. The chapter illustrates some of her findings.

I chose to observe John because I had been involved from the start in devising strategies to help with his language development. From our experience of his difficulties we have set up a language group, which has since gone on to help other children. This help is not only with their early speech, but helps them overcome shyness and improve many areas of individual development. John's keyworker was the first person to identify the concerns about his development. This concern was shared by other members of staff and the next step was to talk to his parents, who were also concerned. We believed that liaison between parent, home and nursery was very important. Not only that, parents are the best people to supply relevant knowledge about their child. Close parental involvement is listed in the Warnock Report (1978) which says that no assessment can be complete without the vital information the parent can give. When John was 18 months old, three areas of his development led to concern. His spoken language up to this point consisted of only a few sounds. He made no attempt to speak. It seemed, too, that his muscle control and coordination were not developing normally. He would run everywhere, bumping into tables, chairs and any object in his way. He would easily fall over and had very little concentration. His social development worried us. He would avoid eye contact and made no attempt to interact with staff or his peers.

We introduced John to many activities to develop his speech and language. We used large picture cards, books, puppets, songs and rhymes. Lots of one-to-one work and including John in all that was going on around him, but still leaving him time for him to explore the nursery on his own.

Over time I noticed some changes in John's learning and development. These are best highlighted with reference to weekly observation notes.

Week 5 – observation notes

John is running towards the slide. He stumbles on the first step. He calls out 'Nika, Nika,' as he moves up the steps, one at a time, holding on to the sides of the slide as he goes. John reaches the top of the slide and sits down, as he looks around the garden. John calls out to Nika. 'Nika down.' John slides down to the bottom of the slide, rolls over onto his tummy and pulls his knees up under his tummy and stands up. John looks at C and smiles as he looks in her direction. John points to the slide. 'Nika come down.' C runs over to John. He moves over to the slide steps. John looks down on the steps. He bends down onto his knee and points with his middle finger at some ants crawling on the steps. He puts his fingers onto the ants. 'No, don't do that,' C shouts at John. C pushes John's hand away. He stands up and moves up the steps to the top of the slide.

John is clearly enjoying the outside play area. His coordination and muscle control are evident as he runs and climbs the slide. He is obviously feeling very confident in every move he makes. He is interacting with C. He shows an understanding of the concepts of up and down. He is much happier now that he is able to communicate with C. The smiles and laughter between them show a contentment in John. He is able to share his curiosity about the ants with C.

Week 10 – observation notes

John is sitting at the table. He moves his chair towards the table and picks up his fork with his left hand. He points towards the bathroom with his right index finger.

John:	Gone in there.
Keyworker:	Who has gone in there, John?
John:	N gone there.
Keyworker:	N has gone to wash her hands ready for lunch. Did you wash your hands, John?
John:	Yes!
Keyworker:	Would you like some water?
John:	Yes! [He picks up his knife in his right hand]
Keyworker:	Put your knife and fork down, John. [He lays the knife and fork down on the table.] I wonder what we've got for lunch? [John looks towards the keyworker and smiles, puts his left index finger in his mouth]
John:	A! Look! [John points to the door] Dinner there.
Keyworker:	Would you like some cauliflower cheese?
John:	Yes! RaRa. [He starts humming to himself]

John is now observing his environment and what is going on around him. His understanding of words is greater than what he can actually say. The questions the keyworker asks he is able to reply to, making himself understood. He clearly enjoys the social aspects of lunchtime, socialising with his peers. I observed John over a ten-week period. By the last week of the study I was able to conclude, on the basis of my observations, that John was taking a big part in the group time. He imitated the actions to the songs, maintained eye contact and interacted with the nursery worker. He observed his environment and watched what was happening around him. His understanding of words, however, remained greater than what he could actually say.

23 'Her eyes are flashing and her ears are sore'

Making sense of life

Lynne Bennett

In this chapter, Lynne Bennett, another student on the Early Childhood Studies Scheme, observed some children at play and then tried to analyse this in terms of what the children knew and could do.

Jonathon, Alice and Daniella were playing in the house. Lynne observed all three children but focused particularly on what Daniella, aged 3 years, 3 months, was doing.

Alice (cuddling a pink toy elephant) says, 'This is a sad elephant because its grandma has died. She was getting old.'

Jonathon is cuddling a fluffy yellow duck. He says, 'This is lovely and soft. I'm Batman and I'm going shopping.'

Daniella comes into the house, holding a shopping basket and doll and says, 'Big sister is going shopping and you look after the baby please.' She puts the doll on the sofa and says, 'She is very sick. Put her there [points to a cushion on sofa] and take her hat off. Her eyes are flashing and her ears are sore.' She puts a spoon in the doll's ear and makes the noise 'sloosh, sloosh' and says, 'Now, that's better.' Stands back and looks at the doll and smiles.

Natasha comes over and sits down on a seat in the home corner. Daniella moves behind her and starts to comb her hair – without asking Natasha.

Daniella says, 'What did you mum say the last time you had your hair combed like that? Did she think it was lovely?'

Natasha replies, 'Well, Stephanie is the dentist and she is going to look at my teeth.' (The dentist had visited us recently.)

Daniella moves over to Alice to give her some medicine and then brush her hair. She says, 'I'm the hairdresser.'

Natasha says, 'I'm going to the ball and I will dance. I don't need anybody – I can dance on my own.'

Daniella has taken a spoon again. She pretends to use the spoon as a torch to look into Alice's eyes. She tells her to blink. Then she says, 'I'm the mummy and I'm off to work. You're the daughter' (points to Natasha). She takes the telephone and lifts the receiver and says, 'Hello, are you a good girl?'

Natasha lifts the receiver of the other telephone and says, 'Yes, mummy. Bring me some crisps home.'

COMMENTS ON THIS OBSERVATION

Daniella is aware of different types of sickness and how sick people are treated. She is assertive in using others in her play. The 'sloosh' sound may suggest she has had her ears syringed or used ear drops. She realises medicine is to make people better. You will not be surprised to learn that both her parents are doctors.

What's more, Daniella is interested in initiating role play. She pays attention to detail regarding sickness. Her vocabulary indicates knowledge in this area. She concentrated on making the patient better and was pleased with herself for doing so.

We have considered how observation gives us information vital to our work with young children. From what we see and interpret we are able to reach an understanding of where the child is and to plan activities and experiences to take the child's learning forward. More than that, observation allows us to assess our provision to ensure that we are actually doing what we set out to do. You will remember the examples given in Part II which showed how close observation of resources, activities and areas gave practitioners important information about equality of access. It is only by spending time observing how an area or a resource is used that we are able to say with confidence that our planning has been successful.

In terms of understanding and explaining what we see individual children doing, a useful technique is to look for evidence of children following particular themes in their play. You will remember Mary Jane Drummond (Chapter 19) talking about how observation can help us know more about the particular schemas children are following. The term 'schemas' comes from the work of Piaget and recent research by Chris Athey (1990) has shown how an understanding of these behaviours – often seen as random – can give another view of children's particular enthusiasms and concerns.

24 Using schemas in the early years

Fran Paffard

Here Fran Paffard draws on her considerable experience as a nursery teacher and on the work she was doing in this field for her MA. This chapter, written while the author was Deputy Headteacher of an inner London nursery school, explains how an understanding of schematic behaviour can influence perceptions of children and also explains how those of us working with young children can use evidence of schemas in order to plan for progression.

I was first introduced to the idea of using schemas in early-years education while retraining as a nursery teacher at the Froebel Institute where Chris Athey (1990) undertook her initial research. Going back to the nursery I began to look at children's play with new eyes. What had previously appeared to me to be random aimless behaviour now emerged as a part of the child's exploration of a particular form or 'schema'. Quyen walked around with books up her jumper; she buried animals in the sand; she built boxes from polyhedrons and put dinosaurs in them; she did beautiful drawings then folded them up and put them in her coat pocket; at story time she always sat under the table. Instead of seeing this as pointless and slightly frustrating behaviour, I could now see it as a part of an enveloping schema.

WHAT IS A SCHEMA?

The word schema can sound like off-putting jargon,but getting to grips with schemas can extend our understanding of how children are actually learning. The word 'schema' comes from the work of Piaget. He saw children's learning as a process moving from actions through to thought. The child, by repeating patterns of actions, is both learning to generalise (e.g. which objects are suckable) and assimilating her experiences into this pattern (e.g. dummies are suckable, coal isn't). These are the patterns of action he called schemas. A schema then is simply a 'pattern of repeatable behaviour'.

Chris Athey, observing three- and four-year-olds in a nursery setting, found that they were engaging in 'patterns of repeatable behaviour' or 'schemas' that clearly influenced their learning. It is this research which has motivated nursery workers to find out how schemas can help in their work.

Athey suggest that there are three main ways in which a schema shows itself:

1 sensory/motor
2 symbolic/representational
3 functional dependency

Sophie, at three, demonstrated her absorption in a circular schema in all these modes.

Sensory/motor

Sophie spent lots of time outside in the nursery, chasing round and round the trees, riding round the edge of the tarmac on a bike and spinning around on an old tyre swing. Given a skipping rope she didn't skip, but spun around so that the rope flew out in a wide circle. In the cornflour tray she used both hands to form wide circles.

Symbolic/representational

Sophie loves the workshop, sticking tissue paper circles together and selecting round plastic lids and corks to use. Her paintings were all of circles, lollipops, suns, flowers and if there was a choice of painting paper she always chose the circles. She enjoyed Plasticine and loved rolling it into balls and sausage shapes. Shopping with her mother she insisted on buying turkey roll 'because I only like the circle ones'.

Functional dependency

In the blocks Sophie chose a cylindrical block and rolled it down the ramps. She showed another child how to position the block 'or it won't go down properly'. She used the model clock in the playhouse shop moving the hands to different points 'now the shop is open, now it is closed time'. When we lost the marbles for the marble run Sophie made some balls from Plasticine, experimenting to get them the right size 'they have to be really round to go down'.

In all these different modes Sophie is obviously interested in circularity and rotation. Her interest led her to explore her own body movements and the movements of objects. It led her into modelling and artwork, into trying to represent her experience in a symbolic way. And it led her into hypothesising, making conceptual deductions about circles, spheres and cylinders. She explored ideas of time, forces, propulsion and one-to-one correspondence, to name only a few. It was obvious watching her that she was very absorbed in her explorations and gaining deep satisfaction from her learning. At the same time she was able to communicate her ideas and co-operate with other children. Athey suggests that through schemas we are able to understand and therefore assist the progression from action to thought for the young child. What began for Sophie as a chasing game in the nursery garden resulted in all kinds of valuable learning across the range of nursery provision.

HOW MANY SCHEMAS?

There is no such thing as a definitive list of schemas. Each schema connects to and builds on a child's existing schemas – for example, a child explores vertical and horizontal schemas before she or he can explore a grid or a cross schema. Children may be exploring a variety of schemas at one time, or a child's schema may not be easy to observe, so we need to be wary of over-simplifying the way in which they work. However, various lists have been produced of some identifiable schemas in children's play and I am including here a list based on the Rumpus Schema Extra produced by Cleveland teachers in early education. This is a list I have found useful as a starting point with nursery workers and parents in introducing schemas.

A schema spotter's guide

Transporting

A child may move objects or collections of objects from one place to another perhaps using a bag, pram or truck.

Positioning

A child may be interested in placing objects in particular positions – e.g. on top of something, around the edge, behind. Paintings and drawings show evidence of this.

Orientation

This schema is shown by interest in a different viewpoint, as when a child hangs upside down.

Dab

A graphic schema used in paintings randomly or systematically to form patterns or to represent, for example, eyes, flowers, buttons, etc.

Trajectory

A fascination with things moving or flying through the air: balls, aeroplanes, frisbees, etc. When expressed through the child's own body movements this often becomes kicking, punching, jumping or throwing.

Horizontality and verticality

A child may show evidence of particular interest by actions such as climbing, stepping up and down or lying flat. These schemas may also be seen in constructions, collages or graphically. After schemas of horizontality and verticality have been explored separately the two are often used in conjunction to form crosses or grids. These are very often systematically explored on paper and interest is shown in everyday objects, such as cooling trays, grills, nets, etc.

Diagonality

Usually later than the previous schemas, this one emerges via the construction of ramps, slides, sloping walls. Drawings begin to contain diagonal lines forming roofs, hands, triangles, zig-zags.

Enclosing

A child may build enclosures with blocks, Lego, large crates, etc. perhaps naming them boats, ponds, beds. The enclosure is sometimes left empty, sometimes carefully filled in. An enclosing line often surrounds painting and drawings while a child is exploring this schema.

Enveloping

This is often an extension of enclosure. Objects, space or the child herself are completely covered. She may wrap things in paper, enclose them in pots or boxes with covers or lids, wrap herself in a blanket or creep under a rug. Paintings are sometimes covered over with a wash of colour or scrap collages glued over with layers of paper or fabric.

Circularity

Circles appear in drawings and paintings as heads, bodies, eyes, ears, hands, feet, etc. They are also used in representing animals, flowers, wheels, the sun, and a wide variety of other things.

Semi-circularity

Semi-circles are also used graphically as features, parts of bodies and other objects. Smiles, eyebrows, ears, rainbows and umbrellas are a few of the representational uses for this schema as well as parts of letters of the alphabet.

Radial

Again common in paintings and drawings. Spiders, suns, fingers, eyelashes, hair, often appear as a series of radials.

Rotation

A child may become absorbed by things which turn – e.g. taps, wheels, cogs, keys. She may roll cylinders along, or roll herself. She may rotate her arms or construct objects with rotating parts in wood or scrap materials.

Connection

Scrap materials may be glued, sewn, fastened into lines; pieces of wood are nailed into long connecting constructions. String, rope, wool, etc. are used to tie objects together, often in complex ways. Drawings and paintings sometimes show a series of linked parts. The opposite of this schema may be seen in separation where interest is shown in disconnecting assembled or attached parts.

Ordering

A child may produce paintings and drawings with ordered lines or dabs; collages or constructions with items of scrap carefully glued in sequence. She may place blocks, vehicles or animals in lines and begin to show interest in 'largest' and 'smallest'.

Transforming

A child may become interested in materials which change shape, colour, etc., e.g. ice melting, potatoes cooking, clay hardening, paint mixing.

One-to-one correspondence

There is often evidence of this in scrap collages and constructions where a child may, for example, glue a button inside each bottle top or place a piece of paper inside each cup of an egg box.

Functional dependency

Although causal relationships are not fully appreciated, interest may be seen in the dependency of one function upon another, for example, a child may draw a lift with a button beside it and say 'You have to press this button for the lift to come' or pretend to turn an ignition key 'so that the engine will start'.

WHY LOOK AT SCHEMAS?

Looking at schemas reinforces some basic principles of early childhood education.

1   It is child-centred and positive. Looking at a child's schema involves starting from where the child is and what the child can do, not what she can't.

2   It is easy to make assumptions about children's capabilities. Schema-spotting helps to avoid these judgements since it depends on close observation. A child who is thought to have a short concentration span because they flit from place to place may be found to be continuously exploring an idea or schema across different areas.

3   It encourages us to respect the child's interests and enables workers to interact with the child in a more helpful way. A child who is in a 'transporting schema' and takes all the home corner cups and plates to the far end of the garden can be given a picnic set to use.

4   Behaviour perceived as negative may be understood to be part of a schema, so that children aren't automatically labelled as naughty and their behaviour can be channelled into more acceptable routes. Danny, who was constantly in trouble for kicking and knocking over children's buildings was as relieved as I was when we gave him his own pile of crates to kick and skittles to knock over.

5   Although schemas and their categories can sound off-putting and full of jargon, I have found that talking to parents about their child's schemas a very helpful way of working together. One worker cannot possibly track a class full of children, but parents are acute observers of their children and are quick to spot changes in the patterns. It also helps parents to share in their child's learning. One patient mum received a soggy folded piece of painted paper with delight every day for a whole term, respecting her daughter's enveloping schema and gave her paper, paints and masking tape to let her carry on at home.

6   As adults we bring to young children the vocabulary and the categories we grew up with. Learning is categorised into subjects (science, history, etc.) and social and emotional behaviour is seen as a separate issue. Schemas, once the initial terminology is understood, provide a new and generally positive way of interpreting the child's actions, in which learning and behaviour are closely enmeshed.

7   Recognising a schema can help us to predict and to offer the kinds of experiences that will extend a child's learning. It may be that we offer a content to fit the form of the schema. So a child in a grid schema may be interested in maps, in peg boards, in windows, in weaving. A child who uses only limited areas of the nursery may be lured into using others by giving her, for example, squared paper in the graphics area, grid or square shapes to do painting and printing, a crossroads for toy cars or trains, long thin strips of card or wood and nails, staples, glue for fixing them, or the task of cutting up a tray of biscuits into squares.

PROVIDING FOR SCHEMAS

If we look at the usual areas of nursery provision with schemas in mind, new priorities emerge:

Materials

Do we provide circles, squares, grids, oblongs, etc. in the paper? Does the home corner have blankets, bags, mixing bowls for enclosers and envelopers? Is there equipment outside for transporting: trolleys, wheelbarrows, rucksacks, etc.? – ropes and string for connecting? – balls and skittles for throwing and rolling? – hoops and old tyres for rolling and spinning? Ideally all areas should provide for all schemas, and obviously the more open-ended the provision the better. Masking tape and paper bags are far more versatile than expensive toys from catalogues.

Rules

Allowing children freedom to explore their schemas is crucial. A child in a dynamic vertical schema probably won't be interested in a butterfly printing activity, but will they be allowed to do the splash paintings they enjoy instead? Do we allow children to fold up their paintings, to wrap things up in masking tape, to carry around shopping bags, to take things from inside out – or provide alternatives outside? This doesn't mean that we shouldn't plan to introduce new and stimulating ideas into the nursery but as staff we need to be ready to follow the child's interests and not try and impose the learning we have so carefully provided.

Interactions

Do we value the action part of a schema, and see the child who is zooming cars across the carpet as just as busily learning as the child producing lots of drawings? Do we talk to children about what they're doing and listen to them, acknowledging their interest and feeding in the language to support it? Do we make connections, suggest other things to look at? Read stories that support their schemas? Do we talk to parents about their child's pattern of play and ask about how they play at home?

Planning

Planning for schemas in the nursery doesn't cancel the need for other forms of planning, but it can add another dimension:

• Planning the nursery environment so that each area has basic provision for common schemas.
• Planning specific activities, outings and experiences with particular schemas and children in mind.

- It is not possible to plan for every child all the time, but possibilities include:

    (a) allowing staff observation time for key children, to identify and support their schemas;
    (b) focusing on one schema and providing for it in detail for one week;
    (c) tracking certain children, identifying schemas and recording the learning going on;
    (d) making the tracing of a child's schema a regular part of whatever record keeping is being done.

WARNING

Not every child is easily identified as being involved in a schema, some may be involved in two or three at once, others may not seem to be particularly immersed in any. Schema-spotting, fascinating though it is, shouldn't become an exercise in 'labelling' children. Its usefulness lies in illumating the child's inner learning, focusing us more clearly on what children are doing, not trying to fit their behaviour into boxes. Identifying a child's schema is only one of many tools at our disposal in observing and supporting children's learning. It is also easy to forget that children move between schemas, sometimes overnight. Thinking that you know a child's schema doesn't mean that you can stop observing, or that you can make assumptions about them. I have also heard some schemas being characterised in a negative way, e.g. the trajectory or dynamic vertical schema being associated with throwing, kicking and destructive behaviour. Schemas can help us to understand and channel some difficult behaviour certainly, but every schema has crucial learning embedded in it which needs to be supported and valued.

Finally I would only add that research on schematic learning in children is relatively new. There is much that we still don't know about them. The more nursery workers critically explore the possibilities of schemas, the more we shall find out.

FURTHER READING

Athey, C. (1990) *Extending Thought in Young Children*, London: Paul Chapman Publishing. (A fascinating, but quite difficult account of her research.)

Nutbrown, C. (1994) *Threads of Thinking*, London: Paul Chapman Publishing. (An accessible read, looking at using schemas in early education.)

Nicholls, R. (ed.) with Sedgwick, J., Duncan, J., Curwin, L. and McDougall, B. (1986) *Rumpus Schema Extra: Teachers in Education*, Cleveland LEA, Cleveland. (A practical basic pamphlet for nursery workers and parents.)

25 Alice drawing

Margaret Boyle

To end Part III, Margaret Boyle, a student on the Early Childhood Studies Scheme, analyses Alice (2 years, 6 months) painting and drawing and shows how her close observation of just what it is that Alice is attending to helps her understand what Alice already knows and can do.

In paying attention to the child drawing, Margaret tried hard to focus on what it was that Alice was doing – the process – and tried equally hard to avoid asking the almost inevitable question 'What is it?'

In reading this piece you might try asking yourself if Alice shows any repeated patterns of behaviour in her drawing – in other words gives evidence of schematic behaviour.

In planning this experience for Alice, I chose the particular medium appropriate for her age and development. She mixed and used thick powder paint in four basic colours – the primaries plus green. She used a medium-thickness paint brush on paper on a table top. She painted alone, as I was trying to concentrate on her processes. The experience was planned more as a chance to provide an observation and a starting point, rather than to teach Alice new skills.

THE OBSERVATION

There was not a lot of spoken language used by Alice. She appeared to be concentrating, and her actions were informative!

Alice is interested in marks as represented by various lines, patterns and shapes. She alternated between horizontal and vertical lines, moving her arm side-to-side and up-and-down regularly. She alternated between pressing her brush firmly on the paper, creating a circular 'splotch' and holding her brush horizontally off the paper and letting the paint dribble down on the paper, creating tiny patterns of splotches (before painting over them). Thus, during the observation, Alice varied her physical movements and noted the effects of her actions.

Alice is hugely interested in the exploration of space. Her arm and hand movements included up-and-down and side-to-side brush movements. She made circular shapes with the brush. She opened and shut the paint pots. She played with the brushes with in-and-out movements in the paint pots. She experimented with brush strokes on-and-off the paper. She tried painting in small areas versus using the whole page.

During this time Alice exhibited an interest in texture. She practised painting her own hands (experiencing the sensations of wetness and feeling the paint dry on her hands). She also showed a tendency to paint until the paper was saturated, laying layer upon layer in varying textures.

Altogether Alice played with and exhibited six of the eight art elements listed by Lancaster (1990): 'arrangement, colour, line, pattern, shape and texture'. Alice is also interested in symbolic representation. Whilst I was taking notes she asked what I was doing and why. I'm not sure what impact I had on it, if any, by my answer. After asking her question she returned to her painting, saying nothing. However, she then made circular movements with her brush, perhaps a precursor to writing?

Comments on this observation

I believe that Alice is a very active learner, as Piaget defined it. She is exploring herself and her environment, taking in all aspects of the art experience. She is assimilating all before her in an 'effort to *deal with* the environment by making it into the organism's [in this case Alice's] existing structures – by 'incorporating' (Donaldson, 1978). Alice does this by exploring space, physical limits, elements of art and cognitive concepts.

She balances this behaviour with Piaget's principle of accommodation – that is 'the effort to *fit the behaviour of the organism* [in this case Alice] *to the environment*' (Donaldson, 1978). This is shown when Alice realises the limits of the paper and that her painting is contained by the size of the paper. Another example of her possible accommodating behaviour may include her realisation that the type of tool used limits her actions. She may have attempted more emergent writing/ symbolic representation if she were using a pen rather than a paint brush.

According to Piaget's stages of development, Alice is consolidating the know-ledge she has gained during the sensorimotor period. By painting her own hands she showed a growing awareness of herself and her boundaries. Alice is now into the pre-operational period where, as Donaldson (1978) explains this 'consists mainly in the development of the child's capacity to represent things to himself'. That Alice was representing her feelings and knowledge is evident. Unfortunately, as Alice did not articulate much during the observation, I can only assume from her concentrated actions, diligence and past behaviour that she had a plan of what she was trying to represent.

From my own personal knowledge of Alice she is greatly concerned with taking her clothes off and putting them on again. Rather than perceiving this as a nuisance, I believe this provides information about Alice. I would suggest this behaviour is part of a schema, supported by this art observation. I have considered the fact that Alice, after painting something 'definite', will more often than not obliterate it, mixing over it so it becomes an indistinguishable shape. It was only by paying attention to her processes that I realised this could be an attempt to erase the original mark – i.e. an on-off-on-off pattern like her clothes behaviour. Her clothes behaviour could also be an indication of her interest in layers and texture!

CONCLUSION

The importance of observation and the application of that knowledge cannot be over-emphasised. These findings can be used to extend Alice's learning about marks and mark-making in a broad and balanced curriculum. I would aim to give Alice an active, independent role in her choices and learning and many opportunities for experiencing, exploring and discussing. I would try to 'decentre' myself – imagining myself a two-year-old waiting for an adult to introduce me to all the fun possibilities that could await me!

REFERENCES

Donaldson, M. (1978) *Children's Minds*, Fontana.
Lancaster, John (1990) *Art in the Primary School*, Routledge.

In Part III we have looked at observation as probably the most important tool in the early childhood worker's repertoire. Observation, which is something we do instinctively when we are interested in children, can give us more detailed, more sensitive and more personal information about each child, about each child's interests and needs and allow us into each child's 'head' to follow the processes the child is engaged in in every activity.

But observation on its own is merely 'fun'. In order to be turned into a useful tool, observations need to be recorded, read through and analysed – and this analysis is often best done with some understanding of how children learn and develop. In the last piece in this part we read Margaret Boyle's analysis of Alice drawing and see how the author's reading influences her understanding of what Alice is doing. Constantly dressing and undressing is no longer seen as an irritating habit, but part of a pattern of behaviour the child demonstrates in different areas of her learning.

By observing children closely the sometimes remote and academic writing of researchers and authors starts to make sense. When you see a child in the home corner acting out the familiar sequence involved in feeding a baby, for example, you begin to understand what Margaret Donaldson means when she talks about situations that make 'human sense' to the young child. Or, by contrast, when you see a young child struggling to complete a work sheet requiring her to colour all the big balls blue, all the little balls red, you understand the meaning of 'disembedded thought'.

More than that, observation of what we, the practitioners, provide helps us critically analyse our provision in the light of how the children respond. For example, it is only by observing the children at play in the home corner that you get any sense of how well the home corner is set up. When you see children engaging in the same routines every day and feel that their play has become static, perhaps introducing something new or taking something away from the home corner will stimulate more challenging play. Or again, the play may have become static because the space is limited and creating a larger home corner may, again, allow the play to take off. But you can only analyse your practice by observing what the children are doing.

Observation is our best tool: the key to understanding and improving our practice and to ensuring that the children we care for are continually learning and developing.

Part IV
Children talking

Introduction to Part IV

The things children say often delight and amaze us. When we analyse carefully the things they say, the meaning – sometimes very complex – becomes clear. You will remember the example of the child exclaiming 'I seed it and I feeled it and it's not a dog!'. Here are some other examples which show how children struggle, through spoken language, to express complex ideas and concepts. Two-year-old Andy, taken to see Monet's 'Water Lilies' at the National Gallery looked at it, stepped back and said, 'He must have used a very long brush!' A simple enough sentence, but within it a clear understanding of the fact that the painting, made up of tiny brush strokes, could only be seen as 'meaningful' when observed from a distance. Hannah, at 22 months, looking at a huge jacaranda tree, said, 'I can climb up and up and up – and down and down and down'. It was only with the knowledge that Hannah had been listening to the story of 'Jack and the Beanstalk' that the impact of her statement became clear.

Three-year-old Daniel, visiting his grandmother, asked where the stray kitten who had been there on his last visit had gone to. His grandmother replied, 'I haven't seen him for a long time and when I asked his daddy where he was, his daddy said he hadn't seen him for a long time either.' There was a pause – then Daniel asked, 'Is his daddy also a cat?' Daniel clearly couldn't make sense of a talking cat, never having encountered one in his short life!

Oliver was not too happy to have a new baby brother, but he knew that he was supposed to be pleased. So he hung around the baby, stroked him, helped feed him and tried his best. But when the baby had had his bath and was being dressed Oliver said, 'Now he's lovely and clean, so you can take him back to the hospital!' Oliver couldn't quite risk telling his parents that he wanted to get rid of the new baby, so he put it as kindly as he could!

Tizard and Hughes (1978) and Gordon Wells (1987) have shown that all children, coming from all homes, are able to use language effectively to make and share meanings. They use talk at home, as equal partners in any dialogue and in real-life situations in which the meaning is embedded. But when young children first start in the nursery class or school they may find themselves in an unfamiliar context – and for many children the language and the expectations of these do not coincide with those of home. At home children are asked questions where an answer matters: 'Do you want some milk? Have you fastened your shoes? Where are your pyjamas?'

But in school or playgroup, sometimes questions are asked merely to test the children and small children are often confused when they are asked a question where the answer is either obviously already known to the adult asking the question or where the answer is irrelevant to the child's life. Many small children encounter adults who fail to tune into the child's interests or recognise the child's experience: their interest is to 'educate' the child. Often this 'education' takes the form of questioning the children, trying to elicit one specific response. You will probably recognise yourself in the example below! We have all done something similar to this – but we need to question whether this type of dialogue enhances children's learning.

Helena has been playing in the home corner for some time, busily enacting a familiar scene. The adult goes over to her and spots what she sees as an ideal opportunity to test Helena's ability to count to five, since the child has made five plasticine sausages.

Helena: Look, I've got sausages here.
Adult: Oh, how many have you got? Can you count them?

At this point Helena walks away.

When we, as adults, intervene in children's play and try and use it as an opportunity for teaching, the child's response often gives us a clue as to whether we have correctly tuned in to the child's interests. Helena, instead of responding to the adult or continuing in her play, walked away. Her interest had clearly not been in counting and the adult, by trying to 'teach' her something had destroyed her play.

The acquisition of one's first language, which happens for all children so seemingly effortlessly, is one of the greatest cognitive achievements of human beings. Children, without being explicitly taught, learn the vocabulary, the grammar, the rules of their own language and discover they have a power-ful tool for communication. When the adults who are with them communicate with them, through talk, and as equal partners, spoken language becomes one of the most powerful tools for supporting and extending learning.

In Part IV we examine the importance of talk in early learning, looking at some of the theory and also at some examples of how adults have structured situations to encourage children to talk.

REFERENCES

Tizard, B. and Hughes, M. (1984) *Yound Children Learning Talking and Thinking at Home and at School*, Fontana.
Wells, G. (1987) *The Meaning Makers: Children Learning Language*, Hodder and Stoughton.

26 Talking with and listening to young children

Bernadette Duffy

In this introductory chapter Bernadette Duffy explains the importance of talking and listening in our everyday lives and gives us examples of how an adult, tuning in to what the children are saying, can arrive at a better understanding of young children's interests and concerns, fears and anxieties, loves and passions. Drawing on a vast body of writings and research on the importance of talk, she gives us some wonderful examples of children talking at the Dorothy Gardner Centre, where she is the head teacher, together with a very detailed explanation of what workers can do to encourage talk as a primary means of learning and accord it the status it deserves in early childhood education.

THE IMPORTANCE OF TALK

We spend the greater part of each day talking and listening. We use speaking and listening to maintain and develop relationships with other people, to communicate our ideas and thoughts, to reason, argue and negotiate. Spoken language is the medium through which we maintain our daily lives. Yet talk is often, in this culture and in our education system, undervalued and far more prestige is attached to written forms of language than to spoken language, even though throughout our lives we will use spoken language more frequently.

As adults we have access to and the ability to use a whole range of styles of talk. We can move from one form of spoken language to another to suit the situation we find ourselves in. We can alter the vocabulary we use (often including the dialect and language), the structure of the sentence, the conversational style to suit our purpose. For example, the way we talk to our families is often very different from the way we talk to our employers. So, as adults we have developed a repertoire of styles.

We need to give children access to breadth and understanding of the spoken language to equip them to develop a repertoire of styles and to ensure that they are successful in life.

THE IMPORTANCE OF TALK FOR YOUNG CHILDREN

Children are born with the desire to communicate. While still in the womb the foetus responds to sounds. For example children are more likely to quieten after birth to music they have become familiar with while still in the womb. Shortly after birth babies can distinguish their mother's voice from that of other female voices. In the early months of life, while feeding, babies learn the rules of conversations: they keep eye contact and take turns in the 'conversation' with the carer (Karmiloff-Smith, 1994).

The vast majority of home environments present a wide range of rich and rewarding language experiences, despite the concerns of some professionals. The research of Gordon Wells (1987) established that all children progress through the same stages of language acquisition, but that different children will progress at different rates. This will depend on these factors:

1   the use of spoken language in the home;
2   the value the family's culture places on spoken language;
3   different lifestyles;
4   family roles and relationships;
5   presence or absence of siblings.

Children's talk offers us an insight into their thoughts, feelings and ideas. Children will often talk through their problem-solving activities and give us an insight into their thinking. Talk enables children to move from the here and now to the past, future and into alternative worlds. It enables them to make sense of the world around them, to elicit meaning, label actions and develop concepts.

Talking and listening give children access to learning across the whole curriculum especially in their early years. Spoken language is the first form of language that children use and, from this, written language develops. By listening attentively to young children we can develop an understanding of their knowledge, not only about language but also about all other areas of experience.

THE LINK BETWEEN TALK AND SELF-IDENTITY

The language children speak, the language they use to express their innermost thoughts and feelings, the language their families speak are obviously very closely connected with their self-identity (Whitehead, 1990). The value that educators place on the spoken language of the child will reflect on their self-esteem. To be bilingual or multilingual is the norm in most of the world, but too often children whose first language is not English are looked on, in this country, as having a problem or special needs. Historically, some language combinations are given more recognition than others. For example, to have access to French and English is seen as an advantage, but having Arabic as a first language is seen as a problem in need of remedial help. Children who have access to more than one language have the opportunity to understand more about the abstract nature of language and it is important that this advantage is built upon by ensuring that the first language is supported and developed alongside subsequent languages (Siraj-Blatchford, 1994).

All children growing up in this country need access to standard English. It is the common shared communication in industrial and professional society in Britain. Children have an entitlement to use standard English. But it is essential that it is taught in a way which does not denigrate non-standard dialects or other languages (Whitehead, 1990).

By giving children as much access and as many options as we can to using talk, we enable them to make real decisions about the spoken languages they wish to use in later life.

EXAMPLES OF CHILDREN TALKING

I would like to share with you some examples of children's talk collected by the staff at the Dorothy Gardner Centre. The extracts come from the records the staff keep of the children and the commentary focuses particularly on spoken language.

We are looking for evidence in answer to the following questions:

1   Are children hypothesising, predicting, speculating, questioning?
2   Are they relating new ideas to previous experiences and understanding?
3   Do they express/justify feelings and opinions?
4   Can they organise, interpret and represent ideas and information?
5   How is the children's knowledge and understanding of the world around them reflected in their talk?
6   How does the adult support all this?

Example 1

Setting: Dean (3 years, 6 months) arrives at the Centre for breakfast and, on his way to the dining room, sees a member of staff who is busy preparing for the morning session.

Dean: Good morning Priya.

No reply

Dean: I said 'Good morning'.
Adult: Sorry, I wasn't listening.

She turns to give him her full attention.

Dean: I don't like it when I say 'good morning' and people don't answer.
Adult: Why not?
Dean: It's not fair, not nice – if I say hello you should say it back.

Adult: Good morning, Dean.
Dean: Good morning, Priya.

Comment

In this extract Dean is showing his understanding of the conventions surrounding greetings and his hurt when adults don't comply with the rules. He is drawing on his previous experience and is clearly able to use spoken language to express his feelings and give explanations. Dean is a confident user of talk and is able to use it to get the response he wants. The adult involved is sensitive and gives weight to Dean's feelings and concerns by taking the time to listen to him talk through them and articulate them. Often it is during the unplanned or routine experiences that opportunities for talk arise.

Example 2

Setting: Felix (3 years, 9 months) is in the reception area with a member of staff opening the door for parents as they collect their children. Louise (2 months) has been left with them and starts to cry.

Felix: Sing to her
Adult: I'm not sure – it might make it worse!
Felix: Say 'Rock a bye baby' – my mum sang that when I was a baby.

Adult sings, baby stops crying.

Felix: See! I told you it would work. I cry when I'm asleep.
Adult: Why?
Felix: There's monsters in my room. There's not really monsters, but I think
             there are when the lights go out.
Adult: When I was little I thought there was a troll under my bed and that it
             would eat me.
Felix: Did you have a toy troll?
Adult: Yes, yes, I did.
Felix: That's why then. You dreamed it. Wasn't real. What did you do?
Adult: I asked my mummy to leave the light on.
Felix: I do that! When Spencer [older brother] is with me I'm not frightened.

Comment

Felix shows an impressive ability to empathise with a much younger child and with an adult and by drawing on his own experiences is able to offer explanations and help. He obviously has a concept of time and its passage as he is able to accept that the adult was once a child with the same feelings and fears that he has. Felix is able to question, hypothesise and offer explanations. His conversational skills are very good. Again, the adult uses an unplanned experience to explore the child's understanding and knowledge, allowing him to articulate his concerns in his own way. Felix and the adult are sharing real experiences that are significant to them.

Example 3

Setting: Katy (4 years, 2 months) and Lauren (4 years, 3 months) are in the art/ technology area using the materials available to make bandages and splints for the 'injuries' that have occurred during their re-enactment of the television programme *Casualty* in the imaginative play area. Approximately ten other children are also involved. An adult is observing while being treated as a casualty.

Lauren: I'm bleeding. Look! Look!

She rushes into the area.

Adult: What happened?
Lauren: I cut myself. The blood's coming out.
Adult: What should I do?
Lauren: Quick to the hospital Nee nee [sound of ambulance] Doctor, doctor, save me!
Katy: It's not real.

She looks concerned.

Lauren: Yes it is. It is.

She uses a felt tip pen to make blood.

Katy: It's not really real. It's pretend.

Lauren comes out of role, voice changes.

Lauren: No, not really real, but pretend real. Put a bandage on.

Katy takes up the doctor's role.

Katy: You have to wait. There are other people first.

Comment

Lauren and Katy show a clear understanding of hospitals and their procedures, including waiting in casualty departments. This is based on their first-hand knowledge of hospitals and on information from television. They are also drawing on a recent focus on 'bodies' in the nursery. During this there had been conversations about blood. They are able to adopt roles in the drama and come out of them to negotiate difficult areas. Their distinction between what is really real and what is pretend real is fascinating. Lauren seems to have an idea about being true to the role she is in, while Katy is concerned with the literal truth of everyday life. The adult has acted as a facilitator making sure that the materials, equipment, time and space needed are available to them. Earlier input of a factual nature about hospitals and blood is drawn on to support their drama.

THE ROLE OF THE ADULT

Children use a wide repertoire of talk and operate at a high level of ability when:

- Adults are aware of what happens in earlier stages of language development and learn from them. For example, mothers, who show the greatest sensitivity during the first months of the child's life, produce the most linguistically able children at one year of age. Interactions between mother and child are sustained when the mother lets the child initiate and end interactions and responds to them (Karmiloff-Smith, 1994).
- Adults are sensitive to the child's current levels of communication ability and are aware of their interests (Wells, 1987).
- Adults have a desire to help and encourage the child by listening attentively to them and understanding the child's meaning.
- Adults extend the child's utterances and reflects what the child has said back to the child.
- Adults are aware of the vital role that the home and family play and enter into partnerships with parents (Tizard and Hughes, 1984).
- Adults and children know each other well (Bruner, 1980).
- Adults ask open, genuine questions (questions they don't already know the answers to) about experiences that are meaningful (Kersner and Wright, 1993).
- Adults do not respond too rapidly to the child's contribution, but give the child time to think and add additional information.
- Adults speak quietly in the nursery. The average volume of the speech of adults in the nursery is above normal! (Kersner and Wright, 1993).
- Adults ask fewer questions and, instead, offer their own speculations and reasons.
- Adults ask questions that require more than a 'yes' or 'no' answer or that offer a choice between two options.
- Adults understand that too many questions lead to tense and depressed levels of performance, less elaboration from the children and less initiative shown (Wood and Wood, 1988).
- Adults are aware of children's willingness to contribute information when asked to do so and welcome this.
- Adults encourage children to use them as a resource (Bruner, 1980).
- Adults recognise the importance of observing, recording and assessing children's spoken language.

- Adults make full use of real, stimulating and meaningful experiences like trips and outings, especially in the local community.
- Adults provide a model of high quality spoken language.

PROVIDING AN ENVIRONMENT WHICH ENCOURAGES TALK

We can provide children with rich opportunities to talk to each other and to adults when:

- The environment is organised to provide small, enclosed areas (Bruner, 1980).
- The environment is homely, relaxed and reflects aspects of home life.
- Drapes and soft furnishings are used to absorb distracting background sound (Kersner and Wright, 1993).
- Unnecessary background sound from radios, tapes, etc. is removed (Kersner and Wright, 1993).
- Adults are spread around the nursery. Even if they are not directly involved with a group of children, their presence encourages children to concentrate (Bruner, 1980).
- The session is not broken up, but allows for long periods of uninterrupted play (Bruce, 1992).
- There are opportunities for children to work in pairs and in small groups (Wood and Wood, 1988).
- The importance of routine tasks like cleaning, tidying away and others is recognised as a way of enabling children to concentrate on talking when they are involved in tasks which require little intellectual challenge.
- Adults give time for talk: time is made for 'chatting', usually when the adult is stationary for a period of time or engaged in low-key tasks like repairing equipment.
- The value of sharing stories is recognised and opportunities are created to do this (Wells, 1987).
- There are policies agreed by all those involved – staff, parents, management committees – which stress the value of talk in its own right and as a medium for learning across the curriculum.

CONCLUSION

In this short piece we have looked at why talk is so important in the early years and at how the adults working with young children can use talk to both support and extend children's learning and to develop trusting and respectful relationships with children.

By the age of 3 or 4 dialogue is as important as physical exploration. At this stage the child explores by means of words as much as through actions

. . . adults can therefore play an important role in advancing the child's understanding through conversation.

(Tizard and Hughes, 1984)

We need to examine our attitudes and ways of working to ensure that uninterrupted periods for talk are available in all settings. We need to make talk a priority. It is too important to be left to chance.

REFERENCES

Bruce, T. (1992) *Time to Play in Early Childhood Education*, Hodder and Stoughton.

Bruner, J. (1980) *Under Fives in Britain* (Oxford Research Project), Grant McIntyre.

Karmiloff-Smith, A. (1994) *Baby, It's You*, Ebury Press.

Kersner, M. and Wright, J. (1993) *How to Manage Communication Problems in Young Children*, Winslow Press.

Siraj-Blatchford, I. (1994) *The Early Years: Laying the Foundations for Racial Equality*, Trentham.

Tizard, B. and Hughes, M. (1984) *Young Children Learning: Talking and Thinking at Home and at School*, Fontana.

Wells, G. (1987) *The Meaning Makers: Children Learning Language*, Hodder and Stoughton.

Whitehead, M. (1990) *Language and Literacy in the Early Years*, PCP.

Wood, H. and Wood, D. (1988) 'Questioning the Preschool Child', in A. Cohen, and L. Cohen (eds) *Early Education: The Preschool Years*, PCP.

27 Louisa makes a plan

Susan Bragg

The second chapter in Part IV was written by Susan Bragg, a nursery nurse who studied on the Early Childhood Studies Scheme. She uses her observation notes to analyse what the children are saying and doing. Her starting point was a technology area she had just set up for the children in the class. Her purpose in doing this was to see how well the children were able to plan, to select and use appropriate materials and tools, to carry out their plans to make something and to evaluate their efforts. You will see, as you read it, how Susan is able to support the children's language and thinking by trying to focus on what it is the child is doing and interested in rather than by trying to 'teach' something.

The background to the observation note starts like this:

The children had just heard the story 'One Eyed Jake' – a familiar story. They had decided what to make and had drawn a plan of this. Four children were involved:

Louisa, aged 5 years, 9 months
Vanessa, aged 5 years, 6 months
Gina, aged 5 years, 2 months
Jonathan, aged 5 years, 5 months

Louisa had drawn a plan. She went over to the tray and filled her hand with small beads. As she walked over to the wood she said to herself 'Now which bit do I need?' Taking a long piece of wood in her other hand she returned to her seat. She placed the wood on the table, saying, 'This is big enough,' and then emptied the beads out of her hand on to the table. Next she took the glue and squeezed little blobs of it along the wood. Onto each blob of glue she carefully stuck a bead. When she had put glue along the whole length of wood she took her pencil and drew lots of circles on to her plan. Then she took a piece of metallic paper. 'This is gold. Look! I'm taking this one,' she said, showing the other children at the table. As she began to cut it with the scissors she said to herself, 'Needed this like this,' and wrapped the metallic paper around the wood. She removed the paper and put glue on the wood where the paper had been. Then she wrapped the paper round the wood again.

Louisa let go of the paper and it fell off, so she threw it into the middle of the table. Walking away from the table she mumbled 'I need . . .', and went over to the tray and put some more beads into her hand. She took them back to the table and turned her piece of wood over, then covered it with glue. Onto the glue she sprinkled the beads. Louisa brushed her hands together to get the beads off. 'I want to saw,' she said, going back to the wood. Jonathan opened the vice for her and she placed the wood into it. 'Do it out, do it out,' called Jonathan. 'OK. Yeah?' Jonathan continued. Louisa pushed her wood down into the vice. 'No, it needs to go up there,' said Jonathan, as he held the wood in position. Louisa giggled and held the wood up as Jonathan tightened the vice.

'It's my piece of wood,' Louisa said as she nudged Jonathan out of the way. Using the junior hacksaw she carefully made forward and backward movements into her piece of wood. After sawing it into three pieces she removed the last piece from the vice and picked up the wood that had dropped on to the floor. Louisa went over once again to the trays and looked through them. 'Ah, feathers, yes! I'll have some of these' she said, as she took a handful back to her place. With the glue pot in both of her hands she squeezed glue onto the feathers. To each feather she stuck a bead. She then helped herself to a long cardboard roll. Using a left-handed pair of scissors she began to cut the roll.

'These are left-handed scissors, Louisa. You are right-handed,' I said. Louisa just looked up at me and smiled and then swapped the scissors for a pair of right-handed ones. With the scissors she cut curved shapes out of the roll.

'Look,' she said to Jonathan, showing him the roll. Jonathan was too busy gluing to look up but Vanessa looked. 'What are you making?' Vanessa asked. 'I'm making a boat, I'm making a boat. He's making a boat, too,' she said, pointing to Jonathan's model. Louisa then stuck the cardboard roll onto the wood. While she held it in place she took a small square of cardboard and placed some glue upon it and stuck it on the roll. 'Ah, it's staying now,' said Louisa, letting go of the roll. She then tried to stick two pieces of wood onto the first piece of wood. She held them for a while, but when she let go of them they fell off. She made several attempts at sticking them on, but then began to lose her patience.

'What do you think we can use to stick it, Louisa?' I asked. Suddenly her eyes opened wide. 'How about that hot glue thingy?' she asked with a large grin on her face. 'If you show me where you want it to go I will stick it for you,' I explained.

While I stuck the pieces with the glue gun, Louisa cut a fringe out of a piece of pink foam. She then covered the foam with glue. I handed her back the model and she wrapped the foam around an upright piece of wood on her model. 'This is a passenger ship,' she said. 'Where is it going to?' I asked. 'An island,' she replied. 'Who's going on it?' I asked. 'Leanne, Andrew and I and my family,' she continued, as she squeezed the foam around the wood. She let go of the foam and it came off.

'Oh I need some more glue,' she said and put more glue on and held it tight. 'If it doesn't work this time I'm not going to use it.' As she let go of it, it fell off. She took it and threw it across the table in anger. 'What about using an elastic band?' I suggested. Louisa agreed and held the foam in place while I put an elastic band over it. 'Good. It worked!' she said, looking at the other children. 'That's good, isn't it, using an elastic band?'

'Where did you get that?' Vanessa asked, pointing to the foam. 'OK. I need an elastic band.' Louisa pointed to where she had got it from. She then began to cut out trolls that were on the back of a cereal box. 'I'm gonna cut three pink ones,' she said, as she cut. As she finished cutting them out she placed them on the table. She then went over to the trays and took some shiny paper. 'I got some paper,' she said, showing Vanessa. She cut it then left it on the table and went over to Jonathan. He was holding up pipe cleaners. 'Look at these, Louisa.' 'Wow!' she replied. She went over to the trays once again to where the pipe cleaners were.

Picking up some sequined fabric Louisa said, 'I'm gonna have this for my boat.' 'Wow!' said Vanessa, looking at the fabric. 'Oh, it feels nice' said Louisa, holding it in her hands. She then rolled it up and put glue on top of it and stuck it on to her boat. Using the purple marker pen she drew a wavy line along the side of her boat. 'Finished!' she announced, standing back, looking at her model with great pride.

'It's wonderful, Louisa. You've put a lot of work into it. Well done!' I said. 'Oh, I nearly forgot,' she said, picking up the purple marker pen. She wrote her name on it. She was writing upside down, but she was doing it so that it appeared the right way up when you read it.

This observation lasted for about 45 minutes.

SOME COMMENTS ON THIS OBSERVATION

- The activity was clearly of interest to the children and this was evident from their sustained activity.
- The activity was open-ended and allowed the children to make choices and to be in control of what they were doing. Whilst they were involved in following their own agendas they were able to talk to one another and to the adult, describing, explaining, negotiating, expressing their feelings and ideas, making judgements, collaborating and solving problems.
- The adult was eager not to 'teach' the children anything, but allowed them to follow their own ideas, offering help when needed.
- The adult tried to tune into the children's interests and to pay attention to what it was the children were trying to do. Through doing this, the adult was able to offer support to Louisa when she became frustrated. This meant that Louisa was able to fulfil her own plans and not give up before she had done so.
- The adult used meaningful praise and comments to support and extend learning.
- Through the provision of varied and interesting workshop materials the adult allowed the children choice of both materials and tools.
- Talk for real purposes was actively encouraged.

28 Cooking together

Angela Tindall

The second set of observation notes comes from Angela Tindall who worked as a classroom assistant in an inner London school. In these notes Angela describes how setting up a restaurant contributed to the children's developing ideas about language and literacy and shows how opportunities for speaking and listening arose out of the meaningful play situations.

Because our topic is food, I helped the teacher change the home corner into a kitchen cum restaurant. This gave several opportunities for providing activities that support oracy and literacy development.

The teacher had already provided menus. I added two illustrated recipe books, one with Malaysian dishes and one with European dishes. I am intending to build on the resources by adding posters, printed materials and a banner advertising the restaurant in the children's community languages. Some parents are keen to help with this as they are encouraged by seeing the value placed on their culture.

Opportunities for writing include writing pads for orders, telephone and note pad for bookings, and recipe books. Opportunities for speaking and listening arise spontaneously from this provision.

Here is a transcript of a conversation I overheard while the children used the resources provided.

Three children Pran, Sunny and Uma playing in the restaurant.

Pran: A book with food. My mum has a book with food.
Sunny: Oh! I'm going to make rice. I'm going to get sand and call it rice.

Sunny goes over to the sand tray and fills a tin with sand. He comes back over to the kitchen area and puts the tin of sand onto the scales. Pran and Uma, who are watching him closely, quickly join in and they too go and get sand to put on the scales.

Pran: Ouch! I think this tin of sand is too heavy. Oh no! Look, it still fits the scale.

Sunny: Take them off now. I want to make soup.
Uma: I like soup – red soup.
Sunny: Yes tomato. I like tomato.
Pran: But we don't have an oven to make soup.
Uma: Let's use a cup.
Sunny: Where's your brain gone? We still can't hot it up.
Pran: I don't want soup.
Sunny: OK, we'll make another soup.
Pran: Well, I'm gonna make Angie tea. Do you want tea? Yes? OK, I'll make you tea.
Uma: I want soup. Let me see that book.
Sunny: We can see the book together.

Uma and Sunny flick through the pages until they find the section of the recipes for soup. Together they decide on the shark fin soup.

Pran: Look! A pan for hotting soup up.
Sunny: That's for fish, not for hotting soup. Anyway, we don't have an oven.
Pran: Oh! Let's make cakes.
Sunny: OK, we'll make from sand.

Together the children are putting sand onto the scale. Uma then tells the boys to stop because the scales are full. Sunny then checks the book and informs Uma and Pran that it's time to cook the cakes.

Sunny: Oh yes, we don't have an oven.
Pran: Let's cook it in here. [He points to the storage shelves.]

COMMENTS ON THIS OBSERVATION

- The children are able to hypothesise, predict, speculate and question, as we see when Pran thinks the tin is too heavy and is surprised that it still fits on the scale.
- They all relate the new activity to past experience – 'my mum has a book with food.'
- They express their ideas and feelings 'I like soup – red soup.'
- They negotiate with one another, as when Sunny suggests they share the book.
- They solve problems and are able to criticise one another safely through their play, as shown when Sunny asks 'Where's your brain? We still can't hot it up.'
- The adult, in this situation, is an observer and her presence, her interest in what the children are doing, help them sustain the play.

29 'Let's make honey!'

Mary Smith

The third set of observation notes in Part IV were written by Mary Smith who worked at one of Islington's Under Fives Centres. She describes what happened in the garden of the Centre as the result of a swarm of bees arriving in it.

As you read her account consider just how she is able to extend the children's learning by responding to what they say in the spirit of genuine dialogue, following up their suggestions and, where appropriate, offering explanations and relevant resources.

A group of two girls and four boys are looking at a small swarm of bees that arrived this spring in our garden, next to the large climbing frame on the grass bank. The bees have made lots of holes in this part of the garden. They go in and fly out all day long. At first the children observing them were a little scared saying things like 'They're monsters!' and screaming, then running away, then returning for another look. One of the boys, Daniel (4 years, 6 months) asked if they were wasps or bees and wanted to know if they could make honey. Together we took a closer look and decided they were the wrong colour for wasps and were also too big. Aaron (3 years, 6 months) said they were monsters and then tried to shoot them with his finger, going 'zap zap' from a safe distance!

Daniel was still looking at them and started talking about making honey. He said we could make some at the nursery. I asked him how we could do it. He replied that we had to pick some flowers together. We went inside to get a tray for the flowers, then back to the garden to collect wild flowers – daisies, buttercups and dandelions. When the tray was full we sat on the grass and studied them. Daniel said, 'We have to pick out the pollen from the centre of each flower.' It took a while to do this, placing it in the corner of the tray. Daniel said we had enough to make the honey and then asked me go get a cup and spoon. I got them. Daniel put the contents into the cup and then stirred it with the spoon saying, 'I know it will make honey!'

After a time I asked, 'What's happening to it, Daniel?' 'Nothing,' he replied, 'We have to add apple juice to it and then it will be honey.' I got the apple juice from the kitchen. Daniel poured it into the cup and stirred, saying, 'Is it honey now?'

'No,' I replied. 'I don't think people can make honey. . . only bees.' Daniel was not convinced and said, 'We have to put more pollen in and then it will be honey.' We added more, but couldn't make honey. At this point I said, 'Daniel, we've tried our best to make honey, but people can't make it. We'll look for a book about bees and that will show us how they make it.'

We found a book and sat for a long time reading, looking and explaining – page by page. As a follow up we went to the shop to buy honey and even managed to get a jar with honeycomb in it. The children enjoyed the experience of spreading the honey on rolls and eating them at tea time.

COMMENTS ON THIS OBSERVATION

- Daniel used a real-life situation and drew on his previous experience and knowledge as he asked questions about bees and honey.
- Because he was following his own interests and was supported in doing this he was very persistent and refused to give up his set task of making honey.
- He was inventive – as in suggesting we use apple juice – and knowledgeable – as shown by him knowing about pollen in flowers.
- The adult tuned into his interests and concerns and supported him as much as possible by taking up all his suggestions. At no point did she tell him he was wrong or imply that he was stupid.
- The adult was able to extend the experience for Daniel, by showing him how books give information, and for the other children by going to the shops to buy honey to put on rolls.

30 Making ice

Sarah Cotter

The fourth set of observation notes in Part IV was written by Sarah Cotter who worked in one of Camden's nurseries. In this piece she describes what happened after the children had listened to the story 'Bear's Long Walk Home' which describes a walk in the snow and which mentions icicles and 'frozen steam'.

I wanted to relate the activity to the story and wanted to try and freeze water outside and not in the freezer. The weather was very cold.

Two bowls were put on the table with a jug of water. 'What do you think happens to water if it gets very cold?' I asked. 'It goes like ice,' Michael said. Rebbeca asked, 'Can we make water go cold and see if it turns to ice?' I replied that that was what I wanted to try. The children poured some water into the bowls: more in one than the other. Michael and Rebbeca carried the bowls outside.

The next morning the children eagerly asked what had happened to their bowls of water. Michael and Rebbeca fetched them. Rebbeca said, 'Look! Look! Mine's not water any more.' Michael brought his in and said, 'Mine's not like Rebbeca's.' Rebbeca looked at Michael's bowl and said, 'You've got too much water.' 'But it was cold outside,' said Michael. While saying this he put his hand into the bowl. 'Look, I have got some hard water.' 'Ice, silly!' said Rebbeca. 'But I've got cold water underneath,' said Michael.

I asked Rebbeca what she thought she would find if she broke the top of her ice. 'I don't know. I can try,' she said. I gave her a fork and she started breaking up the ice. 'It's all ice,' she said.

'That's right,' I replied. 'You had less water so it all got cold enough to freeze. Michael had more water in his bowl so the top got cold enough to freeze, but the rest of it didn't.'

Rebbeca asked if we could add hot water to the ice to see what happened. I went and got some hot water and poured it slowly for the children to see. 'The ice has gone,' Michael said. 'The hot water warmed it up and melted it,' I explained. 'Can I feel it?' Rebbeca asked. I tested it first to make sure it wasn't too hot. When Rebbeca felt it she said, 'Mummy says I'm like hot and cold water.' 'What do you mean?' I asked. 'Hot and cold make warm water, like black and white skin make brown skin, like me.'

COMMENTS ON THIS OBSERVATION

I chose to set up this activity because I had the confidence and knowledge to extend it through the children's questions. As Harlen (1985) says, 'Research has clearly indicated the need to relate scientific activities to real-life experiences of the children.'

The story I used as the starting point for this activity clearly introduces scientific concepts to the children. However, for them to understand these they need the opportunity to explore for themselves. Early on in the activity I provided an opening question which demonstrates a 'cognitive demand': 'What do you think happens when water gets very cold?' The answer Michael gave, 'It goes like ice' is scientific. If Michael had not been given that information from the story he may not have come up with that answer. So Michael may have been drawing on his previous experience of ice or on his understanding of the story.

Later I used the skills of observing, understanding, and listening to be able to collect the children's findings and help them come to a conclusion. For the children it was a fun learning experience, finding out about hot, cold, hard, soft, quantity.

The links Rebbeca made between hot and cold and black and white show how children always draw on real-life experiences.

The children were interested in the activity and talked through it, offering ideas, suggestions and comments and, in Rebbeca's case, using talk to demonstrate her feelings of being special.

REFERENCE

Harlen, W. (1985) *Primary Science: Taking the Plunge*, Heinemann Educational.

Chapters 26 to 29 have, we hope, given you things to think about. Often we hear people say that young children learn, primarily, through using their senses and their physical skills. This is true, but they also learn through using and hearing spoken language. Chapter 26 showed clearly how important talk is for young children and for their learning across all areas of the curriculum. Talk is important, also, for those of us working with young children. Talk gives us a window into the processes the child is exploring – just as observation does. Sometimes talk is in the form of monologues – children saying aloud to themselves what they are thinking. Vygotsky showed the close links between thought and language and suggested that thinking can be regarded as 'inner speech'. Very young children often need time for thinking to become internalised.

The observation pieces in these chapters give poignant evidence of children using talk to make sense of their world and to communicate their thoughts and ideas to others. We read, in these examples of how the adults have tried to engage with the children in sustained and mutually satisfying conversations. The 'enabling adult' plays a number of different roles, always being sensitive to the particular needs of the child at the particular point in time. In the examples given here it is particularly noticeable how the adult tunes into the child, listens intently to what the child is saying, avoids asking 'testing' questions and allows the child time to come to a response.

Encouraging talk is one of the most important aspects of our work as early-years professionals. As Bernadette Duffy points out:

> Talking and listening give children access to learning across the whole curriculum . . . By listening attentively to young children we can develop an understanding of their knowledge, not only about language but also about all other areas of experience.

When we think about the importance of speaking and listening, we need also to think about the importance of telling and listening to stories. Storytelling is universal in all cultures, through all ages. Through structuring and sequencing events and telling others about them, we begin to make sense of our experiences. Skilled storytellers are able not only to retell the events of their own lives, but able to create whole worlds and, in these worlds, address issues and themes which are sometimes too difficult to face in reality.

Telling stories, then, is one way in which we are able to make sense of the world and represent our thoughts, ideas and feelings. When children make and tell stories they are in the unique position of being in control of what happens. The only other place where this is true for them is when they play. In stories they create their own world, people it with figures of their own choice, pose and solve problems and explore difficult and dangerous areas through the safety of the imagination. Research by people like Carol Fox has shown that very young children, who have had experience of hearing stories read and told, are able, within the context of their own stories, to solve complex problems that they would not be able to solve otherwise. In one of the many stories she collected from young children she found that a child could solve a complex multiplication problem within the context of the story – a problem that the child would have been quite incapable of solving in reality.

The work of Vivien Gussin Paley shows how, when children are enabled to make and enact stories whenever they choose, they are able to perform at an extremely high cognitive level and solve problems, learn to negotiate and deal with conflict, address problems of stunning enormity and express complex feelings.

31 Storytelling to young children
The way and how of it

Betty Rosen

In this chapter, Betty Rosen who is a teacher and storyteller, writes about the magic of storytelling. For those of us who feel safe with a book in our hands, reading this chapter may give us the confidence to let go of the book and engage in the dangerous but immensely rewarding task of telling rather than reading.

STORYTELLING AND IMAGINATIVE PERCEPTION

I had finished telling my story ten minutes before. Most of the children were playing outside or had gone into the dining hall. The classroom door opened and Sumita, aged six, armed, literally and metaphorically, with her best friend, sidled up and inched her way between me and the class teacher. 'Was that true, then, miss?' she whispered, 'Was it true what you told us?'

True? I might have been telling them stories about myself from my own child-hood days – or motherhood days, or grandmotherhood days, or personhood days. Such stories we all have. They may not be true in detail – memory or wishful-thinking or both can play tricks on us – but they are true in principle, which is what counts. Such stories make storytellers of us all, every day – you and me and them. Such stories have the right to a daily place in the nursery and infants' schoolroom: adults must tell their own stories if they are to elicit stories from the lives occupied by the children they care for. Personal experience is the class- or nursery-room's strongest resource. Each child has expert knowledge of her/his own life: it's easiest to become articulate about what you know best. And you *know* your own life is real. But the story I had just told Sumita's class was a different sort. This one was about a lonely fisherman who stole a mermaid's magic garment as she sat singing on a rock. He fell in love with her, of course, even though she had her back to him, for such was the beauty of her lovely voice. He knew, like all the people in that part of Donegal, that without her magic cloth she was but a woman, unable to return to the water and obliged to follow the thief, even to the end of the world. But this mermaid needs to walk on her two little feet only as far as the fisherman's thatched, whitewashed cottage in the hamlet on the cliff top where the other fisherfolk live.

There she becomes a wife, and as the years pass, the mother of three children, two girls and then a boy. Far from the sleek cool waters she once called home and the sweet smell of the sea spray, she bakes her bread and sings her children to sleep at night, until the day the magic garment returns to her hands and becomes again a second skin to her body . . .

Mermaids? A magic garment woven from the blue of the sea, the green of the sea weed, the brown of the wet sand? How can it be true, I ask you?

I did my storytelling apprenticeship in a secondary boys' school near the Broadwater Farm Estate in Tottenham. There, 15-year-old streetwise lads (who were, before my storytelling days, very well able to reduce me to a tearful jelly on occasions by the time I set off homewards in my yellow Mini at the end of a harsh day) had their own way of asking Sumita's question. After listening in uncharacteristic total silence and immobility for up to three-quarters of an hour to a story, which might include a dog with a fleece of gold, gods dining on nectar and ambrosia, a father who serves a banquet made from the chopped up pieces of his murdered son (who is himself later magic-ed back to life just as he had been before but for a brand new left shoulder bone made of ivory), a victim of the terrible punishment of eternal thirst suffered in the underworld swampland of Hades . . . someone in the classroom would ask, 'Do you believe that story then, Miss?' His mouth would be smirking just a little to hide the seriousness his eyes reveal. The others giggle a bit or guffaw but almost immediately fall silent and poise themselves for the reply which they need to hear.

There's only one truthful answer to such a question: 'You'll believe the story while I'm telling it.' I know, but refrain from adding, 'and you, my questioner, believed it, too, in your listening.' That's how the imagination operates. It extends the arena of both makebelieve and reality. Within the most fictional of tales, there must be elements which relate to the experiences the children have had already. Older children make such connections silently in their heads during a storytelling though, thankfully, are usually so relaxed by the story they will share their thoughts during later discussion time. The younger the children, the more vocal and immediate their responses are likely to be. These may be picked up and incorporated in to the emerging tale by a skilful teacher – even one who is just learning her trade, as I've observed when my youngest daughter, Rosalind, was setting out on her career as a childcare worker. Or she may use such 'interruptions' as an instant resource which spreads the message that a story that is told becomes the property of the listener, who is empowered, even enlightened, by affecting the progress of a story as I shall try to show later on. But perhaps even more significant are those aspects of the story which enable the listeners to reach out towards experiences which are yet to come, both within their own lives and in the experiences of other people whose lives are entwined with their own.

Maybe mermaids and magic garments are not exactly central to human experience. Yet in this particular story they rub shoulders on equal terms with much that has very recognisable truth which may be already important in the lives of the children and certainly will be in the operation of their growing awareness of what's going on outside themselves. It is a story about loneliness; about longing; about love, between man and woman, child and parent; about conflicting loyalties and decision-making; about yearning for one's roots and unease within the alien scene; about reunion bringing ecstatic joy and about the searing fear of parting from someone you love . . . and much more. Inevitably, strands and stitches in the texture of such stories link up with recollections belonging to individual listeners and have special meaning for them. The whole of this tale occurs within the magic of moonlit seascapes or the comfortable warmth of the family kitchen of small community living. A good story, even a much simpler one than the two I have referred to here ('The Fisherman and the Mermaid' and 'The story of Tantalus'), operates on more than one level. There is infinite space for connections to be made with each unique listener's world. The imagination verifies the world we know and creates new worlds for truth to inhabit. It utilises previously grasped truths in the perception and creation of new ones. If the most powerful nourisher of the imagination is a good story, the greatest impact is made when it falls from the lips – yours or mine – of a storyteller.

STORYTELLING AND IMAGINATIVE RESPONSE

I have written extensively in my books about the extraordinary way adults and children are capable of retelling a story I've just told them, in totally new ways which indicate truly amazing creative powers within themselves, both visual and linguistic. Most of the evidence I have quoted has come from their written versions of stories. Here I want to concentrate on oral contributions for younger children I have worked with.

First, here are a couple of story outlines upon which I shall base my examples. They also happen to be good tales which you might like to take up yourselves by changing anything in them, adding plenty, and certainly by providing them with what they patently lack: a precise setting – perhaps one that you know from childhood days or where you've lived for a long time or where you have spent holidays.

Story 1

Once there was a small town where the people had everything they could wish for. They should have been content, and would have been, but for their fear – a fear they rarely spoke of though they all shared. It was of something terrible that lurked in the place beyond. There was no path because no one in living memory had ventured there. They knew that if it should learn of the existence of the people in the town that would mean the end of them all. A little girl, more curious about the world than most, decided she would go and find out what was there for herself. She made her way to the place beyond and there, indeed, she saw the terrible thing, huge and lumbering. She could not see it properly so she took up all her courage and moved closer and closer. To her amazement, the nearer she got to it, the smaller it became! When she got right up to it, it had become so small she could pick it up in her cupped hands. 'Who are you?' the little girl asked the tiny mannikin.

'My name is Fear', he replied.

I set this story in a Welsh village by the sea (I grew up in Wales). I usually call the heroine Gwyneth or Megan and the terrible thing is a giant over the mountain, Mynydd Gareg Wen, which towers over the western edge of the village. I also draw upon other details from my limited Welsh language repertoire which increases the precise cultural flavour and can prove particularly useful in multilingual class-rooms, not least as a tacit validation of bilingualism.

Story 2

There once was a valley full of quarrelsome folk. Two of the gods looked down – as gods will – wondering if the people deserved to be punished for their bad ways. The gods disguised themselves as travellers and went from house to house in that valley to see if anyone would give them a bed for the night or, at least, a bite to eat. No one did, as you may guess, until they arrived at the very last home, a humble cottage on the mountainside away from the land below. An old couple asked them in, made them comfortable by the fire and fed them simply but well. Suddenly the old woman noticed that while they ate their meal the jug of home-made wine never emptied, no matter how often the wine was poured. 'Alas, you must be gods!' the old woman cried, and rushed out into the night to catch their pet goose to kill it and cook them better fare. But the gods smiled and protected the goose. Soon they all took their night's rest. While they slept there was a great storm. The whole valley was flooded and everyone in it disappeared. All to be seen in the valley the next morning was a great lake, with a bright rainbow arching over it. The old people were rewarded with riches but, most important of all, with the granting of their only wish: that they might die in the same moment so that neither should live without the other. At the end of their days, they turned into two trees, side by side, with their branches intertwined.

This is the Greek story of Baucis and Philemon. I would just add that in my version I let the people in the valley wake up in the storm, gather what they can of their belongings together and scurry away over the mountains, never to be seen again! I don't always include the ending but let the children tell me how the two old people might wish to be rewarded. This often leads to prolonged and intriguing discussion. Try it.

Now to some infant responses. Take first Story 1. Telling it to secondary-age children means they sit and listen to the whole thing – forty minutes or so – and no one says a word. I know better than to expect the same from nursery-age or infant-school children and can readily make a virtue of necessity these days! My telling to one particular class of reception children, for example, was received with motionless attention (a very busy mental occupation) interspersed with patches of vocal and physical activity. The first major vocal episode occurred when I expressed Gwyneth's doubts as to how to get up the mountain without being seen. These are the children's outbursts:

Go up at night

When the mammies and daddies are asleep

And she could take a rope (me: why?) to pull herself up

She could get a torch

She could have a candle

The moon

Moonlight

A full moon

And when the stars are out

All these offerings were taken seriously, discussed, and I provided the 'truth' e.g. that the only torch she had didn't work; that she was afraid a candle would keep blowing out. Sometimes their suggestions 'became' the actuality of the story.

Story endings are moments for prolific oral involvement. I wondered aloud what might happen when she got back to the village, setting these ideas in motion:

He might get bigger

He wouldn't because she wasn't afraid

He was fierce

It's not very scary

He can't eat people up if he's small

I've got a wobbly tooth (That, too, was accepted and didn't throw me off course as it once might!)

He got bigger. He was a great big giant again

He got smaller still

This led into a discussion about the best size for a giant to be. Well, not exactly what you'd call a discussion – more a shouting match. This big! This big! This big! You can imagine the sort of thing, involving one or two feeling the need to stand up, very close to me indeed, to make their points the more positively. The Head-teacher said she wondered what Gwyneth's mother would say when her daughter appeared:

You naughty girl!

Where were you?

I've been up there! (pointing vigorously)

She wouldn't tell her mammy where she'd been

She'd have to walk over the sea . . .

Swim over the sea

You can imagine how these were discussed and how I had to do some geographical back-tracking to explain that the village was beside the mountain and on the other side of the village was the sea, so no walking on water was required! However, an extraordinary mental picture was suddenly evoked in the head of one little person. He said, 'In the middle, at the top of the mountain, there was a little rock pool, at the top of the mountain.' I know he saw, in his head, Gwyneth negotiating it.

Thus are new versions created between listening ears. Picture books (not that I'm against them!) and television have ready-made pictures.

Finally . . .

When she got to her mammy's house the giant scared her mammy

Gwyneth would say, GET SMALLER!

That big!

This big!

This big!

But I've been through all that before, remember? Time for lunch . . .

Afternoon school, and I moved to Year One with, as requested for shared project purposes, the same story again.

At the end of it I told them about some of the things I'd been afraid of during my life, especially when I was little, and some teachers and parents present joined in with me and the children. We talked about fear itself, and how it can often fall away when the source of it is confronted. This took almost as long as I'd taken to tell the story itself. The discussion (which my instinct tells me was reassuring to the participants and might have been made more of had it taken place in the normal course of classroom events with a trusted teacher, and followed through over the ensuing days) involved stated fears from the infants listed below:

Spiders

My daddy (this turned out to be fear FOR her airline pilot dad's safety)

Concorde

Monkeys jumping at me (Does it happen often? I ask. When I go to the zoo, he says, making instant better sense. Truth can often hide behind bizarre comments children make. It's important for them to feel secure in the knowledge that no spoken offering they make will be rejected.)

The dark

Monsters

Shadows in the moonlight

My dog

A dog chasing us (This gave rise to a detailed story of a particular event)

My cat dying

Death

Crocodiles under the bed

Snakes and crocodiles

Injections

When I kicked a ball over the fence (. . . another story).

Now the point of all this is, first, that all the discussion emerged from a storytelling. Second, even though I was a stranger in their midst, the initial communal experience of enjoying a story freed them to be open and voluble together. It made it safe for them. Everyone was given space. Each child's individual fears were comfortably explored and the anxieties of others were spotlighted and comprehended. The imagination does not simply invent fictions; its main function is to make new rounded sense of information already at its disposal.

On to a different reception class and Story 2. The children were mainly Asian in origin and English was not the first language of most of them. In addition to the sort of interaction I have described above, I was able to spend time hearing retellings of the story I told by small groups of children outside the classroom. The first lot were conveniently videotaped by a member of staff; this time I had to make do with my small tape recorder.

I will limit myself here simply to a few examples of ways in which these little children put their own stamp upon the events of my story either through imaginative flights of fancy or through visions in their heads which were moulded by their preconceived notion of the world. You choose:

Hamidur: The gods knocked on the cottage door and the lady said come in and the man turned the heat up. (I had said that the old man put more logs on the fire.)

Vinay: The wine jug started to fill up and bubbles were floating on it, going blublublublub.

Rajpreet: Once a pulla time there was a woman and a man. They lived in a cottage. There was a goose and a goat who lived in their house . . . [I had said the goat and the goose lived beside the pond but I suspect Rajpreet's 'their house' referred to that of the goose and the goat. A misinterpretation? Or is it a piece of intertextuality born of imaginative involvement in other stories such as 'The Three Little Pigs' told by their teacher? The next quotation suggests so.]

Sheena: Then the old woman ran out and she knocked on the goose's house and when he opened the door he went outside and they ranned around and around the pond.

These children had only just joined the reception class so were barely 5. Yet in spite of having no experience in the classroom of telling fictional stories themselves (by the end of my visits they'd had plenty!), they managed the following group-retelling of Baucis and Philemon. In the effort of this feat some of the juicier bits, e.g. blublublub, disappeared, alas.

Once upon a time there lived an old man and an old lady. They had a goose and a goat and they lived in a cottage. Then the gods started to knock on the doors but nobody, nobody . . . some people slammed the door and some people said no, you can't, we don't have strangers in the house. So . . . so the lady opened the door and she said, come in. Then he put the heater on. Then she poured some wine into two cups and when she done that the jug got full up, got back full up again and the bubbles were floating about. She went in the sitting room and she said, YOU ARE GODS! The gods . . . then the lady said, we could make the goose hot and the lady caught the goose . . . The lady and the goose runned around, the lady couldn't catch the goose. The goose runned around the pond. And the lady couldn't catch the goose and was very tired. The goose ran back in the house then the lady ran back in the house and the gods said, just go to bed. The goose went in the kitchen and the lady thought he was there and the lady went inside and there was the goose.

The lady saw the cherry tree moving about (next morning). The wind was blowing it. The wind was blowing the valley away. The valley started to go up and down and up and down and then the children were running about. The river growed and growed. They ran to somewhere where it couldn't come up to. They went up to the mountains. The valley fell down. Then all the people ran away. The wind was blowing. The water started to grow. The wind stopped and then it went back down. There was all water.

I have tried to indicate with these examples of children's talk something of the imaginative stimulus that storytelling can provide. What you cannot see was the drama work. I fleetingly watched on in the playground as thirty-plus children I'd been with during the morning crept stealthily and silently about, scrambling over logs, stooping low under the climbing frame, squeezing their way through concrete hoops, arms thrusting aside invisible undergrowth, feet sucked at by invented bogland, eyes searching upwards to discover how much of the mountain was left before the time came to meet with the giant over the mountain. (For a nursery curriculum based around the daily dramatisation of stories told by the children themselves I know of nothing better – or more readable – than the books of Vivian Gussin Paley.) Neither, alas, can you see the extraordinary art work achieved by the children in the Story 2 school under the eye of a professional artist with whom I had the good fortune to work for several days: watery landscapes topped with a rainbow shouting its colours; a tottering church steeple nudged by the snouts of fish; a cottage poised on the brink of a plum pudding mountain; and the most amiable, brilliant-white goose that's ever escaped the oven. These, and more, turned into so spectacular a mural (or, to quote the painters, muriel) it was later displayed in the Design Council in the Haymarket. And I haven't even mentioned new stories composed within a collective storytelling environment created initially by the perseverance of a teacher/storyteller as a long-term commitment. Music and storytelling which were so closely linked in old traditions have become separated, yet songs, and instrumental music-making for background effect, can prove a wonderful source of creative fun to heighten the pleasure of story making. An invaluable collection of stories with songs is *The Singing Sack*, though you don't need a book for the imaginative invention of jingles that little children can learn (incredibly fast, it seems to me: I've found they're often ready to join in when a song pops up in a story even at the first hearing). Being linked with a story gives music a new meangingful dimension.

WHAT ELSE?

Have you ever heard someone say, 'These kids just can't listen!'? Well, of course they can. I've watched even children with impaired hearing in my audiences straining to listen by their own means. I've watched hyperactive children settled throughout a good tale. Once I watched a whole staff, who had been dragooned into a Friday evening in-service session by a bossy headteacher, hang on every word. Narrative is the easiest form of discourse to listen to. Sometimes, especially with adults, I begin my sessions with a bit of patter, perhaps about how I have got to be where I'm at, perhaps about notions of storytelling, perhaps about the place of storytelling in history, or whatever. Then I begin a story. An instant change takes place in the appearance of the group. Don't ask me what infinitesimal signals beam out to me; whatever they are, the result is a kind of expectant stillness in the very air. Invisible antennae have transmitted the news to them that something different and perhaps worthy of undivided attention has just begun. I don't believe that so-called listening skills need to be taught. We simply need to provide that which actually invites listening – and there's nothing like wanting to know what's going to happen next.

Every good teacher of very young children knows that you can't compartmentalise talking, listening, reading and writing. They are subtly and inextricably linked together. To love books you must learn to love stories. To write stories you must begin by hearing them told and read; authorship must not be seen as something that occurs elsewhere. Surely the most joyous and stressless encounter with a story is when it is attached to a storyteller.

Having spent thousands of hours over my professional life reading aloud in classrooms I would hardly be likely to dispute the value of bringing the printed word to children in this way. The pleasure of it is most manifest when it's a well-illustrated book for the very young. But the complementary activity of telling, rather than reading, a story has distinct advantages of its own: there's continuous eye contact, body language, variation of pitch and speed and expression of voice to correspond with the words you have selected yourself as you go along, which do not have to conform to somebody else's choice. Most of all, it is an interactive process, adapting to the moment by moment visible responses of the audience.

A story told is a gift presented by the teller to the hearers. A book was around yesterday and will be there tomorrow (there are advantages in this, of course). A story told is for this present moment only. Your storytelling comes from inside you and no one else. If you transmit the magic of it – and we can all learn to do so if we care enough for the tale – children feel warmed by the spell you have woven for them alone. You have moved forward at one stroke in creating a mutually trusting community within your own four walls.

SO HOW IS IT DONE?

I don't need to spend long over this bit. In my view, there is no mystique attached to telling a story well though there are those who would have you believe so. The mystique is in the story itself – and its amazing capacity to mesmerise listeners, even occasionally to put them into a trance-like state. Sometimes I feel perturbed if members of an adult audience say to me, 'I could never tell a story like that'. On the one hand, of course it's flattering and I like praise as much as anyone else; but on the other, the last thing I want to do is to make people feel that you've got to have some special skill or training or vast experience to be able to hold an audience. Unless you have ambitions to do a turn at the South Bank, you have all that's necessary within you already. As I said at the beginning, we all have life-long practice in telling others about incidents and experiences from our own lives. It isn't as though telling a story is something to be taken up as a new venture, like painting in oils or playing the mandolin. And a major portion of our thinking time is taken up with narrating – the row we might have had but couldn't find the words, the interview we are soon to be attending, what we imagine ourselves doing on holiday, etc., etc. I'd say 60 per cent of the battle is finding the right story for you. If you don't like a story a lot, don't try telling it. And a story does not have to be elaborate to grab you. Sometimes even four little lines can attract you:

Here I am

Little Jumping Joan

There's nobody with me

So I'm all alone.

I really like that! – always have – you may not. There are so many wonderful stories for young children it's inconceivable that those who choose to work with the under-eights would not find personal treasures in the repertoire, including stories remembered from childhood.

Thirty per cent is the effort you put in to make that favourite story your own. You can change it in any way you fancy, to suit yourself or your children. And don't be afraid to use snippets from your own memories to help the reality of your tale: in my version of The Giant over the Mountain I have farmer Bassett and his daughter, Molly, delivering milk to the villagers – just as they did in Clydach, South Wales, when I was little; I have Gwyneth's mother shaking up her pillow at night at bedtime, just as my mother used to do; and Baucis and Philemon own a goat as well as a goose because a nursery man I know in Wiltshire who owned one of each told me that the goose would lay his head on the goat's belly and go to sleep: a nice idea for five-year-olds to contemplate! To remember your story, whether you make notes, draw diagrams, list key words, write it out first (resist temptation to learn it off by heart – if you do you'll be struggling for the 'correct' word you've learnt and the spontaneity will be lost, along with your cool!) or list the main episodes or whatever, is up to you. Practise in the bathtub or on the bus to work or whenever. I find the most useful aid is to *visualise* the events in the story so I am merely describing the moving pictures in my mind.

Which leaves 10 per cent. Fill that as you will – with your own tricks and tactics that suit you and the children you know. Whatever you may learn from others, there's no substitute for your own strengths which are fostered by your learning experiences, day in day out, with the children who learn alongside you.

Then tell your chosen tale as if it is the first time it has ever been told.

REFERENCES

Corbett, P. (ed.) (1993) *Tales, Myths and Legends*, Scholastic Collections (many good stories including my version of Baucis and Philemon).

East, Helen (ed.) (1993) *The Singing Sack*, A & C Black (with audiotape).

Paley, Vivian Gussin (1981) *Wally's Stories* and *The Boy who Would Be a Helicopter*, Harvard University Press.

Rosen, B. (1988) *And None of it Was Nonsense*, Collins Educational (Chapter 5: 'Selecting and preparing material for storytelling'; Chapter 6: 'A story read and a story heard', including Tantalus).

—— (1993) *Shapers and Polisher*, Collins Educational, (reprint; this contains much reference to telling stories to young children and includes various versions of 'The Giant over the Mountain' and other stories for telling).

Through her powerful and poetic writing Betty Rosen recreates the magic of storytelling and of listening to stories. For those of us involved with young children this presents us with wonderful opportunities to grab children's attention, open up to them imaginary and fantastic worlds, introduce them to the conventions of book and story language and supply them with a store

in their heads of known stories. With a wealth of story language in their heads together with the characters they encounter in stories and a growing store of 'tunes on the page' they are able to create, explore and expand their own skills as storytellers and story makers. The more opportunities children have to hear stories read and told, the more they are able to organise their own abilities to tell stories and eventually to write stories.

The power of poetic and book language is sometimes startling. Hannah, at 22 months, would re-tell familiar stories paying close attention to the sequence of events and to certain phrases that impressed her. So the Three Bears always went for a walk 'one early morning' and most stories started 'wunsaponatime' and when her mother commented one day on a very darkly stained nappy, she started saying 'it's a dark, dark poo in a dark, dark nappy'!

The stories young children tell start off being very simple – e.g. 'I went to the park' and as their experience and exposure to stories grow they are able to elaborate these simple 'proto-narratives' into recognisable story forms.

Tamara, at the age of 6 wrote this little story:

> One nite I saw a kangaroo darnsin round a sarcoll and I shoutit as loud as I could, but she couldant hear. So I tucht her. She saw me. I said Hallow. Larst nitht I saw the sam kangeroow asleep and I was vere cwiat. The next morning the kangeroow fanisht

You can see that Tamara, who had had stories told to her since her babyhood, was able to draw on the sort of language she has encountered in books and stories to help her create her own 'voice'. The language she used in this written story is very much the sort of language she will have heard in the stories read and told to her.

Fiona, also aged 6, drew on different things within the stories she has heard in this story.

> One day a little girl met a little boy. The little boy said, 'Do you want to come to my house and have tea?' And the little girl said, 'Yes, I would like to come to your house and have tea there. Where do you live?' The little boy said, 'I live at 37 Lawers Road, London N6 QRD. My mum said anyone can come to tea.' The little girl said, 'I'll ask my mum if I can stay to have tea. I will ask if I can stay the night.' The boy said, 'My mum said anyone can stay the night as well.'
>
> So the little girl went home and asked if she could have tea and stay the night. Her mum said she could but only if she would be good. The little girl said she would be good. So the little girl went to the boy's house for tea and she stayed the night. In the morning the little girl went to school with the little boy. She sat next to the little boy when she was working.

She played with him at playtime and sat next to him at lunch time and did the same thing in the afternoon. It went on and on and on until they were grow ups. Then they got married and hugged and kissed and had a baby and lived happily every after.

Fiona's story draws on both her everyday experience and on the repetitive phrases she will have heard in stories. And it has, of course – as all the best stories do – a happy ending!

Geraldine Lanigan (whose work you have already come across) told her group a story rather than reading one. She was astounded at the reaction and recorded some of the stories the children told:

Octavia (4 years old):

Once upon a time when I was little in my garden, there were a earthworm coming out of my plant.

A perfect story – with a beginning, and an end and set in a meaningful time frame – Rachel (4 years, 4 months):

Once upon a time, in a faraway kingdom, there were lots of big houses and there were some very, very pretty ladies in them. But one was the most beautifullest in the town. She was the most beautifullest in the whole kingdom. And the queen and king invited the most beautifullest girl in town to their palace. Well, of course they gave her a pretty bedroom too, and, of course, she had pretty dresses and she always, always had breakfast when her alarm clock rung. But she were indeed a very good one too. One day, when she was sleeping, she heard some galloping horses riding by. And one of them was the most handsomest one in the world. He knocked on the door. It swung open and he went in and up the winding staircase and found her lying there on the bed. Well, when she woke up, she found him waiting there and they lived happily ever after.

Rachel, who is the same age as Octavia, builds on her store of known stories and creates a world, peoples it with characters and ensures that there is the traditional happy ending. Look at how she uses comparison and superlatives – 'most beautifullest', 'most handsomest in the world'.

Damian (4 years, 6 months):

Once upon a time there was a big bear called Bernie, and he worked at a building site. He went up to the building site on his red motor bike. The other people were waiting for him and they were going too. Now Bernie drove a concrete mixer. That's the end.

Damian, draws on his own experience and on his interests – a building site, a red motor bike, a concrete mixer and a big bear called Bernie.

You might want to start your own collection of children's stories. Write them down, date them and keep them. Over time and as you refer back to them, you will be able to see the children growing and developing almost in front of your eyes. And, while you do this, try your hand as a storyteller yourself.

In Part IV we have looked at the importance of speaking and listening and of storytelling – which involves both. In Part V we extend our look at language by considering how young children make sense of the world of print and what we, the adults, can do to foster both a love of reading and writing and the necessary skills and knowledge to enable young children to become readers and writers.

Part V

Understanding the written world

Introduction to Part V

All of our young children live in a world where the written word is prominent. They see words written all around them – in shops, on street signs, on food packets, on television, in books. They encounter people reading these words – sometimes for pleasure, sometimes for information, sometimes for other purposes. As young children struggle to make sense of their world, they try to understand just what it is the adults they see around them are doing when they 'engage with print'.

Because the development of early literacy is so important, this is a very long section and contains both articles and observation notes which we hope you will find both interesting and informative.

32 Talking in your head

Young children's developing understanding of the reading process

Gillian Lathey

Part V opens with a chapter by Dr Gillian Lathey, Senior Lecturer at the Roehampton Institute, describing a piece of research she carried out in a nursery in West London. The author has been a teacher for many years and developed an interest in young children and their acquisition of literacy. Being bilingual herself, she developed a particular interest in children's literature in translation, which was the focus of her doctoral research completed in 1997.

As a very young child listening to stories read by his mother, Jean-Paul Sartre tried to explain to himself what was happening. His mother lowered her eyes, appeared to fall asleep and used unfamiliar language with confidence. Who was speaking? And to whom? Sartre's conclusion was that when reading to him his mother acted as a medium, and that the book was speaking through her. When alerted by Elizabeth Plackett to this remarkable insight in Sartre's account of his early development as a reader and writer in *Les Mots* (1964), my decision to investigate young children's understanding of the reading process was confirmed. I hoped to find out more about what young children (3 and 4 years old) think the act of reading entails and how they think fluent readers process print. Having worked with young children for many years, I was quite aware that insights like Sartre's may only be momentary, and that children's perceptions of such a complex process are likely to be shifting and changing all the time. In her essay 'The Development of Initial Literacy' (1984) Yetta Goodman describes children's active search for understanding:

> During early development, children may construct principles which they later have to discard. Some of these principles may actually interfere with the development of others for a period of time. The principles will overlap and interact, and the children will have to sort out which principles are most significant to meaning and which are not very useful.

The principle which the young Sartre had constructed, the delightful notion of the reader as medium, was the invention of a mind eager for understanding, and would be modified as his understanding grew.

In order to uncover some of these 'principles' constructed by young children, I spent some time in a nursery with a wide ethnic mix, close to Portobello Road in West London, armed with picture books as well as my own reading material and a mini tape recorder. Anyone who has tried to do so will know that it is well-nigh impossible to 'interview' three- and four-year-olds, and that the best material is often gained by chance. After my first visit – spent entirely in the sandpit – I became a permanent fixture in the book corner for one afternoon a week ready to read stories, and to talk about books and reading when the moment seemed right. I had an agenda of questions and possible approaches, but soon found that my own personal reading material proved to be a rich source of interest, comment and speculation. I spent time reading silently and asking children for their reactions, as well as asking them to demonstrate for me what it is that silent readers do.

WHAT GOES ON IN A SILENT READER'S HEAD?

After talking about my book and reading silently for a while as a group or an individual child watched, I usually started by asking the children whether they thought I was reading or not. Responses were mixed. On two separate occasions Ben told me that he did not think I could be reading because I was not 'talking'. I then tried to find out what he thought *should* happen.

Me: You know when I'm reading something like this, what do you think, what do you think happens? How do I do it?

Ben: By talking like this: [He holds the book and runs his finger backwards and forwards along the flyleaf] chatter, chatter, chatter, chatter, chatter, chatter.

By his delightful use of the word 'chatter' Ben is telling me that only reading aloud counts. Like Ben, Michelle felt that I could not be reading: 'Because you're not talking.' However, later in the same afternoon I talked with Michelle about her mother reading at home. She told me that her mother read 'books, not stories' – a nice distinction! I then asked her to show me how someone at home would read a book like my novel. She held the book in both hands and commented: 'They – they would just sit quiet.' Despite her earlier answer, Michelle does know more about silent reading which she has observed in her home. Even more revealing is her final comment: 'I like them being like that.' To be present while adults sit and read quietly represents for Michelle a calm and pleasant experience. Michelle's understanding of silent reading is context-dependent. Silent reading is a familiar practice at home, but in the nursery adults always read aloud to children. My silent reading in the book corner created an artificial situation which no doubt influenced her reply.

Some children were, however, quite clear about what was happening. Hannah claimed that I was reading: 'Because you're just reading it in your head.' Samya, who was walking purposefully to another part of the nursery during one of my silent reading sessions stopped for a moment to ask in a loud voice: 'Are you talking in your head?' Alice also told me that I was reading in my head because, 'Nobody hears.' I asked her what might be going on in my head and she replied with much laughter: 'I don't know. The wheels are working.' Alice had no doubt picked up the notion of wheels going round in the head from an adult, and is glad to have a way to satisfy me! Joshua resorted to fantasy when asked the same question. He talked about a 'stick in my head'.

Me:	And what's that stick doing?
Joshua:	It's going down in your trousers and going in you shoes.
Me:	It's going down my trousers and in my shoes?
Joshua:	Yes [touching his own legs]
Sally:	[To me] You've got tights on.

Joshua happily uses my question to allow his imagination full play, and may be thinking about puppets, or recalling a conversation about the brain sending messages through the body. Who knows? This whole conversation, including Sally's final comment, is a perfect illustration of the connections made by young children in their thinking, and how amusing and fascinating these are.

Joshua's 'stick' comment highlights the difficulty of gathering evidence in any systematic way, yet a revealing discussion on the nature of silent reading did develop quite unexpectedly, as the following scene illustrates. I am sitting in the book corner talking with Sade and looking at books. Ben and Oleuwaseun join us. I am looking at my novel.

Me:	I'm just going to read this bit to myself. You watch me. [There is an interested silence as I read.]
Me:	Now, then. Do you think I was reading that, Ben?' [Ben shakes his head]
Me:	Ben doesn't think I was. Do you think . . . [Sade and Oleuwaseun nod]
Sade:	Yes I think you . . .
Me: (to Ben)	Why do you think I wasn't reading it?
Ben:	Because you weren't talking.
Sade:	No, because you didn't *hear* her talking.
Me:	But sometimes, you know, when grown up people read books like this, they don't talk, do they? Or do they always talk, do you think?
Sade:	No.
Oleuwaseun:	They don't have to. They can if they want.
Me:	And what do you think is going on in their head when they're reading silently like that, Seun?
Oleuwaseun:	Some people read quietly.
Sade:	They . . . they're reading it in their head they are.
Me:	They're reading it in their head, are they?

Sade:	In the brain. They go dm dm dm dm dm dm dm . . .
Me:	Do they?
Sade:	. . . talking . . .
Me:	So they're reading in their brains and it's going dm dm like that inside, is it?
Sade:	Yes.

These three four-year-olds are reflecting on the reading process as demonstrated by a fluent reader reading silently. Ben did not think that I was reading because he could hear nothing, while Sade and Oleuwaseun have a much more sophisticated understanding of what a silent reader does. Sade contradicts Ben on a fine point of logic. He should, she asserts, say simply that he did not hear me talking, not state categorically that I had not been talking at all. The thinking behind Sade's contradiction becomes clear later in the conversation. Sade states that people reading silently are reading in their heads, and then further refines 'head' to 'brain'. She even makes sounds to represent this voice in the head and describes them as 'talking'. She understands reading silently as an internalisation of the voice used when reading aloud, a voice which can be physically heard in his or her head by the reader. In order to reach such a conclusion she must have had considerable experience of watching silent readers at work. Oleuwaseun emphasises the choice a skilled reader has – to read silently or out loud. He tells me that some people read 'quietly', but is clear that this is their choice. Both Sade and Oleuwaseun have developed an understanding that reading involves inner mental activity, and Sade makes this concrete by describing the sounds made by the voice in the brain. Nigel Hall in *The Emergence of Literacy* (1987: 32) describes how the children he talked to perceived reading as an oral activity, and some believed that even animals could learn to read and write. He found that it was not until five to seven years that children started saying animals could not read because 'they are not human' or 'they haven't got brains'. Hall concludes:

> The idea that reading is a distinctly human activity or that it involves inner mental processing appears to be a much later development and may be due in part to instruction and an increasing metacognitive ability.

I would suggest that the understanding shown by Sade and Oleuwaseun and other children who described 'reading in the head' at such a young age is unlikely to be the result of instruction, but has rather developed from experience of observing silent reading. These children are cousins, they are familiar with at least one West African language and one parent of each child is a student. They have had plenty of opportunity to observe silent reading, to watch their parents write, and to learn that it is possible to communicate in more than one language. They have, with 'increasing metacognitive ability', begun to draw their own conclusions about the processes involved in reading and no doubt in all language models.

THE RELATIONSHIP BETWEEN THE READER'S CONSCIOUSNESS AND PRINT

Closely related to an understanding of what happens in a silent reader's head are children's concepts about the relationship between the reader's consciousness and print, sometimes revealed quite incidentally. On one visit to the nursery I started reading a popular picture book to a small group. Yassin walked up to us holding the model he was working on. After a while he looked at me, clearly puzzled, and asked: 'How come you know the story?' He was familiar with the book, had heard it read to him many times in the nursery and possibly at home, but was unable to understand how I, a stranger, could possibly know the same story. For Yassin the story was attached to particular people and contexts. At that moment he did not consider the story to be 'fixed' to the book, permanently there to be read by anyone. The book and the pictures were important, but somehow the story belonged to the people who told it.

Unfortunately Yassin had gone to finish his model before I could answer him or pursue the discussion further. A remark like this is a perfect opening for reflection on how books and the reading process work.

A colleague undertaking her own research, Sally Ginnever from Sir Thomas Abney School in Hackney, related a similar incident which happened in her reception class. A teacher from St Vincent had told her class a story about growing plantains. Some time after she had gone, Paul asked where the story had come from. Other children replied that it was in her head. Paul then wanted to know whether she had a book in her head! Paul's understanding appears to be the reverse of Yassin's. He may have limited experience of storytelling, and believes that stories must always be attached to books. Luckily this discussion did continue, and Sally describes how Dougal answered Paul by telling him that the teacher did not have a book in her head, but that everyone has words in his or her head and puts them together to make stories. Dougal has helped Paul to begin to distinguish between story reading and storytelling by explaining to him something about the process involved in telling a story without a text.

Understanding the relationship between text and reader is an important part of learning to read, and can be a source of puzzlement for some children. Sartre's belief that the book was speaking through his mother is another example of how a child's thinking can develop, as is Alan Garner's account (in *The Signal Approach to Children's Books*: 322–3) of his misunderstanding of first person narrative.

> the only time my father ever read to me was a total failure because it was 'Robinson Crusoe' and he never got beyond the third page . . . somewhere round there . . . because I kept saying 'you didn't'.

Garner could not dissociate the words he heard from his father, who presumably made no attempt to discuss the relationship between the book and himself.

IMITATING SILENT READERS

Discussing my silent reading sessions with children revealed their developing understanding of the processes involved, as did incidental comments such as those made by Yassin and Paul. Another window onto children's thinking was opened by asking them to take my book and *show* me what a silent reader actually does, so that I could observe their physical gestures and actions. In their investigation into pre-school children's silent reading, Ferreiro and Teberosky (1982: 155–60) found that there was a development from a belief that reading had to be accompanied by talking to an understanding of the importance of 'looking'. I asked Luca to show me how an adult would read my book. He flicked through the book and then looked hard and long at the cover and various pages, opening his eyes wide in an exaggerated fashion. On another occasion he again spent some time looking at the front cover, then looked at a page silently and uttered a loud sigh. Luca recognises the importance of looking at the book's cover to gain some idea of its content; of focusing the eyes and looking closely at the page, and of registering a reaction from time to time – in this case a sigh! Leona held my book to show me what I had been doing.

Leona: When you go like this [looking at the text in an exaggerated manner] it still means you're reading it.

Leona knows that you do not have to use your voice to read, but that 'looking' is essential.

A hypothesis which would prove to be less 'useful' (Goodman, 1984) was demonstrated by several children who seemed to believe that following the text with a finger is an indispensable aspect of silent reading. I spent considerable time one afternoon with Fadua, who can speak both Arabic and English. After I had read silently, Fadua told me that she did not think I was reading, and when asked what she thought *was* happening she replied: 'Because you do that with your finger.' I had not been using my finger to follow the text, so presumably Fadua was implying that I ought to. Later she wanted to have a go at reading my novel, opened it at the first page and sat in silence looking at the text and running her finger slowly and carefully underneath each line. Suddenly, half way down the page she noticed a two-line quotation at the top of the page which she had not 'read' and was determined to start again. Again she sustained this 'reading' activity for a long time, until I asked a question:

Me: How did you learn – how did you know how to read like that?
Fadua: My sister knows.

Fadua then continued until she began to tire, at which point she moved faster down the page and flicked through the book looking for a page she could 'remember', the word she was using to stand for 'reading'. I wanted to investigate her understanding further, and after once more reading silently myself, asked my usual question:

Me: What do you think goes on in my head when I'm reading it? What do you
           think's happening when I'm reading it? You watch me. [I read silently, *not*
           using my finger.]
Fadua: cause – cause – you – fingers [speaking very slowly and deliberately]
Me: Mmmmm . . . what have I got on my fingers?
Fadua: [distracted by noise] It's a bit louder – a little bit come . . . over there.
Me: What happens if I'm not using my fingers?
Fadua: Because . . . can't read it.
Me: I can't read it? Do I need to use my fingers?
Fadua: What?
Me: Can I read it without using my finger?
Fadua: Yes.

Fadua, through watching her older sister read, has developed the notion that
following lines of print with the finger is an essential part of reading, even for
silent readers. As she learns to read herself, this will no doubt be a helpful strategy
for a time, but she will realise that it is not essential. Indeed she seems to change her
thinking during the course of our final conversation, probably as a result of my
questions. When I ask what is happening, it is the use of the finger which is her first
concern. Fadua seems to be saying that I could not read without using my finger,
yet when asked a direct question realises that of course, I could. Here is an instance
of the development described by Yetta Goodman (1984: 105) when a child has
constructed a principle which may:

> actually interfere with the development of others for a period of time.

Fadua does not, for example, make exaggerated eye movements or mention the
importance of 'looking' as other children did. She is concerned with one principle
for the time being, yet her thinking is already beginning to shift. Fadua's concentration and absorption when following lines of small print were quite remarkable,
as was the length of time she spent on this activity.

CONCLUSIONS

Talking with young children about their understanding of the reading process has
proved to be a fascinating and often entertaining area of research. At times my
questioning forced children to invent spontaneous answers (the 'gems' we all love
to hear), and in some cases acted as a trigger to develop a child's thinking a stage
further. Indeed, it became increasingly clear to me as the study progressed that
discussing children's perceptions with them can play a vital role in their developing
understanding.

This understanding rests, of course, on children's experience of literacy inside
and outside the nursery. Fadua has watched her sister follow lines of print with her
finger, Michelle enjoys the sense of security and peace when her mother reads
silently, and Sade and Oleuwaseun have seen their parents reading and studying at

home. The influence of these models is apparent in the children's behaviour and comments. One child who expressed disgust at the sight of an adult novel may have a relative with literacy difficulties. Understanding that reading can be separated from speaking is an important development in children who are not yet reading as Ferreiro and Teberosky (1982: 159) have pointed out, and the models they have observed have helped Sade and Oleuwaseun to achieve this understanding.

Children need to observe adults and older siblings reading in order to be able to imitate their reading behaviours. They will inevitably see adults engaged in functional reading – shopping lists, street signs, adverts on television, and so on. They also need to observe sustained silent reading, the recreational or purposeful reading represented in the home by the variety of newspapers, magazines, pamphlets and books. To extend this experience into the nursery is difficult because of lack of time, yet there is no reason why adults working in the nursery should not take along their personal reading material to show children and talk about the pleasure and purposes of reading in their own lives. Talking generally about reading, and about the models children have seen, can only serve to further their understanding of the reading process.

The current debate about the place of 'knowledge about language' in the curriculum has at its centre the importance of reflection on language. Thanks to the explosion of research into early literacy development, we now appreciate the *active* nature of children's developing understanding of the reading process. Children's thinking is changing all the time as Yetta Goodman (1984: 102) points out:

> children discover and invent literacy as they participate actively in a literate society.

Children construct principles based on their observations – for example, that speaking out loud is essential to reading, that 'looking' is important in silent reading, or that you have to follow lines of print with your finger to read. We need to be aware of these developments and to encourage discussion and reflection on the reading process so that principles which are not productive can be discarded.

It is surely an important part of our role as teachers of reading to encourage discussion and reflection when children do voice their developing understanding or indeed their confusion. Yassin's chance remark: 'How come you know the story?' made when I was reading a familiar book, would have provided a good opening for discussion, and Fadua's notion of the importance of the finger began to change as I talked to her. Children have a great deal to learn about reading, and their thoughts on the processes involved are fluid and changing. Their perceptions and attitudes by the age of 3 or 4 will influence their future development as readers and indeed as writers and talkers. All adults working with children have an important part to play in fostering children's confidence as readers and encouraging them to reflect on what it is they have to do to become readers in the fullest sense. Understanding how silent reading works and the pleasure an adult experiences when absorbed in a book or magazine is a vital stage in this development. The relationship between reader and print is an enormous intellectual puzzle which continues to tax the best adult minds – children need all the help they can get.

NOTE

With thanks to the children and staff at Ainsworth Nursery.

REFERENCES

Ferreiro, E. and Teberosky, A. (1982) *Literacy Before Schooling*, Heinemann Educational.
Garner, A. interviewed in *The Signal Approach to Children's Books*, Thimble Press.
Goodman, Y. (1984) 'The Development of Initial Literacy', in Hillel Goelman *et al.* (eds) *Awakening to Literacy*, Heinemann Educational.
Hall, N. (1987) *The Emergence of Literacy*, Hodder and Stoughton.
Sartre, J.-P. (1964) *Les Mots*, Editions Gallimard.

As workers in the field of early childhood education we often need to consider ways of ensuring that young children encounter literacy in situations that make human sense to them. All young children try to make sense of the world, to find the patterns and work out the rules. The world of literacy is part of their world and they approach literacy in exactly the same way that they do any other area of experience. They watch, listen, consider, try things out, get them wrong, try again – and so on. In the observation notes in Chapters 33 and 34, written by students on the Early Childhood Studies Scheme, you will find some examples of children actively exploring the written world, sometimes trying to work out what the purpose of writing is, sometimes writing themselves, sometimes working out the rules governing print, sometimes playing at reading. We also read about what the practitioners do as they plan for literacy and try and engage with the children about their discoveries and theories.

33 Ade plays at reading to Charlotte

Jacqui Perry

At the time of writing the observation notes, the author lived on a North London council estate with her husband and two sons, who were then aged six and fourteen. She and her husband ran a Kid's Club for the children on the estate and she worked part-time as a nanny and helped out at her younger son's school. She said of herself:

I love working with children, as they are always such an inspiration. I never thought that studying for a degree could be so enjoyable and rewarding. I feel that children have so much to offer and it is up to us, as child care workers, to learn as much as we can in order to help children develop their skills and understanding of the world around them.

Five-year-old Ade is playing with some cars on the floor and Charlotte, who is 18 months old, is sorting through a pile of books.

She picks up *Fox in Socks* and goes over to Ade. She uses a lot of body language to tell Ade what she wants. She gives him the book, then takes him by the hand. Ade seems to find this amusing and follows her lead. Charlotte keeps saying 'Boo! Boo! There! There!' (She says 'boo' for book.)

She pulls him over to an armchair and only lets go of his hand when she is sure he is going to sit with her. She repeats 'Boo Boo?' in a questioning tone, as if to say, 'Well, are you going to read to me?'

Ade smiles at her and says, 'Do you want me to read to you, Charlotte?' Charlotte smiles back. 'Boo,' she repeats. Ade places the book on his lap and, before he gets a chance to turn the first page, Charlotte is doing it for him. She sits quietly and listens to the story, looking at the pictures and turning the pages. She occasionally looks up at Ade, smiles and remarks on something. Ade, not really understanding what she has said, nods and smiles and says things like, 'Oh, yes!' or 'Really, Charlotte?' (which is something I tend to say to her); then he continues reading.

The strange thing about this is that Ade, although he knows the book fairly well and can, in fact, read most of it from memory, sometimes using the pictures as clues, does not read the story in English. He reads the whole story, with Charlotte listening intently at his side, in a language I can only describe as 'gibberish'!

When he has finished the story I congratulate him on reading so nicely to Charlotte and, just as a matter of interest, I ask him what language he was reading in. With no hesitation he answers, 'African, of course!' (Silly me! I should have guessed.)

I later found out that he had listened to a Nigerian storyteller in the school assembly. His class has been learning about different cultures and languages and he is interested in hearing other languages.

I asked Ade whether he would like me to read the same book again to both him and Charlotte, but he says, 'No!' (His eyes look upwards and he tuts!) 'We've just had that one,' he says, indignantly.

'Would you like to choose another book, then?' I ask.

Ade chooses another book (strangely enough, it happens to be a French story book) and Charlotte also picks up a book and hands it to me. I sit between the two children and read both books. They both sit still and follow the pictures. Ade occasionally asks me to point out a French word and explain its meaning.

COMMENTS ON THIS OBSERVATION

In this observation I was fascinated to watch Ade taking on the role of the adult in storytelling and seeing him read in a similar way to me. Charlotte was never concerned that she didn't understand the words being read to her. She seemed quite happy to sit and listen and study the pictures. She also had Ade's full attention, which was what she wanted. She managed to make her needs clear to Ade, using body language. Finally, it was fascinating to note that Ade followed each word he 'read' with his finger, although he was not, of course, reading the actual printed words on the page! This observation is fascinating for a number of reasons. Let us examine what it tells us first about Ade.

Ade clearly has the confidence to be a reader and a clear (although not necessarily accurate) idea of what is involved in reading. Moreover, he understands that languages other than English can be written down and read and he draws on his previous experience of hearing a story told in another language. It is extraordinary that he chooses to 'read' this story (which he knows well and can read from memory) in a made-up language.

What about Charlotte? What does she already know (aged only 18 months) about literacy? It is clear that Charlotte understands something of how books work. She is able to choose the one she wants, to turn the pages, to tune into the sounds and use the pictures to provide the meaning. Even when she cannot find the meaning (as in the French story book) she is content to be in that warm situation, with a book and the undivided attention of another person.

When Jacqui tries to discover why this has happened she suggests that he

is drawing on a recent experience of hearing a Nigerian storyteller in school. Ade plays the role of adult in the session and imitates the way in which adults he knows read to children. Interesting, too, is the fact that he runs his finger underneath the text in the French story book, although he is not paying attention to the actual words on the page. (Go back to Chapter 32, for more on this.)

34 Making a big book

Nancy Coyne

In the second set of observation notes, Nancy Coyne, who worked as a nanny for two small children describes how she chose to make a 'Big Book' for the children to see how they responded. 'Big Books' are enlarged formats of books, first introduced in an attempt to match the intimacy that occurs when an adult reads to one child (usually on her/his lap) with a group of children. A child on a lap is in close proximity to the text and the pictures: using an enlarged format of a book allows this to happen for children in a group.

I decided to make a big book for the two children I look after because I found that, while reading a smaller book with both of them, Mark – who is 14 months old – wanted to touch the pictures on every page. He would cover up the words so Louise – who is three-and-a-half – would complain that Mark was 'spoiling the story' because she liked to look at the words and point out the letters she knew or ask about words. So I thought the solution would be to have a big book with pictures on one side so Mark could look at it and touch it and attempt to say what the pictures were, while Louise could sit on the other side of me and 'read' the book by herself, eventually.

So, with this in mind, I told Louise what I wanted to do and asked her to help me. This made her very excited and she came up with the title 'When Goldilocks Went To The House of the Bears' because we had recently been to a stage production of this fairy tale and both children really enjoyed it. So, while Mark was having his daily nap Louise and I began to make the big book. I drew lines on the right-hand side of the paper first and while Louise sang the song aloud I wrote the words. Then I got Louise to look through some books and find some pictures of chairs, beds, bowls and bears so that I could draw them.

I drew three of each and Louise helped colour them in and glue them to the page. Louise got very excited making this book and kept saying, 'Are we nearly finished yet?' Eventually, after about two weeks, the book was finally finished and we sat down to read the book. Louise was adamant that she sat on the side with the writing and Mark on the side with the picture. Mark loved the size of the book and touched every picture and said something like 'da da' and when he saw the page with Goldilock's eyes he pointed to his own eyes and then poked mine, which made Louise laugh. Louise, on the other hand, pointed to each word and read it and recognised letters that were in her name. She knew that the words went from left to right and from top to bottom. The last page, where the three bears growl, brought giggles all round, with shouts of 'Again! Again!'

The big book is now a firm favourite in the household and is read at least twice a day. It proved to be a success in that Louise, having helped me make this big book, wanted to make a small book for Mark all about fruits which she didn't want any help with. She completed about 90 per cent of the book herself and during that week told everyone we met she was going to be an author when she grew up. Someone asked her what an author was and she was able to say, 'They write books.' I think this understanding of what authors do is clearly linked to her own experience of helping me to make my big book.

COMMENTS ON THIS OBSERVATION

- The adult, through noticing what each child was doing when they shared books, used this information to help her solve the problem of the two children having different needs.
- She took a familiar story to enlarge and allowed the children to draw on their previous experience, both of the story itself and also of their visit to the theatre to see a dramatised version.
- She involved the older child in the process of making the book and clearly talked to her about what an author does – as revealed by Louise's later comments about authors. As she watched the children interact with the big book she was able to come to some conclusions about where each child was with regard to understanding books, pictures, texts and the conventions of print.

35 Learning to read made easy

A study of one child's development as a reader

Evelyn Slavid

Chapters 35 and 36 are 'biographical in nature': both were written about real children and are based on observations made about the children in the first case by the child's mother and in the second by the child's grandmother. The tradition of keeping notes on one's own children's progress is a long one and the literature on reading is full of pieces like these. In Chapter 35 Evelyn Slavid (following in the tradition of Halliday, Baghban and Bissex) studies her own child and describes how Jess became a reader. As a small child Jessica is already aware of the pleasure offered by reading; she is able to reflect on what it is she does as she reads and has a tremendous interest in books and in how they are constructed. She was able to read by the time she went to school. She had been immersed in books and stories at home and showed, from very early on, an interest in books and in how they work. By the time she went to school and started to learn 'phonics' she already understood that reading involves taking the writer's meaning from the page. She had already developed what Margaret Meek calls:

> an orientation to literacy: a set of expectations of what reading and writing can be like: the pleasure of a story, a way of playing with language, a notational device for drawing action instead of words.

Evelyn Slavid has been a primary teacher for many years and has recently completed an Open University degree in psychology. She is currently supervising students and lecturing part-time at Kingston University. Her interest in children and in literacy started long before Jessica's birth.

Jessica is 5 years, 10 months old. I have just tested her reading age using a test called 'New Reading Analysis' (NFER Nelson) and found that her reading score comes out at about age 11 and her comprehension age at the same. I do not hold great store by tests like these and the fact that I administered the test myself could, of course, be open to criticism. However, Jessica spends a lot of time reading and really enjoys it. I was interested to see if this was reflected in the test score.

If I examine her favourite books at present I discover that they are quite diverse: Enid Blyton adventure stories; 'Milly Molly Mandy' stories and lots of poetry including works by Michael Rosen and Brian Patten. I have never stopped her from reading anything she has been given or chosen, but will always talk to her about the stereotypes some authors display. She is, I feel, learning to be critical about the books she reads. She often chooses to read books with her friends. They take turns to read stories to each other. She also swaps books and they often talk to one another about what they are reading. So reading, for Jess, is not just a solitary activity, but a social one as well. Jessica has just passed through a stage where she would read stories but not in the order in which they were written. I found this very strange and when I asked her why she did this she said that certain chapters sounded more interesting than others and so she read those chapters first. I then asked her if she thought that the author would mind, but she said no, because she read the whole book in the end. It was fascinating for me to hear the author P.D. James talking about how she writes her books and to hear that she doesn't write them sequentially, but starts with the scenes or actions that interest her most at the time. So maybe Jessica is onto something!

When I was asked to write about Jessica's reading development, I didn't know where to start. As a working mother I felt that I hadn't done anything different from any other parent. But when I observed other parents and thought about how much I had learnt as a teacher, I realised that, when it came to teaching my own child to read, I possessed knowledge that other parents may not have had access to. I was lucky in that I was teaching at a time when reading schemes were being removed from the school I worked in to be replaced by 'real books' and when Waterland (1985) and Bennett (1979) were compulsory reading for primary teachers. It was also a time when reading was regarded as a developmental process along with walking and talking. Armed with this information I then became a parent. I did not find parenting in general an easy process and found I did not have a great deal of time to observe my child's progress. Many friends suggested I should keep diaries of her progress. I never managed this in any detail, although I wrote down certain milestones.

What I did do with Jessica was to talk to her about print. We would look at the writing on things like cereal boxes, etc. I provided her with lots of books – plastic books and material books, but mostly picture books which might have been deemed more suitable for older children (mostly hand-downs from friends). She had an alphabet frieze in her room. But the most important thing we did was to read to her as often as possible from when she was about 9 months old. When she first started speaking I played games with her using books – e.g. showing her a picture with a word underneath, covering up the word and saying, 'What do you think the word says?' I would then uncover the word and we would both be pleased that she had, of course, guessed the correct word. All that this game did was to draw her attention to print. It was fun – and it distinguished between picture and word. I have to emphasise that I would never suggest covering up the pictures and expecting the child to read the words. The important thing about it was that it was in the context of a game which Jessica enjoyed and in which success was guaranteed.

Another thing I did at this very early stage was to make Jessica a book about herself. I would love to be able to say that this was a well-produced and finished item. In reality it was a scrap book where I stuck odd photographs of Jess and her friends and family and wrote simple, descriptive sentences – e.g. 'Jess is pointing at her dad' or 'Where is Jessica's mum?' She loved to 'read' this book and learnt it off by heart and would want to 'read' it to other people. It was during this 'reading' that I observed interesting comments from some friends and family. They would actually say, 'She's not reading. She knows it off by heart.' This seemed a strange reaction from people who happily interpret the most unintelligible utterances as 'words' and the first hesitant steps usually ending up as a tumble, as 'walking'. This book is still a favourite of Jessica's and she still enjoys showing it to friends and family. What I also did with this book was to sometimes point to words on the page, such as 'I' and say 'Can you see that it's the same here?' (pointing to another 'I'). This helped Jessica realise that the same symbol or set of symbols always says the same thing.

Before she could read I never tried to teach Jessica the sounds that letters make, but she learnt the alphabet by singing songs. It was only once she started reading that we talked specifically about the sounds that letters make.

It was coincidental that I became aware that Jess actually realised print–word correspondence because, when she was about 19 months old, she was videoed by a relative. He later sent me a copy and in this video Jess can be clearly seen pointing to the word 'I' and then pointing to her own eye and saying 'I'. Now there is clearly some confusion for her about meaning, but, at this very early age, she was able to identify a symbol as having a meaning of some sort.

Some of Jessica's favourite books were those where she could join in and make noises or help by finding things in the pictures. She often wanted to 'read' the story to me, which was great, and, although she was really telling me the story, I would once or twice draw her attention to print by saying things like 'Can you see a word that starts with the same letter/sound as your name?' I need to stress that I would not interrupt the flow of the story, but wait until the end before doing this.

I continued reading stories to Jessica – interesting picture books and sometimes the same book night after night after night. She usually chose, though sometimes, in desperation, I would hide the book that had gone on for too long and introduce something different. As Jess got older she would talk about the picture more and more and recognise more words. It was at this later stage that I started talking to her about the sounds that different letters make. I always used the name and the sound of the letter as I believe that even at an early stage children are able to understand that this, for example, is letter 'A' and it usually makes the sound 'a' as in 'apple'.

One of the other special things that has happened for Jessica is that, from when she was very young, her father has made up stories for her. They started when she was about 2 years old and involve the same core characters, with additional characters brought in from time to time by Jessica or by Peter (her father). I see them as a sort of soap opera! Many different issues are dealt with in these stories (known as the 'Emma' stories). Even though the core characters remain the same, it was only last week that I discovered that one of them was blind. Jessica has always loved the 'Emma' stories and, if given the choice of being read a story or told a story, it will be told a story every time. Jess has learnt a great deal of what she knows through these stories – about plants, animals, love, jealousy. There is so much that children can learn through the medium of stories.

When Jess went to a childminder I was adamant that I did not want her to be taught to read, and it was the same when she went to nursery. The childminder read her lots of stories and sang rhymes to her and when she went to a nursery they read a wide selection of stories. They did many activities based on nursery rhymes, sang songs and used many aids and props whilst telling stories. It was a nursery that did not teach children to read, although many nurseries in the area pride themselves on the fact that they do!

When it came to choosing a school for Jess, I was determined that we needed to choose a school where she would not be put off reading. I visited many schools and was shocked by the number that insisted that children work their way through a reading scheme, regardless of ability or interest. I was amazed when one parent at a local playgroup where I was giving a talk on early reading, expounded the virtues of a school where her child had read 120 books in the same reading scheme. I felt so sorry for the child! I eventually found a school where, although they used reading scheme books, they allowed children to choose what they wanted to read from a wide selection of books. The school provides an atmosphere in which reading is valued. All the children (aged 4–11) have a quiet reading time during the day. Fiction and non-fiction books are present in all the classrooms and are easily accessible to the children.

More recently I have turned my attention to the way that Jessica's enjoyment of stories has carried over into her writing. I was, originally, very sceptical about emergent/developmental writing. But I now realise how it gives children the freedom and confidence to write. Jessica and her friends, both at home and in school, often choose to write and make up stories for and about each other. I believe that this is due to the fact that, at school, they have been given the chance to be successful writers (in terms of composition), without fear of being criticised for incorrect spellings. The stories Jess writes are often based on the stories she has read or been told. She knows how to get help with spelling, but for her, the essential bit of writing – the meaning of her stories – is allowed to develop.

I want to conclude by saying that I don't feel that anything I have done has been difficult. Jessica says she doesn't remember how she learnt to read, although she does remember one or two favourite books (like *The Very Hungry Caterpillar*) that she spent time looking at when she was little. She says that she learnt those books off by heart – and was then able to read. This is, of course, an oversimplification of a complex process. But learning to read was easy for Jess – maybe because it was pressure-free, fun and because she always understood the purpose of reading and the pleasures to be found in books.

REFERENCES

Bennett, J. (1979) *Learning to Read with Picture Books*, Thimble Press.
Waterland, L. (1985) *Read with Me – An Apprenticeship Approach to Reading*, Thimble Press.

36 Hannah and her books

Sandra Smidt

This chapter by Sandra Smidt charts the development of Hannah's interaction with spoken language, books and stories from her birth to the age of 22 months. Evelyn Slavid and Sandra Smidt worked together for many years and it was Jessica's development as a passionate reader that largely led to Hannah's parents reading to her from birth.

INTRODUCTION

Babies need books. No one would argue with that nowadays. One has only to look in bookshops to see how many books are being produced specifically for babies to see how a potential market has been exploited. One has only to talk to parents who have been involved in some of the 'books for babies' projects to appreciate how true this is. But what do babies get from books? Why are books important not only in the early years, but in the early months?

In this piece we look at how one baby, growing up in a house full of books, interacts with books and try and explore what it is she is learning from this experience. Hannah is almost 10 months old. She crawls, pulls herself upright, babbles to herself as she explores her world, climbs up on her mum's knee for a cuddle and greets each new day and situation as something to be explored and enjoyed. Like other babies of her age she is intensely interested in everything and will spend considerable amounts of time exploring new objects and achieving goals she sets herself. As an only child she has the benefit of a great deal of adult love and attention. She also has the advantage of having been introduced to stories, rhymes, songs and books from birth.

Her books include board books, waterproof books, hardback and paperback books. She has flap books, books with photographs of babies like herself, counting books and story books. We examine how Hannah interacts with the books and with the adults around the books to try and understand what she is interested in and how this helps her understand her world.

WHAT IS THIS THING AND HOW DOES IT WORK?

Hannah sees people around her reading books, papers and newspapers. She also sees people holding the books they read aloud to her, turning the pages and often pointing to words or pictures on the page.

When she was nine-and-a-half months old, her mother reported that she had spent something like two hours exploring her box of books. With her back turned to her mother – who was sitting at the opposite end of the room – she spent the time taking the books out of the box, choosing some to pore over and rejecting others. Her exploration of the books seemed to relate to turning them over and over, sometimes holding them upwards, exploring the pictures and print on the cover, paying great attention to some picture or pattern. At first her mother thought she was selecting the books she knew well for further exploration, but it emerged that this was not the case. Her selection of books appeared random – although it almost certainly wasn't. But quite why Hannah rejected some of the books remained unclear.

A few days later (and after more similar play with the books) Hannah was seen sitting upright on the floor and holding a book just as she had seen adults do. She tends now to get the books the right way up and to start from the front and move to the back. She peers at the pictures and turns the pages with skill and care.

We guessed – and it can be no more than that – that her exploration of the books had helped her sort out the orientation of the books and to achieve her goal of holding a book 'like a reader'.

PICTURES AND NAMING

Like most young children Hannah's life is bathed in language. Those who care for her talk through the routines of bath time and nappy changing; they sing her songs and chant rhymes; they play finger games and peekaboo. Embedded in this sea of words Hannah finds meaning by tuning into individual words or phrases which she now recognises, and which are always set in meaningful contexts. Like all babies Hannah uses the context to get at the meaning. Her recognition of individual words and phrases has led her to the point of 'requesting' names for things she is interested in. She makes her meaning clear by pointing, eye pointing and vocalising.

When she looks at her books she makes little noises to indicate recognition. When she sees a picture of a cat, for example, she makes a sound – looks at the adult, who almost invariably scaffolds her learning by saying something like 'Yes, it's a cat, isn't it?' – and beams. It is easy to understand this naming when it relates to the real objects in her world – things like a cat or a baby or a flower. But she also demands the naming of things which are totally 'unreal' to her. *Rosie's Walk* by Pat Hutchins is full of things Hannah has never seen or experienced. She has no knowledge of foxes or hens or goats, yet she requests the naming of these creatures and will then select one for special attention. She will leaf through the pages of the book until she comes to the page she wants (most often the one showing the goat) and study the picture with intense concentration as she plays her 'name it for me' game.

As Hannah encounters images in books she is able to discover that not all cats look exactly like her cat: yet they are still cats. She is beginning to classify. Very recently Hannah came upon the picture of the camel in *Dear Zoo* (Rod Campbell). Her grandmother said, 'It's a camel – and look, Hannah, here's another camel', and showed her a picture of a camel in *Where's Julius?* (John Burningham) and then a drawing of a camel on a cigarette package and a stuffed camel made by a child in Egypt. Hannah looked carefully from one to another: one would guess she was trying to find what features made all four images share the label 'camel'.

When Hannah was a small baby her parents bought her a set of books based on the theory that young babies respond to high contrast images. She did pay some attention to these black and white images, but showed no preference for them over other images she was introduced to. From the age of about three months she showed intense interest in paintings and objects in her environment. The pictures she encounters in books clearly also interest her and for a long time she seemed very tuned in to images on a dark background – the cat on the wall against the night sky in *Peace at Last* (Jill Murphy) and the animals going home in the dark in *Where Does Brown Bear Go?* (Nicki Weiss). She demonstrates her interest in these pictures by paying prolonged attention to them and requesting names for the images she focuses on.

Browne (1994) found that her daughter Rehana was interested in complex, bright pictures until the age of six months, but then, for a short while, preferred simpler images. Browne says:

> In common with many other children, however, oversimplified images or pictures lacking depth or movement were quickly discarded.

Hannah shows evidence of this by the intense concentration she lavishes on pictures both in books and on the walls. At the moment she demands to be shown two Chagall prints which are complex, colourful and full of movement. So she will now point to 'the sun playing the violin' or 'the red horse with a fish and a bird in its head'. It is fascinating to speculate on what sense Hannah is able to make of such eye-catching images, representing things fantastical and way beyond her experience.

BOOKS AS TOYS

Hannah uses books for different purposes. She now, at the age of 10 months, is very used to flap books and is able to turn down the flaps with great dexterity. Her favourite of these is *How Many Bugs in the Box?* (David Carter). For a long time she wanted to interact physically with the book, turning down the flaps, opening them and showing glee when the 'bugs' were revealed, but when she reached the page where the seven space bugs have to be revealed by grasping a small piece of ribbon and lifting it, she sat back and waited for the adult to do this. After several weeks of watching closely exactly how this was done, she suddenly pushed my hand out of the way, grasped the ribbon very deliberately and accurately and lifted the flap. Her delight was palpable!

Often, in books, she is looking for and at human faces. Her interest in photographs of people she recognises has been apparent from when she was very small and to capitalise on that she has been given a specially made photograph album containing pictures of her and her family and friends (rather like Jessica's scrap book). She will spend a long time smiling with recognition and turning the pages to find a particular photograph. One has the caption 'Hannah's got a serious face' and when she reaches that page she always looks up at the adult and composes her normally smiling features into a 'serious' expression!

THE POWER OF STORIES

When my own children were babies they were given books, but most of these were books based on the idea that babies relate to simple images of realistic things. The whole purpose of sharing these books was the naming of the objects. Hannah, by contrast, has had stories told and read to her from when she was very tiny. At first she would glance at the pictures and respond to the sound of the human voice reading aloud. But her interest and attention were limited. Gradually, however, she has begun to not only enjoy hearing stories read and told, but has begun to 'demand' them. She now adopts a particular position – leaning back against the adult reader in a position of great warmth and comfort. She listens raptly to the words and pays great attention to the stories. At ten months she can listen to stories with extended texts – such as *So Much* by Trish Clark, *Peace at Last* by Jill Murphy and *Where the Wild Things Are* by Maurice Sendak. She will listen to each of these from beginning to end, held snugly against the adult and focused on the pictures.

What can such a young child be getting from this experience? The meaning cannot possibly be central to her since the books explore ideas and concepts way beyond Hannah's experience. She is interested in the pictures and pays attention to these as the story is read. It is clearly a very warm and loving experience – held close to an adult, having that adult's undivided attention, adult and child focused on the same thing and bathed in language. But there seems to be more to it than that. There is something about the very language of the books, the themes they explore and the complex and vivid illustrations that captures and holds Hannah's interest. Each of these books is very different and it is worth trying to examine what it might be that Hannah gains from each of these.

Where the Wild Things Are was perhaps the first story book Hannah had read to her. She would listen to the words and sometimes glance at the pictures and if someone recited the text of the book to her without showing her the book she listened with complete absorption. She clearly doesn't know what wild things are, what it means to feel lonely or understand how to work through anger and fear. There is something about the very language of the book – something about the rhythm and lilt of the words – that means something to such a young child. Maurice Sendak in using such poetic language has clearly tuned into one of the things that young children attend to. In addition, the sensitive and complex illustrations – very unlike the oversimplified images often encountered in books for babies – engage Hannah's attention for long periods of time.

Peace at Last was first read to Hannah at about the same time that she began to crawl and to encounter the word 'no'. Her mobility brought her into situations that were potentially dangerous and her parents started using the word 'no' and shaking their heads. Hannah quickly imitated the shaking of the head and did it every time she heard the word 'no', whatever the context. So when she heard *Peace at Last*, every time the reader got to the refrain '"Oh, no" said Mr Bear', Hannah would frantically shake her head and grin. In this book she is particularly tuned in to the sounds represented in the book and to the repeated patterns of language. She was given a miniature version of the book and her first response was to throw it away in disgust. When it was then read to her she kept her eyes fixed on the reader's face with an expression of disbelief on her face. When she was then shown the large and small versions of the book at the same time and shown that they are identical in everything but size, she was extremely interested.

So Much! is about a black baby celebrating a birthday party with his family. The illustrations are graphic and sensitive and the language – like that of the Sendak book – is poetic and rhythmic with the added feature that it is in dialect. The book is full of features designed to attract a small child. On each page we encounter the baby waiting with his mum for a ring at the doorbell and the entry of a family member. The text ends with 'It was . . .' encouraging prediction and the build-up of anticipation. Hannah has had a lot of experience of predicting what will happen next. Some of this comes from her knowledge of rhymes and games and finger plays; some from the rough and tumble games she plays with her dad; and some from her experience of flap books. In this book each family member wants to show their love for the baby in some way – by kissing or squeezing or fighting the baby. Hannah waits for these moments of physical interaction with the reader and shows her enthusiasm by kissing and squeezing back.

Hannah will listen to each of these stories and at the end demand a repetition. She is able to sustain her interest and attention over a long period of time.

WHAT THIS TELLS US ABOUT EMERGENT READERS

Like many children Hannah's first exposure to literacy has been within her home and family. The literature activities she gets involved in are set in the context of all of Hannah's activities – playing with everything she encounters in order to understand the world she inhabits. Her parents and the other adults she encounters around these literacy events are all following Hannah's lead. They allow her to select the literacy activity (does she want to be read to or to explore the books?) and follow her lead – sometimes leaving her to explore, other times naming things for her and yet again reading the stories she has selected. In this reading of stories Hannah is not a passive recipient. She indicates by her pointing, her vocalising and her body language, the features of the story or pictures which interest her. There have been many studies of young children's responses to stories and books: most of them focus on the years when children begin to respond verbally. Although we can have no definitive answer to what is going on in a young child's mind, the physical evidence of total involvement in the world of books is persuasive. Hannah will spend prolonged periods of time physically exploring books with her hands and with her eyes: she will watch with enormous concentration what the adults do with books and then imitate these actions, spending time on perfecting her physical skills: she will get deeply engrossed in the pictures and shapes on the page and will, again, spend time searching for something she particularly wants to see: she adopts a particular physical stance when she wants to listen to a story and remains alert, attentive and responsive throughout these reading sessions. No one who has met Hannah has any doubt that she will acquire language and begin talking. She will not need lessons in how to talk. As she engages with print and fantasy through her play and exploration and is able to watch competent readers reading, she is developing a positive orientation to literacy. She expects books to be interesting, exciting, fun and comforting. It is more than tempting to suggest that if she is allowed to play with books and languages in this way she will become a reader, just like Jessie. Watch this space!

FOOTNOTE

Hannah is now 22 months old. She is talking non-stop, combining words into sentences and showing, in her wide vocabulary, how much of her learning about the world and about language itself has come from books. She now acts like a reader, sometimes 'reading' the books to her teddies who are required to sit on her lap and 'listen to the 'tory'. Often she re-tells stories with remarkable accuracy, remembering the sequence of events and turning pages with agility. If she, by mistake, turns over two pages at once, she reminds herself 'one at a time'.

She was given a set of magnetic letters and told the names of the ones she showed interest in. Now she not only pays attention to the pictures, but often, also to the print. She will point to letters she knows and comment 'S for Sana, H for Hannah, M for mummy', and so on. She notices the difference between capital and lower-case letters – as when she commented, when finding a 'h' – 'Oh, a baby h for Hannah'. (Since the birth of her baby brother all large objects are classified as 'mummy' and all small objects as 'baby'!)

Hannah is also beginning to understand some of the different forms and purposes of writing. Stories retold by her often start with 'wunsaponatime', but a letter or a card is read as 'Dear mummy, mmmmmmm, love from Hannah'.

Hannah's ability to make links between fantasy and reality is fascinating. When listening to a story she will rush off, in the middle, to fetch things from her real life that appear in the book – a teddy, when she listens to *Peace at Last* or an animal that occurs in *Bringing the Rain to Kapiti Plain* or *The Honey Hunters*. She also now comments on things she remembers from the stories – saying 'in the book' – making clear that she is able to distinguish reality from fantasy.

A new book is viewed with excitement and some uncertainty. She demands to hear it again and again before she will attempt to join in or spend time looking through it on her own. Words are her passion and, as with a book or story that is new, a new word has to be repeated and repeated until Hannah with astounding understanding uses the new word in a different context – but always preserving the meaning.

REFERENCES

Browne, N. (1994) 'I'm Three Years Old and I Can Read', in *GAEC Newsletter No 6*.
Hall, N. (1987) *The Emergence of Literacy*, Hodder and Stoughton.
Meek, M. (1991) *On Being Literate*, Bodley Head.

Children's books referred to in the text

Aardemam, V. (1981) *Bringing the Rain to Kapiti Plain*, Macmillan Children's Books.
Burningham, J. (1988) *Where's Julius?*, Picture Piper.
Campbell, R. (1982) *Dear Zoo*, Picture Puffin.
Carter, D. (1992) *How Many Bugs in the Box?*, Orchard Books.
Cooke, T. (1994) *So Much!*, Walker Books.
Hutchins, P. (1968) *Rosie's Walk*, Picture Puffin.
Martin, F. (1994) *The Honey Hunters*, Walker Books.
Murphy, J. (1992) *Peace at Last*, Picture Mac.
Sendak, M. (1964) *Where the Wild Things Are*, Bodley Head.
Weiss, N. (1989) *Where does Brown Bear Go?*, Picture Puffin.

We have looked at children working out the rules surrounding reading and asking themselves questions like these:

- What is it that fluent readers do?
- What carries the meaning?
- What do the little marks on the page mean?
- Why is the story, read aloud, always exactly the same?
- Do I read it from top to bottom, from left to right, from right to left?

We cannot talk about children exploring literacy without realising that children ask themselves similar questions about writing. As they discover their own abilities to make marks and, through their exploration of the marks they make, begin to realise that the marks can convey meaning, a whole new set of questions arises:

- Is writing different from drawing?
- What is that person with a pencil in her hand doing?
- Can the marks I make be read by someone else?
- Are the spaces between words important?

It is important to remember that understanding about reading goes hand in hand with understanding about writing. The two are inextricably linked. Books are, after all, written and writing can be read.

37 Early writing

Gillian Allery

In this chapter, Gillian Allery examines some of the current theory about how best to support children's writing, together with some examples from her practice.

Although the whole subject of literacy in the early years is of great interest to me, I decided to write on the subject of early writing. Views of literacy and especially of early writing change continually as more research and study produce new theories. There is so much to cover that I have limited my chapter to comparing my experiences in the nursery with what I have learned from the professionals in this field. I am interested to see what the children know and how I can help further this learning in the nursery setting.

Young children will see writing going on in their homes before starting school – shopping lists, birthday and Christmas cards, forms to complete and letters written are part of everyday life. At first, children copy what they see – making marks with anything to hand on anything they can find – often, to their parents' horror, with a crayon on the wallpaper or table. Long before they are able to write, children realise that writing communicates meaning. For example, when mum leaves a note for the milkman and he does as she asks, mum is happy and the child recognises the note must have carried a message.

> The most significant piece of meaningful writing in every child's life is probably her or his first name.
>
> (Whitehead, 1990)

This is very true and a good way of encouraging the child's recognition of her or his name is to begin by labelling children's property and the pictures and marks they create. This leads to easy recognition of initial letters. Grouping together names of the children with the same initial letter, on the wall for instance, will help the child to become familiar and at ease with the letters. Emergent writers often spot letters in their environment that they have in their name. It's quite usual to hear a child say

'I have one of those' speaking of a letter of the alphabet, long before he or she can recreate that letter on paper.

The emergent writer's first step becomes apparent when he or she starts to make a distinction between his or her drawing and writing. Sometimes letter-like marks appear on drawings, or lines of made up writing are produced. Before long children are interested in putting 'kisses' in the form of 'x' at the bottom of greetings cards. Then, perhaps, they may try to add something to the bottom of the shopping list, occasionally using a symbol or a drawing to represent the item, or indeed using letters of their own name. The early writer is making attempts at thinking coherently and putting her or his thoughts on to paper, even though we, the adults, are unable to read what is written. It is worth remembering that when a young child picks up a pencil it might not be a drawing that he or she will produce.

This came to my notice recently when Sienna (2 years, 5 months), after a visit to the local farm, was drawing a picture of her outing. She looked as if she had finished and sat back and surveyed her work. She then chose a pencil and made some marks at the bottom of the paper. 'That must be the farm, Sienna,' I said. She replied, 'No, it's writing.' 'Oh really, what does it say?' I replied. 'It says there's two horses at the farm.' She then took a brown felt pen and made more marks.

'More marks?' I enquired. 'Mmm, it's Snap and . . . mmm . . . the other horse,' Sienna said, trying to think of the horses' names. I wrote what she said below her writing. She was pleased with that. 'Mummy can read it now,' she said.

In these few minutes I realised that Sienna, at 2 years, 5 months, was making a clear distinction in her own mind between writing and drawing. She used spatial organisation, putting the words under the drawing. She also seemed to grasp that, by my use of her dictated text underneath hers, her mother would now be able to read what she'd said – realising both that writing conveys meaning and that, for it to be readable by someone else, it has to be written in the conventional form. Marian Whitehead, speaking of emergent writers, said:

> At any time they are operating along a continuum always being somewhere on the line from oral to graphic expression.

I believe emergent writers are learning to do things alone and independently. We must, as workers with young children, find time to appreciate and display children's early writing attempts.

A wonderful example of a child's recognising the importance of writing came when Carl, aged four, was playing at writing notes for the other children. On investigating why he was playing this game, I found out that his mother had been asked by a neighbour to write a letter for the school. Being Bengali she had no written English. Carl was doing the same for his friends, although he thought it strange that the neighbour, being an adult, couldn't write. I explained that perhaps she might be able to write in Bengali and suggested he ask her if she had time to write a note for us to see. Two days later we were all thrilled when Carl brought in a note in Bengali from his neighbour which apparently said how glad she was to have neighbours like Carl and his family. All the children agreed with Carl that she must be very clever to write like that.

After this wonderful episode we asked all the children with parents or friends who had another language to bring in examples of these. All of the children were interested to see other scripts and together we made a welcome board with all the different languages.

It is essential that alphabets and texts from other cultures should be seen to be respected in the nursery. It is worthwhile making an effort to collect stamps, packets, signs, books and newspapers from other cultures and have them in the home corner, book corner and on display in the nursery. I think any practitioner should also make a point of letting the children know that we, as adults, don't always understand what is being said in print in other languages and scripts. We could perhaps suggest that we try to find out, possibly by asking someone speaking that language or even try to guess what is meant. It is good for the children to see that we don't know everything.

Intervention of the adult into the child's play is a controversial thing. Peter Heaslip (1994) saw that the form of intervention had to be carefully considered, because what is right on one occasion with one child is entirely inappropriate with another child, or even with the same child at another time. Having said that, the child's knowledge of literacy would be slowed somewhat without the adult's part in setting up print-rich environments, a place to write, basic resources such as pens, paper, books – all these things contribute to the child's learning. For children to write they crucially need to see writing in action. Therefore spending time writing with the child or sharing literacy with the child will encourage them to develop or to make sense of text. It is worth remembering Vygotsky's words:

> What the child can do in cooperation today, he can do alone tomorrow.
>
> (Vygotsky, 1978)

My third example is Joe, who at four-and-a-half, has written all that he knows on a piece of paper.

Joe is aware that the writing cannot be read and that he would need to re-group the letters he knows into recognisable text, but that, at the moment, he needs an adult to help him. He mixes upper and lower-case letters, writes from light to right and fits 'Joe' into the writing. He is using recognisable letters of the alphabet. There is the omission of word spaces, but he knows the names of the letters although he hasn't yet arrived at the alphabetic principle recognised by Clay (1979). Her analysis showed that emergent writers appear to work on certain principles, moving from recognition of symbols that can be read as a message, through a recurring principle, whereby children use any letters and words they know over and over again making up words, to an understanding of the alphabetic principle as their knowledge grows.

The children in my examples have shown no sign of having been forced into literacy. On the contrary, they have, in most cases initiated their own writing. Learning to write, far from being a solitary task, should be as social and pleasurable as playing in the home corner or playing ball. Just as spoken language is a social act, a dialogue between people who are both listeners and speakers, so early writers need someone to write to, someone to read what they have written and someone to recognise their wonderful attempts at written words and to show them how valued they are. When a child is not listened to, she or he is unable to learn how to listen and this deprives him or her of an essential partner needed in a linguistic act. The absence of a partner, or listener, could force the child into silence or continued monologue. The same could be said of early writing. Much of the early learning about the written word occurs in a social context, and the child's effort being supported by adults and extended by them will give a valuable point of entry into literacy. If we, as carers and educators, can nurture their early experiences, we can help make their journey into literacy a rewarding one.

REFERENCES

Clay, M.M. Relo (1979) *Reading Begins at Home*, Heinemann Educational.
Heaslip, P. (1994) 'Making Play Work in the Classroom', in J.R. Moyles (ed.) *The Excellence of Play*, Open University Press.
Vygotsky, L.S. (1978) *Mind in Society*, Harvard University Press.
Whitehead, M. (1990) *Language and Literacy in the Early Years*, PCP.

38 Extending literacy through play

Josie Steed

Josie Steed was a student on the Early Childhood Studies Scheme working at the time in a private school. Here she analyses her observation notes which arose from an attempt to introduce literacy through play by converting the home corner into a school corner, filled with materials for writing and mark-making.

> In a play situation children can practise and extend everything they see around them . . . the insatiable curiosity shown by human children means that they are thinking about and experimenting with writing long before they start school. The teacher's task, therefore, is to build on what the child has already discovered about reading and writing.
>
> (Jones 1990)

I certainly found in the task of extending literacy through play that self-initiated writing activities seem to produce much more fluency than some teacher-initiated tasks. I think this is because the child is in control of their direction and their task becomes meaningful to them.

I transformed the home corner into a school corner, incorporating lots of literacy materials. The children were very enthusiastic and produced some wonderful examples of writing and stories. Some inspirational books were generated in the book writing and bookmaking area that I set up.

The school corner was very quiet and industrious most of the time. Some surprising 'teachers' emerged. Normally placid children unable to speak in a large group became quite extrovert and forceful in the teacher role. There were some predictable leaders who kept their class in order and were very bossy.

Jonathan is very unwilling and unmotivated to write or do mathematics. In the school corner he was quite happy to do both and also enjoyed being the teacher. It was interesting that he doesn't conform to class rules – i.e. sit readily and always attend, but he insisted his 'pupil' did, playing out all the rules and class routines.

I think the writing produced was so exciting because it was their choice and made fun by the play situation. The children were relaxed because there were no expectations and no pressure to produce anything and no pre-set standards or required achievement and no peer group competition or comparison.

39 Heroes and baddies

Jacqui Perry

The power of collaborative writing is brought out in Jacqui Perry's chapter in which she describes how making a Big Book allowed children to explore their ideas about heroes and also about how print works.

I was working with a group of children in the reception class, and allowed them to explore their feelings of aggression after a rainy playtime spent indoors. My inspiration for doing this in order to support their developing literacy was taken from the work of Margaret Meek. Meek says that where a child makes up a story for someone else to transcribe:

> because these are his own words the child knows what they say . . . Then children share what they have written by reading to each other. . . The learner gains insight into the relationship of reading and writing in ways he can control.
>
> (Meek, 1991)

The children took turns to tell a small part of the story, which they made up as they went along. As each child told his or her part of the story I wrote it down at the bottom of a large page (leaving space above for their pictures). They advised me on where to put capital letters and helped me to spell words that they knew. I talked to them about the formation of the sentences and it was obvious that they understood there should be a beginning and end to the story. I gave them the option of going round the group a second time so that they could make the story longer, but they knew exactly where they wanted it to end.

This shared experience gave the children plenty of opportunity to cooperate with each other in taking turns and sharing ideas. The writing was meaningful to them because they had chosen the words.

Here is the story the group made up. It is called 'Heroes'.

King Arthur was fighting the baddies because they were trying to get into his castle. King Arthur's knights kicked and punched the bad knights and there was a lot of blood everywhere. The baddies kicked the other knights in their tummies and made them fall over. King Arthur was hiding under his chair. King Arthur told the good knights to dig a big hole and then the baddies would fall into it. The baddies didn't see the hole because they were too busy looking for King Arthur. He was still hiding under his chair. The baddies fell over and slid into the hole. The baddies had to stay in the hole for the weekend and then King Arthur would let them go and told them to be good, otherwise he would put them in the hole again. They didn't give King Arthur any more trouble. The end.

A week after this session took place, four of the children who had been in the group brought in their own self-made books that their parents had helped them complete. This gave further proof of how successful the story-making session had been and how shared writing can be the starting point for individual writing.

REFERENCE

Meek, M. (1991) *On Being Literate*, Bodley Head.

40 YDUDT – Why did you do it?

Young children writing

Sandra Smidt

In this chapter Sandra Smidt examines how young children explore the principles of writing just as they explore the rules governing the physical world.

In our highly literate and visual society children encounter writing events in their natural lives in a huge range of contexts and situations. The postman delivers a letter to the door. Dad writes out a list of things he must remember to buy from the shops. Mum needs to buy a birthday card for her sister. Amita sits at the kitchen table, writing her homework. Dad puts out a note for the milkman. Junior leaves a message for mum on the notice board. Eva marks off the days on the calendar. Mum writes a cheque at the supermarket. The census form needs to be filled in. The traffic warden writes a parking ticket. The doctor writes out a prescription. There are magnetic letters on the fridge, a message pad beside the phone, a diary in Susie's bedroom, a log book in the car. Children try to make sense of all this – and they do so by watching, looking out for patterns, trying to find the rules and by playing at writing for themselves. As they play they include writing in their play. And as they do this they start to reveal the assumptions they are making about how writing works.

They may notice that if you write with your finger on the window pane, the mark you make disappears – but if you make a similar mark with a pen on the wall, it doesn't. They may also notice that nobody seems to mind much if you write with your finger on the window pane, but you get a very different response if you write with pen on the wall! They may notice that some of the marks they make look like something real, something recognisable: others look like squiggles. As the children experiment they begin to distinguish between marks that might represent real things – which they call pictures – and marks which stand for things – which they call writing. Gabriella, a bilingual four-year-old, when asked if she was drawing her picture in Hebrew or English, replied scornfully that she was not writing! At the age of only four she clearly knew that drawing was not dependent on language, whilst writing was.

Adults could, theoretically, write out a shopping list by drawing pictures of all the things they are going to buy. But they don't do that, they use a simpler way of recording; they write down a word, which is a symbol for an object. Children begin to realise that writing serves a number of different purposes.

Baghban (1984) studied the development of her own little girl, Giti, from her first attempts at writing to being a confident 'writer' at the age of three. The little girl, growing up in a literate family started to incorporate mark making into her play from very early on. By the age of 17 months she preferred writing with a ballpoint pen or a felt-tipped pen to writing with a crayon. After all, how many adults write with crayon? By the age of 25 months she was including some of the letters of her own name in her strings of writing. As her discoveries about the world of writing developed she showed that she understood that English writing goes from left to right and from top to bottom. She understood that some letters tend to be repeated, some things get underlined and that print carries meaning and can be used for different purposes.

Ferriero and Teberosky (1979) studied pre-school children in South America and found that very young children assumed that the written form of something must relate in some way to the object it symbolised. So they assumed that the word for 'elephant' would be very long and the word for 'mouse' very short. They also found that children believed that for something to be a word it needed to consist of at least three letters and that all three letters need to be different. These very young children were generating rules about written language, just as children do about spoken language.

Many people like to talk about emergent writing rather than terms like pre-writing. Emergent writing is a term that emphasises the process children go through as they work out just what writing is, how it is done, what and who it is for. The term makes clear that children, when trying to make sense of writing, behave just as they do when they are trying to make sense of spoken language or of the physical world. Through the processes of abstracting, hypothesising, constructing and revising, children come to understand the rules of the world. Let's look at each of these in some detail to see how they apply to writing.

By abstracting we mean trying to extract the essential feature, or pattern, that gives us the rule. Young children, as they acquire their own language, spend a long time listening, watching and sorting things out. An example of a rule they have abstracted is the assumption that all verbs in the past tense, in English, add 'ed'. This leads to the familiar errors 'I goed' and 'The birds flied' – forms of spoken English that no child would have heard from a fluent adult speaker of the language. In terms of writing, one of the rules very young children extract is the example of the minimum number of letters it takes to make a word, cited above.

After abstracting the rule children go on to hypothesise about what something is, what purpose it serves. We see evidence of this in children's exploratory play, when they encounter something new and spend a considerable amount of time exploring the new thing through all means available. In terms of writing, the child selectively imitates aspects of writing behaviour they have observed and been interested in. So Gita chose to use a ballpoint pen rather than a crayon when writing – imitating the adults around her and their writing behaviour.

After the exploration of 'What is it?' comes the constructing of 'What can I do with it?' Here children again imitate selectively aspects of 'expert' behaviour. The young child in the home corner who acts out the sequences familiar from home is putting together her acquired skills and knowledge and trying them out 'like an adult'. Similarly, with writing, children will play at writing for different purposes, for different audiences. So young children, finding slips of paper in the home corner might write a 'shopping list'. Revising happens all the time, in all aspects of learning. As adults respond to the babble of small babies, the babies refine and modify the sounds they produce so that they become closer and closer to the sounds of 'real words'. With writing, as children make marks which become close to recognisable letters, the response of supportive adults encourages the child to repeat these symbols intentionally.

All of this happens within the context of the child's social and cultural life. Where the child encounters adults who are interested in what she is doing, who treat her as an equal partner in the exchange and who recognise and value the cultural and linguistic input the child brings from home, this 'active, thinking, hypothesising child' (Whitehead, 1990) can try out her developing ideas about writing through play. It is important to remember that writing involves a range of activities. There are the skills of transcription – what you need to do physically to make the marks on paper. There are the skills of acquiring the rules of written language – things like how words are spelled, that sentences end with full stops and that a question ends with a question mark, for example. And there is the skill of composition – deciding what to say and how to say it. If we allow children to explore writing through play we find that they explore all of these aspects of written language.

The earliest thing children explore is what they need to do physically in order to make marks on paper. Even at the age of 2 or 3 young children demonstrate that they will use different physical movements for writing from those they use for drawing. Karmiloff-Smith (1994) observed that these young children, asked to mimic drawing, used large movements, keeping their crayon close to the paper. When asked to 'write' they tend to make smaller marks and lift the tool from the paper.

As children explore the conventions of writing they start to explore the arrangement of the letter shapes on the paper. Very early writing appears to cover the page randomly, sometimes going from left to right, sometimes from top to bottom, sometimes around the edges of the paper. Three-year-old Christopher seems to be exploring the whole page, in Figure 40.1.

As children mature, their attempts at writing start to consist of strings of letters, some of which are shapes resembling real letters, some of which may be letters familiar to the child – usually from her or his name. At first the strings of letters are not demarcated in any way, but as children begin to realise that writing is speech written down, they begin to explore ways of putting some sort of marker into their strings of writing. Javelle, at the age of four, would put a star between each of his letters (Figure 40.2).

Other children use a dot or a line or even another letter shape.

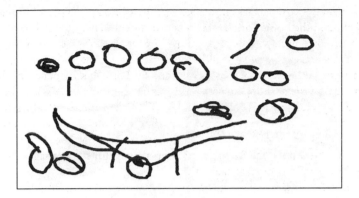

Figure 40.1

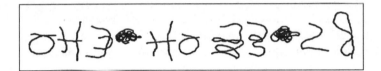

Figure 40.2

It is important to say, at this point, that children's early attempts at writing will reflect closely the alphabets and scripts they are familiar with from home. Young children whose first language is Bengali may include a lot of horizontal lines in their writing.

Urdu speakers may include more dots and curls than are familiar from English. It is important for us to know which languages the children are familiar with so that we can understand their early attempts at writing.

As children play at writing they begin to show, to the observant adult, all they have already worked out about writing. In the following example four-year-old Kirsty explained that she had written 'Baa baa black sheep'. She shows, in this, that she knows that writing conveys a message, that it goes down the page in lines. She also shows some familiarity with some familiar formats for print – newspapers or comics, perhaps (Figure 40.3).

Children also begin to explore the rules of our spelling system. English is not a phonetic language and children struggle to work out the rules of how the sound system relates to the symbolic written system. Research shows that when young children first start to write in order to communicate they often use the name of a letter to stand for a word or a syllable. Glenda Bissex (1980) gives the example of her young son, Paul, who at the age of five wrote this:

RUDF

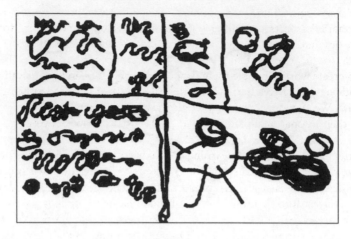

Figure 40.3

The message? Are (R) you (U) deaf (DF)?

Similarly, another Paul, also aged five, wrote this riddle for his mum:

YDUDT

Why (Y) did (D) you (U) do (D) it (T)?

Paul uses the name of a letter where it sounds like a word – Why, you – and the initial or the last letter for other words. He does not yet leave spaces between his words.

Six months later Paul wrote this:

WN U ST I GT SD

and explained that it said 'When (WN) you (U) shout (ST) I (I) get (GT) sad (SD). In a short space of time Paul has elaborated his earlier hypotheses about writing. He had spaces between the words and was beginning to use the initial and the last sound of words, combined with letter names, to convey meaning. At six Paul was writing things like this:

WEN YOU GO FISHING YOU NED A FLOT

This is sufficiently close to conventional spellings for it to be easy to decode. Paul has learned to recognise and write some useful words like 'you' and 'go'; he asked for help with the word 'fishing' and used the rules of spelling he had generated to write the remaining words. By the time Paul left the Infant School he had little trouble writing perfectly comprehensible pieces.

But there is more to writing than transcription, grammar and spelling. Writing is, crucially, also about composition. Frank Smith (1982) drew a distinction between transcription and composition, explaining that transcription refers to the 'secretarial' aspects of writing – things like spelling, punctuation, formation of letters, orientation on the page, and so on. Composition refers to what is written – it relates to the creative side of writing. Writing then offers children the opportunity to create worlds, people them, write for an audience and express their ideas in myriads of ways. Myra Barrs (1992) describes written language as being 'stored in the ear'. We experience the characteristic rhythmic structure of texts or genres through their intonational patterning, and when we write we draw on the store of tunes we know and on our sense of how such tunes are made. Part of learning to write is therefore a question of learning how to write the tune, and of learning what resources there are at our disposal to enable us to create tunes for our readers. *What* children write is at least as important as *how* they write it. If we accept that writing involves drawing on a store of intonational patterning, it seems obvious that anyone concerned with children's early literacy will spend a considerable amount of time helping children acquire a store of 'tunes' in their head by reading to them and telling them stories and poems and rhymes. The greater children's exposure to these, the more material they have to draw on when composing for themselves.

Yet what children want to say seems to matter little in many of our schools. Still common, in today's schools, is the habit of asking children to write their 'news' each Monday morning. My own children, more than twenty years ago, found this a trying ordeal and would agonise over the weekend about what they were going to say. Each week they would come up with a simple sentence

We went to the shops with my mum.

Gaynor came to play.

We went on the swings.

When I suggested they made up some fantastic adventure to write in their 'news' they would scornfully dismiss this, saying 'That's story. This has to be news.' Asking children to write their news can be both a traumatic and divisive experience. Some children may have been to McDonald's or a birthday party or to somewhere exciting; other children may have been indoors all weekend, sometimes just waiting for Monday morning and school to come round.

The writing of news serves no purpose for the children. There is no real audience and the writing becomes a meaningless exercise. While my children were writing those limited sentences in school, they were furiously playing at writing at home. They wrote invitations to friends to come and play, notices to stick on their doors, books for one another, letters to grandparents. They played schools and wrote registers. They played libraries and catalogued their books. And they wrote long and fanciful stories, peopled by creatures real and fantastic. There were wicked stepmothers and beautiful princesses and fiery dragons and lost children and magic wands and potent spells and tragic events. In these books they used direct speech and description. They developed actions and characters and time. They managed events, decided who would live and die. Here is one of the stories Sammy wrote when she was five – invented spellings and all.

> THIS IS A WICH WOO HAS CAUGHT A CLOWN AND SHE HAS STUK A NIFE INTO THE CLOWN. WHY SHE MIXIS THE MAJIC POWRS TO KILL THE FUNNY CLOWN. SHE IS KILLING HIM JUST BECUSE HE IS FUNNY. BUT THERE WAS A RESUN WHY SHE IS GOING TO KILL THE FUNNY CLOWN BECUSE SHE DUSUNT LIKE FUNNY THINGS AND ALL CLOWNS ARE FUNNY AND SPESHALIY THAT ONE. EVRY ONN LIKED HIM BUT THAT WICH. EVUN THE OTHER WICHS LOVED HIM DELLY. THEY ALL THUT HE WAS GRET EXEPT FOR THET ONE WOO WAS THE ONLY WICH IN THE WULD WOO DIDUNT LIKE FUNNY THINGS. SHE RELLY DID HATE FUNNY THINGS. BUT EVRY BODY LOVED THEM. AND THAT IS THE END OF THE STORY ABOUT THE WICH AND THE CLOWN.

It would be interesting to speculate on why Sammy was wanting to get rid of funny things, but in her writing she reveals what rules she has worked out about spellings: she uses 'book language' (we only say things like 'loved him dearly' in books, not in everyday speech). She had the power to create a world, express some very dangerous ideas safely and resolve it in her own fashion. How different from 'We went to the park.'

It is, of course, important for children to have access to a range of genres for writing. They do need to write factual accounts and descriptions as well as narrative and fantasy. But, for very young children living rich fantasy lives through play and story, surely getting 'the tune' on paper should be the starting point.

In this story, written by six-year-old Peter, you can see what 'tunes in the head' he is drawing on.

The Boy Who Broke His Laser Beam.

> Long ago, before motor cars were invented there was this little boy and his name was John and this boy named John liked to go in the forest to see his grandparents and on this particular day he was walking through the forest when, just when he walked through a clearing of four trees, a giant net sprang on to him. The next thing he knew was that he was flying to a nearby cave by the claws of a bat. When he got to the cave he told them everything to let him go. He told them of his father's psychology work. He told them that his father could make laser beams. So they let him go and the king of the animals, who was, of course, the Lion roared 'Show this great laser beam of yours to me!' and the boy said 'I will' and went off home. He told his father about what the Lion had said. After the talk the father did let him have the laser beam. When

the boy was in the Lion's cave he threw the laser beam to all the animals and what a fright the animals got when it blew up and the boy and his father lived very happily ever after. The end

Children find out about writing through their play and through their interactions. They move from what they understand, getting closer and closer to conventional forms and, in doing this, are able to work out the rules of these conventions. Margaret Meek (1991) insists that they do this by persisting, reflecting, learning, correcting, ordering and refining not only their writing (or spelling), but also their thinking. Glenda Bissex sums it up:

When we speak of children's development in writing, we mean development towards those forms selected and refined by our culture. Often we do not appreciate the forms used in other times and places, that children independently explore but must unlearn as part of their schooling. We tend to see our writing system as given, and children developing towards it. Yet if we step away to gain a broader perspective in time, we see the writing system itself developing: we see that the child's literacy learning is cut from the same cloth as mankind's written language development.

Children through play, through interaction, discover that literacy is not just about imitation or about memorising what people tell you. It is rule-governed and the rules, like those of spoken language, can be discovered, applied, overgeneralised, corrected. It is also creative. Children who play at writing find that, in writing, what you want to say and the way in which you say it matters more than copying what someone else has said. Those of us working with young children need to respect their endeavours to do this.

REFERENCES

Baghban, (1984) *Our Daughter Learns to Read and Write: A Case Study from Birth to Three*, International Reading Association.

Barrs, M. (1992) 'The Tune on the Page', in K. Kimberley, M. Meek and J. Miller (eds) *New Readings: Contributions to an Understanding of Literacy*, A. & C. Black.

Bissex, G. (1980) *GNYS AT WRK: A Child Learns to Write and Read*, Harvard University Press.

Ferreiro, E. and Teberosky, A. (1979) *Literacy Before Schooling*, Heinemann Educational.

Karmiloff-Smith, A. (1994) *Baby It's You*, Ebury Press.

Meek, M. (1991) *On Being Literate*, The Bodley Head.

Smith, F. (1982) *Writing and the Writer*, Heinemann Educational.

Whitehead, M. (1990) *Language and Literacy in the Early Years*, PCP.

A great deal has been written about early literacy. The works of writers like Margaret Meek, Frank Smith, Nigel Hall, Glenda Bissex and a host of others have influenced and will continue to influence teachers and practitioners in their daily practice. Nowadays most playgroups and nurseries and crèches understand how important stories, songs, rhymes and books are and how children's attitudes to reading are often formed during their early years around their encounters with books and stories. Moreover, most learning sites nowadays have some sort of writing area where children can try out for themselves the forms, functions and purposes of writing. Many teachers and others are using Big Books and techniques like shared reading and shared writing to support and extend children's learning. Early literacy is now firmly placed on the early-learning agenda.

In Part V we have looked at how children, through play and exploration, come to understand the rules that govern the written world. We have seen how correcting young children's early spelling or punctuation is a waste of time and energy: just as children have to go through a phase of overgeneralising the rules of spoken language, so they do with written language. It is only when they understand, that real learning takes place. Remember Lilian Katz's argument earlier in this book that we can teach young children to do anything, but should we? We need always to keep in mind what will benefit the child and his/her learning.

It is worth emphasising this point particularly with regard to early reading and writing. Parents who have happily allowed children's spoken language to develop without trying to 'teach' them to talk, lose sight of this when it comes to reading and writing. Perhaps because these skills are seen as essential for success in schooling – and indeed they are – parents become anxious when their child 'can't read' or 'can't write'. Like talking and walking, reading and writing are developmental processes and children need to work through the rules they generate in order to come to understand how the written world works. So children need to 'read' a book by memorising it: they need to use the pictures to help them find the meaning; they need to write strings of letters before they can write words. This does not mean, of course, that the adults alongside them should stand back forever and allow children to become stuck at one particular point. The role of the adult in both supporting and extending literacy comes through observation, an understanding of the processes involved, sensitive intervention and scaffolding and showing respect for the intense efforts children make.

In other words, we need to tune into what it is the child is doing, what her/his ideas are. It is only when we are able to use the errors children make as windows to the workings of their minds, that we are able to help them take the next step.

Where young children are invited to play at being readers and writers they take control of the situation and, in situations which allow them to build on what they already know and where the purpose is clear, they reveal just what it is they are pursuing at that moment. It is then that we see children, in Vygotsky's famous phrase: 'standing a head taller'.

Part VI

Representing and explaining the world

Introduction to Part VI

Once young children have explored their world and arrived at some explanation that satisfies them, they begin to represent their findings in some way.
When children represent something by making a mark or a shape, an object
or an action they are making one thing stand for another and are able,
through expressing their ideas in speech or action or images, to show their
thoughts and feelings. As John Matthews puts it:

> when they represent anything (using a mark, a shape, an action or an
> object) *they make something stand for something else and through
> expression* (in speech, action or images) *they show emotion.*
>
> (Matthews, 1994)

In previous parts of this book, we have encountered children representing
their findings and ideas through talk, through making and telling stories,
through writing and through play. In Part VI we look particularly at how young
children explore their world and represent it through drawing and painting. It
is important to remember that painting and drawing are only two of the many
forms of expressing ideas and emotions open to children. Sometimes, when
we see children shouting and singing, running up and down or turning round
and round, their behaviour looks random and trivial. Matthews points out that
these behaviours are highly relevant to children's drawing and painting and to
the education of children as a whole. Actions and movements are, as we
know, prime means of exploring the world around young children and con-
sequently are important for the growth of thinking and of feeling.

In Part VI we look, too, at how the adults with young children are able to
scaffold their learning in a range of ways. The emphasis is on the adults
paying close attention to what it is the children are doing and trying to
intervene sensitively, where appropriate, to help the child make the next
cognitive leap. We avoid considering stages of children's drawing because
we feel a stage theory tends to focus on what it is that children cannot yet do

rather than on what they can do. And we suggest there is a tendency in our culture to always regard children's attempts at mark making or modelling to be representative. Our argument is that this is not always true. Often young children are more interested in exploring the quality of the paper, the texture of the paint, the effect of a circular motion with a pen in the hand, the feel of the glue than they are in making a house, drawing a sunflower or making a collage hen! Yet adults, so used to considering the end product and so conditioned to painting and drawing being representational, often intervene inappropriately, asking children 'What is it?' rather than saying things like: 'Oh, what wonderful colours' or 'I really like that diagonal line'.

All the articles in Part VI have been written by students. Some of them were in their first two years of study and some were more advanced. All write passionately about children representing and describing their world.

REFERENCES

Matthews, J. (1994) *Helping Children to Draw and Paint in Early Childhood*, Hodder and Stoughton.

41 Talking through the process

Beata Clarke

Beata's first language is Polish and she was thrilled to discover that she could write fluently and with feeling in her second language, English.

Amy took a sheet of paper and wrote her name on the top of it with a pencil. She drew a big rectangle with quite smooth movements of her hand and fairly straight lines. She was making comments during the whole time, as follows:

'Now, all right; a house; I will put a little square and a little round. It will be a bath there,' and drew three small rectangles and a little circle on the level of the first floor of her house. 'And – what else? Kitchen?' as she was thinking, and biting her pencil with her teeth. 'Up the stairs. . . . Ye, ye, yep!'

She stood up and with a quick motion of the pencil drew a zig-zag mark while nearly lying on the table. 'This is stairs. I have to do this . . . kitchen, kitchen, kitchen.' She drew a row of separate inverted U shapes in the middle of the house followed by a long loop under this row. Then she added another little mark resembling a V shape.

At this point Darren came to the table, took a sheet of paper and a pencil and started drawing. He kept the pencil quite firmly in his right hand and was 'sliding' the pencil tip on the paper in all directions with a lot of circular and some zig-zag movements. He was exploring all the surface of the paper and applying a lot of pressure with the pencil.

Amy stopped drawing and asked him, 'What are you going to do?' Darren didn't answer. She then asked again, 'What is it? A house?' (no response), looking at him all the time. 'Is it a horse?' (No reply again.) She seemed to be quite fascinated by his drawing and kept asking: 'What is it? Is it a writing? What is it?' (insisting). 'I will tell you in a minute,' said Darren.

Darren drew a few more lines and then wrote several letters from his name in the top right corner of the paper. 'It isn't real letters, is it?' Darren again ignored Amy's question. 'That's it!' he said. 'Finished!' and he put his drawing in the box but then he picked it up again and came to me. 'Did you do my name?' he asked. 'I thought that you wrote it yourself.' I pointed to the letters on his picture. 'But if you want I will do it again in a moment,' was my answer as I was taking notes while talking with him. I then wrote his name on the back of his drawing.

When Darren left the table Amy went back to her drawing. She first filled one little rectangle (a window in her house) with lines drawn with the pencil applying quite a lot of pressure to it. Then she put the pencil on the tray and looking at the tray said: 'And . . . what have I got? All colours. . . . It will get beautiful,' she continued. 'Beautiful, beautiful!' Amy had drawn some colourful marks on top of her pencil marks and she turned to me: 'Is it a nice house?' she asked. 'Yes, it is. A very colourful one.'

'I will do my name,' said Amy, as she turned the paper over and wrote her name a second time. She then placed her picture in the box and walked away.

I was so interested in what children were exploring as they drew and painted that I went on to observe another child.

'I HAVE DONE A MOON'

During my observations of children making marks, one child, Alex (3 years, 10 months) showed noticeable enthusiasm and confidence in painting and drawing. So this child was chosen for close observation of her work during a morning session in December 1994.

The observation started with Alex putting on an apron and standing at a table on which there was a sheet of paper and a tray with seven pots containing brushes and paints. She picked up a brush with red paint and then began to make marks.

With a few short push pull strokes she made a rectangular mark followed by a large continuous rotational movement to produce a closed oval shape. She then added a circular mark connected to the oval, just outside the closed area. While she was doing this she seemed at ease and confident.

After putting the red brush back in the pot she took the brown brush, wiped off some excess paint on the pot edge and, with single strokes, placed a vertical line at each side of the oval. Later, after adding more colours, these lines were widened to become like large brown patches. At this point her work displayed some symmetry.

Alex continued to add more shapes outside of the oval by adding a series of mainly horizontal blue lines in between the brown lines, made by a combination of long and short strokes. This was followed by a large orange patch placed above the blue lines, produced by zig-zag movements. After pausing for a moment, Alex suddenly said, 'Oh, I didn't put my name'. She took a pencil and wrote 'xelA' (Alex reversed).

Continuing with her work Alex picked up the yellow brush and painted an irregular shape below the oval. After that she started to paint shapes in the inner area of the oval, first by colouring most of the lower inside region with yellow wavy lines (partly blending with the red outline). Then she selected grey paint and filled in some of the upper area within the oval followed by some smaller shapes just outside. Next she dabbed on some blue dots to fill in more of the space in the inner area of the oval and then placed two green ring shapes near the corners in the outer area. She then moved the green brush into the area within the oval to add a dot there.

Finally Alex completed the painting by placing a small red blob followed by an orange one within the oval and adding some wavy strokes of orange to fill a remaining outer space on the right. The painting was then placed on the drying rack.

Immediately afterwards Alex began to paint another picture. For this she picked up a pencil and first wrote her name (again in reversed form). She then drew two shapes with continuous motion of the pencil to produce a crescent and a long curvy snakelike line from the top to the bottom of the sheet. Next she covered the top part of the snakelike line with brown paint, making a thick patch. This was followed by a careful but smooth downward movement of the brush along the curved line, done in three stages. When she reached the bottom of the paper she applied several horizontal strokes to create a large brown patch and said suddenly: 'This is a painting,' which seemed to be particularly directed at herself.

She then exchanged this for a brush with grey paint and followed the curves of the crescent all the way round with the brush beginning from and ending at the top. After that she placed a blob at the bottom of the crescent and the expression on her face changed as if she suddenly saw something unusual. 'I have done a moon!' she said joyfully and looking at me, she repeated these words twice. Alex appeared to be very content with the result of her work, even proud of herself.

She put the picture aside and, surprisingly, picked up a new sheet of paper to make some more marks. Possibly she did this because she was enjoying the activity so much and maybe to show me what else she is able to do. This time she changed the technique. She picked up each brush and while holding each one in her right hand she splashed the paint off the brush with her left hand and onto the paper. Eventually a series of splash marks of different colours were left on the paper.

Another child, who was standing at the opposite side of the table asked her: 'Alex, is it going to be a butterfly?' 'Yes' was the answer, as Alex folded the paper in half, pressed on it and then unfolded it. She looked at the result of her work for a long time. Finally she placed the picture on the drying rack and walked away, taking off her apron.

From the observation it is evident that Alex has developed some skills and knowledge in painting and drawing. These abilities have progressed some way beyond exploration of materials and colours. She experiments with different types of marks, most of which have not got any clear visual meanings for the observer, but which probably reflect or convey her mood. Furthermore, as Eng (1970) says:

> The child's spontaneous drawing reflect his feelings and interests. They tell us what it has at heart and what it finds meaningful and interesting. Even if the child's drawing seem stiff and lifeless in the eyes of the adult they may none-theless be the expression of emotions to the child himself.

An important factor influencing the content of children's drawings and paintings is the experience they have had with the materials. Alex clearly showed confidence in using these materials. She knew how to hold brushes properly and avoid putting excess paint on them for painting. She also seemed to plan her work to some extent. In her first painting she started her work in the middle of the paper and then extended outwards to cover virtually the whole of the sheet, but in a later painting she restricted the marking to the middle area.

She displayed control over a variety of motions on the paper. These actions were organised and coordinated arm movements, not involving whole body as is evident in younger children. The variations of movements suggested rapid, complex decision making.

The rotational movement of the brush used to form the oval in the first painting shows an ability to make closed shapes which is an important visual structure in drawing development. In this way Alex created two different regions on the picture and placed separate or different marks in the inside of the closed shapes compared to the outside. This can be seen as the beginning of classifying different marks and the start of mathematical knowledge, as is stated by John Matthews (1994). He also indicates that the closed shape separates a portion of space from the surrounding area and that young children learn to use it to represent inside and outside relationships, as is evident in Alex's first painting.

John Matthews also states:

> Sometimes patches of paint or shapes just happen to correspond to shapes of objects, and the child will see a relationship between the shapes appearing on the drawing surface and shapes in the world.
>
> (Matthews, 1994)

I noted this to be the case with the crescent in Alex's second painting which was a new shape that Alex had learned recently from some previous work. Similarly, the 'butterfly' shape was made because she had learned the technique previously.

Referring to writing, Matthews (1994) says:

> Sometimes in early writing, letter forms are reversed or inverted.

This can be seen in the way Alex signs her paintings.

In general, observing Alex's paintings and drawings, it can be seen that they are all two-dimensional. She is able to rapidly fill up spaces with a variety of shapes in two dimensions. But she has not yet reached the stage of development where she is able to add depth (three dimensions) or perspective to her drawings. Also her drawings do not show clearly recognisable representations of aspects of reality.

In reading this work you will be struck by two things. The most obvious is just how skilled at observation Beata is and how much detail she observes and records. The second is her ability to analyse what she sees according to what she knows about child development. Beata relates what she sees to what she

has learned from her reading. This is an extremely well-researched piece of work and indicates just how useful it is to link theory to practice.

Beata shares with the reader her understanding of what it is the child already knows. Alex knows how to use the materials and this allows her to be confident. She displays control over a range of movements. She experiments with various techniques. And throughout it all the adult is an attentive observer, watching closely what it is that Alex is doing and what this tells her about Alex's developing ideas and concepts.

REFERENCES

Matthews, J. (1994) *Helping Children to Draw and Paint in Early Childhood*, Hodder and Stoughton.

42   Scaffolding Caitlin's learning

Emma Stoddart

Many of the themes from Chapter 41 are picked up here by Emma Stoddart as she explores in detail what she learned about Caitlin (her ideas and thoughts, her skills and ideas), as she watched her draw. Caitlin was 2 years, 11 months old at the time and Emma was particularly interested in the influence the adult had in this situation.

As an early-years worker and an adult who considers myself unable to draw, I am interested in how young children, making marks, are influenced by the adults around them. How can the attitudes and responses of these adults support them in positive ways and what has gone wrong when a child gives up painting and drawing and grows up to believe that she 'cannot draw'? In this piece I wish to explore how a child can be offered an environment rich with opportunities to encourage her to make marks. I will do this by examining my observations of one child making marks and by evaluating my responses to her actions in the light of relevant research.

I will define making marks as drawing or any other action which leaves a visible mark on a material. All children have a compulsion to make marks; whatever their culture they have a desire to leave a record, whether it be with crayons on paper, with a stick in the earth or with any other materials available to them. Making visual representations in this way is vital to a young child's development, both as a means of self-expression and because experience of symbolic representation is needed by the child as she actively tries to make sense of the world around her. We live in a symbolic world in which abstract symbolic representation in the form of written, spoken and sign language are central to our communication with each other.

Piaget suggested that children learn from their environment without interaction with adults or other children; he suggested that making marks starts with random scribbling, developing into intentional drawing only when an accidental mark, recognised as being a representation of a familiar object, is then repeated. By contrast, Matthews (1994) proposes that children make intentional marks right from the start to represent shape, movement and emotion in a way that is meaningful for them. By focusing on the child's process of mark making rather than the end product, adults can interact with the child in a way that is sensitive and supportive. Indeed, this interaction is not only possible, but essential if the child's mark making is to thrive.

I chose to observe Caitlin because I find her evident enjoyment of making marks very exciting. The observation took place in the playgroup in which I work. On this particular morning I had provided felt tips, biros and coloured A4 paper on a small table. I had also put out carbon paper for the first time because I wished to offer the children a new material to explore. Other graphic materials, clearly labelled and within reach, were available to the children.

When Caitlin first begins to make marks on her chosen piece of paper, I sit beside her attending to what she is doing attentively, but in silence. I do not ask her what she is drawing, even when the image emerging on the paper starts, as I guess, to resemble the face and body of something or someone. At a certain point in her drawing she offers me the information herself, commenting first 'A head!' and then, after further development of the image, 'A monster!' Thus my initial inter-action with Caitlin supports Schirrmacher (1988), who suggests that when we notice a child's drawing we do not give our opinion of it immediately; rather, we should pause before we speak, to give ourselves space to think of an appropriate comment and the child space to voluntarily offer us information or start a discus-sion herself if she wishes.

As Caitlin draws (Figure 42.1), she makes an enclosed shape by placing a baseline across the open end of an inverted U-shape: thus she represents the monster's body, a physical entity separate from the space on the rest of the paper. She adds features to further define the head and body; she draws two parallel lines and a further two lines travelling down from the baseline to form two V marks; she then draws a single vertical line on each side of the monster's body, parallel to, but not

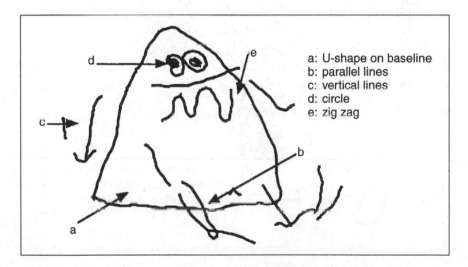

a: U-shape on baseline
b: parallel lines
c: vertical lines
d: circle
e: zig zag

Figure 42.1 Caitlin's monster

touching it. I guess that these lines represent the monster's limbs and that the circles at the top of the head represent eyes, but since I do not ask Caitlin I cannot assume this. If I were to comment 'I see you are drawing some lines down from your monster's body,' or 'Look, you've drawn two circles in the monster's head,' I would indicate my interest in the added features without imposing my guesses on her, and she might well offer me more information.

To use the terms of Matthews (1994), Caitlin demonstrates in her first drawing that she can intentionally use a 'U-shape on a baseline', 'closure', 'zig-zags' and vertical lines. She can distinguish between the physical movements required of her to produce each different shape. She has drawn these shapes from her mark-making vocabulary and combined them in a way that is meaningful to her, to represent her monster in two-dimensional form. When she starts to draw on her second piece of paper, (Figure 42.2), she demonstrates additional marks in her vocabulary: 'waves' and 'variations on right-angular joints'. Finally, on the carbon paper, (Figure 42.3) she makes a 'loop', 'travelling zig-zag' and, by 'continuous rotation', forms more closed shapes.

Throughout the observation I give Caitlin little feedback about what she is actually doing. Had I talked to her using informative language, scaffolding her progress (Bruner, 1980) with comments on her zig-zags, closed shapes and other marks, I could have helped her to become more aware of how her representations were working. She, however, spontaneously offers me information from time to time. By listening, I become aware of a sense of order among her marks and of her interest in forming letters, numbers and patterns. By tuning in to her processes, I

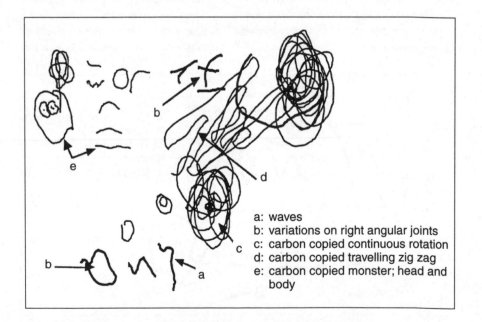

a: waves
b: variations on right angular joints
c: carbon copied continuous rotation
d: carbon copied travelling zig zag
e: carbon copied monster; head and body

Figure 42.2 Caitlin's waves and right-angular joints

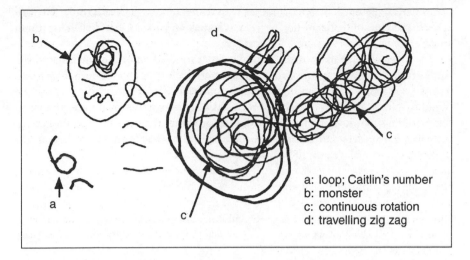

a: loop; Caitlin's number
b: monster
c: continuous rotation
d: travelling zig zag

Figure 42.3 Caitlin's loops

become aware of her vocabulary of marks, her mark-making schema, which I observe her repeating again and again.

Throughout the observation Caitlin demonstrates the ability to use both 'symbols' and 'signs' (Matthews, 1994 after Piaget). Her representation of both her monsters are symbolic, since she intends her images to reflect their actual physical appearance. By contrast, she is also concerned with signs – i.e. letters and numbers which are abstract representations. She shows this when she comments on her loop 'I did that number on mine' and 'I can do writing' as she proceeds to draw travelling zig-zags. Although this latter zig-zag is a sign, the zig-zag on her first monster is probably part of its overall symbolic form. She is free-flowing (Bruce, 1991) between making signs and symbols.

When Caitlin comes to use the carbon paper she is exploring a material that is new to her. I show her its duplicating property. When she asks for explanations, I try to use language which is accessible to her; she is, however, only partially able to grasp what I say. She needs time to experience epistemic play (Hutt, 1979) to gain knowledge and skills of how carbon paper works through hands-on experience at her own pace.

When the observation is over, I plan to extend Caitlin's learning through mark making from her present point of competence to a future point, i.e. through her zone of proximal development (Vygotsky, 1978). Prentice (1994) points out that an adult can communicate support for a child's mark making through both verbal and non-verbal responses. I can articulate my support to her verbally by continuing to use reflective listening and by speaking of my pleasure in her creations. My non-verbal support includes both my attention when she is mark making, an indication of my interest, and the physical environment that I provide for her. I base my planning of the environment on her current interests and skills and decided to offer her a wide range of opportunities with different materials and tools, through which she can consolidate her present schemas and explore and develop them further.

To conclude, a child's mark making will thrive when the environment she interacts with contains supportive adults who focus on and value her process, while providing exciting and appropriate materials. Caregivers should allow the child to initiate activities herself and proceed with them at her own pace, and when commenting should emphasise what she can do rather than what she cannot do. In this way her understanding of representation will flourish and enable her, as she endeavours to make sense of her world.

REFERENCES

Bruner, J.S. (1980) *Under-fives in Britain (Oxford Pre-School Research Project)*, Grant McIntyre.
Matthews, J. (1994) *Helping Children to Draw and Paint in Early Childhood*, Hodder and Stoughton.
Prentice, R. (1994) 'Experimental learning in play and art', in J.R. Moyles (ed.) *The Excellence of Play*, Open University Press.
Schirrmacher, R. (1988) *Art and Creative Development for Young Children*, Van Nos Rheinhold.
Vygotsky, L.S. (1978) *Mind in Society*, Harvard University Press.

In reading this well-researched account you will notice how Emma's role as an interested, observant adult helped scaffold Caitlin's learning. Emma describes how her first response to Caitlin is that of silent, interested observer. She does not ask her what she is drawing, but waits for Caitlin to offer information herself. In doing this she reinforces the important point that adults need to take time themselves to think before commenting. Emma goes on to analyse what she might have said in response to what Caitlin was doing – all the time trying to validate the child's experience rather than to impose adult-centred values.

43 'The workshop table – a stepping stone in the visual arts'

Duane Hernandez

The last piece in Part VI has been written by Duane Hernandez, a teacher currently working in a nursery in East London. He was, at the time of writing this, a student on the Nursery Certificate course at the University – a course designed specifically to prepare teachers to teach young children. He had, at that time, been teaching for five years and said: 'I have thoroughly enjoyed my teaching and found it most challenging working in the nursery.'

In this chapter Duane explains in detail the changes he made to an area of the nursery and what happened as a result. It emphasises the importance of observation and is illustrated throughout by cuttings and examples from his working diary.

SETTING THE SCENE

Provision within the nursery curriculum for the visual arts is one of the most sensitive areas facing a practitioner. This view is acknowledged in the writing of Kenneth Jameson (1974) and Naomi Pile (1973) who vigorously defend the 'child's side' and offer support to educators who wish to build children's confidence in this area.

Developments in the promotion of a child-centred curriculum, far from being the 'latest trend', have their roots as far back as the early pioneers such as Froebel. This way of viewing nursery provision is one of the salient features in the wider recognition of the most fundamental principle of nursery provision for the under-fives, play. 'Play' has at last received the attention and status it deserves through the presentation of ideas in the works of Tina Bruce (1987, 1991) and Janet Moyles (1989, 1994) as well as others. 'Play' is viewed as a central process in the child-centred approach and interactionists add to this the role of the adult. It is therefore curious that, within the nursery in which I work, although the above ethos and practice have permeated many areas of the curriculum, it is sadly lacking in the visual arts. This also seems to be the case in other nurseries I have visited and information I have gleaned from other practitioners. Indeed, Roy Prentice (1994) readily concurs that, although many nurseries have developed creative environments and climates which maximise the potential of play, in art 'such practice is uneven'.

The general approach to the visual arts within the nursery at which I work has been the main table 'art activity'. A special and quite expansive area is set aside for this and provision varies on a daily basis. Generally, the activities presented are based on the adults' ideas and assumptions and are adult-led. The dangers of this kind of approach are only too clear in the light of such works cited above. The following observation highlights all my concerns:

Extract 1

A vase containing daffodils has been presented to the children with the intention of a still-life study in either paint or collage materials – green and yellow only provided. Meanwhile . . . on the main art activity table Yvonne, for the second time, has spread glue on the back of her card and stuck it to the newspaper on the table. This time round she is writing her name (all the letters perfectly), covering the whole A4 card presumably on what she considered to be the back to the tune of 'Oh Yvonne! You've stuck it to the table . . . Look, let me show you.' Yvonne, having heard the explanation from the adult now spreads glue all over her name and starts to stick scraps of materials (the colour of daffodils) on to her piece of A4 card.

Yvonne's main preoccupations were, in the first instance, simply spreading the glue – and, second, as evidenced from previous observations where she painted each letter of her name in huge letters at the easel on successive occasions, a celebration of writing her name. It is sad when adults cut across the child's potential for learning and expression like this. We are all guilty of this from time to time. The most worrying aspect is that some of us may not even be aware of it. The key to resolving this kind of dilemma is careful observation of what children are doing. Bruce (1987) cites a study by Bennett *et al.* (1984) which succinctly puts this in context:

> Teachers in this study had a strong tendency to decide what task they were setting children, and to 'go for it' regardless of whether or not the children were coming along with them. They found it difficult to look at the child in relation to the task. Instead they centred on the task, and on getting the child to master it. They often demanded huge leaps forward in the children's understanding as the task progressed. Careful child observation, careful identification of where children are in their understanding (in the process), rather than focusing on performance (the product), would overcome this inefficient way of going about things.
>
> (Bruce, 1987)

What are the consequences if we choose to ignore the child's central role in her/his learning in the visual arts? In the short term, I concur with Jameson (1974) in that children lose their 'spontaneity' and 'motivation' and may well become dependent on direction by the adult. This is heightened in children of nursery age, who are powerless in comparison to adults and all too eager to please them. In the long term, Prentice makes it very clear:

> Prescribed procedures and preconceived ideas squash the spirit of spontaneous exploration fuelled by curiosity: thus imaginative possibilities dwindle.
>
> (Prentice, 1994)

If this is the case, why do such practices prevail in the visual arts – at least in my experience? At a basic level I guess some adults feel that this is the best way to 'teach' basic skills in the traditional sense. I shall explore this notion later in my consideration of the workshop table and its outcomes. Others would suggest that pressures from above, including, more recently, the trickle-down effect of the National Curriculum. While this may be true, I suspect that Bruce (1987) comes closest in her suggestion that adults can become preoccupied with the products rather than the process involved. Indeed, a sample of a child's visual artwork is likely to be the first tangible and concrete product a parent has of their child's experiences at nursery. Needless to say, there are many ways in which children's experiences and learning can be shared with parents – e.g. by talking to parents, keeping notes and photographs, etc. – without this polarised need to rely, misguidedly, on a 'product'. Indeed, the values with regard to good learning and practice are not served well in this way and parents may be receiving the wrong messages with regard to this.

What is the way forward? First, Bruce (1991) makes it quite clear that open-ended provision is crucial to children maximising their potential within the first-hand experiences we offer. In practical terms (Blenkin and Whitehead, 1988; Lally, 1991; Hurst, 1991) the way forward is a room planned as a workshop, making resources available to children at all times. The latter is particularly important since how can children link interesting experiences if they have to wait a week or so for, say, another gluing activity? Choice is important also because it promotes self-determined behaviour (Prentice, 1994). Second, the adult's role is extremely important. The research of Bruner (1980) demonstrates that experiences tend to be prolonged, extended and developed by the child more frequently when there is an interested, responsive adult at hand who supports, consolidates and affirms what the child is doing.

THE WORKSHOP TABLE – A RE-EVALUATION

The workshop table? This needs some explaining here. What used to be on offer in our nursery's creative areas was: sand, water, dough table, painting at the easel, graphics table and a main art activity table. Essentially, the bare bones of a workshop environment. Caught up within the main art activity provision was a whole host of experiences that needed fleshing out to produce a more worthwhile environment for the children. The teacher before me had attempted to do this and failed and I was not confident of my ground here with regard to the other educators in the nursery. Hence, I decided to create opportunities for writing/ graphics in other contexts – e.g. developing space elsewhere and in context, for instance, within sociodramatic play. I nevertheless held on to the graphics side of what was the graphics table, but developed its scope to become what I called the 'make and do' table. Here there were opportunities for the children to make three-dimensional creations, to cut and stick (with stickers), use hole punches, etc. A fairly limited step in the differentiation and accessibility of activities usually associated with the main art activity. The children responded as expected, with enthusiasm. The adults went some way to accommodating success here.

However, at the start of the new academic year, we completely changed the nursery so that the creative area was now based in the other room. Nevertheless, I had managed to secure a shelved unit for the 'make and do' table, which, it was hoped, would create better opportunities for choice. Initially, things appeared to be working well, but it was soon apparent that enthusiasm had begun to wane. On observing the situation, I discovered that one of the reasons for this was that adults were pre-structuring the table. Materials and resources would be put out that the children did not necessarily feel inclined to use – e.g. chalks and chalkboards – and those who were committed had to proceed with such things in their way to achieve their goals. This was happening more and more, and, before Christmas I even found holly and red and green pens specifically selected for the purpose of making observational drawing.

To take stock of this situation I decided to perform a little experiment. I sought the cooperation of the adults in the nursery and for three days, nothing was added to the table in this way. The children were free to select what they liked from the shelves – but few did. Those who did asked permission or were encouraged to do so as they approached the table. Hence, part of the reason for the table's demise was that the message children were getting was that adults selected the materials and resources and some children, understandably, came to depend on this.

As mentioned, it also took an interested adult to encourage and guide children in making choices and hence use the table again. The role of interested adults has been briefly mentioned and will be revisited. Needless to say, they were crucial here. Since this was lacking before, another message children were getting was that little value was placed on their experiences at this table.

Finally, to take things forward, the resourcing and presentation of the area needed sorting out. Things had landed up on the shelves that were of no real interest to the children – like left-overs from cut-out photographs. What the children needed were the materials and resources that really set the imagination going – things like wire paper ties. Also lacking was a suitable way of presenting three-dimensional 'junk' materials. A wheeled vegetable trolley was the solution. We also made sure that basic tools like scissors, stickers, hole punches, felt pens, etc. were readily at hand.

The 'make and do' table lost its name and became the DIY table. This embodies the new spirit, but neglects the important role of the adult. The scope of the table is limited, but the intention has always been that it becomes a stepping stone towards a more diversified workshop environment.

THE LEARNING/CREATIVE PROCESS: WHAT THE CHILDREN SHOWED US

The most rewarding aspect of all this was that the workshop table took off very quickly and became a centre for a certain kind of creativity and learning. I would like to share some of this with the reader – looking particularly at autonomy, agendas, play, motivation, self-expression, technological thought, basic skills, communication, cooperation, gender issues and the role of the adult.

Autonomy was encouraged in that the children were self-determining in the selection and use of materials and resources to pursue their own agendas. Many children had a clear goal or agenda – e.g. making cards and gifts for brothers and sisters.

Extract 2

Zayba made a pendant with a piece of memo paper and raffia, using the hole punch. She then wrote on it lots of letter-like symbols. She explained that it was for her sister, Ifrah. After the story when I called her name she pointed her sister out to me and then gave her the present she had made.

Other children seemed to be pursuing a key area of intrigue/interest, for some this may have been a particular schema.

Extract 3

Enclosure enveloping: Aneesa has made a border round the edge of her piece of card (with felt pen) and then coloured right into the middle. (She had been making borders in other contexts.) Next she made a border of stickers on top of this and subsequently filled the area inside completely with stickers.

John Matthews (1988) draws attention to the child's preoccupation with the dynamic and configurative aspects of actions and shapes as well as events and objects in the world. An example of this is the inside–outside relationship. To illustrate this, during the course of many art activities, Charlotte has shown a predisposition for emptying the complete contents of, for example, glue pots. This was mirrored by a determined approach to hiding objects inside containers on the workshop table.

Extract 4

Charlotte covered a container at both ends with stickers and other embellishments – spent a long time on this. At a later point it was discovered that a tiny figure she had brought in was hidden therein.

Play was observed in its role as an 'integrating mechanism' in which children could draw upon their experiences and 'wallow' in ideas (Bruce 1991).

Extract 5

On the main art activity table the children have been presented with egg-shaped coloured paper on which they're 'supposed' to stick milk bottle tops to make an 'Easter egg'. The adult concerned has left the room and Lianne has just dutifully made an 'Easter egg'. She takes one of the egg-shaped papers over to the DIY table, and punches four holes in it. Next she cuts some wool and asks me if I can make a knot. 'I'm making a raining hat' (it had been raining that lunch time). When her creation has been completed she asked me to try it on. I did so trying my best to hook the loops under my chin. 'Those bits are supposed to hook under your ears,' she retorted, since I had been putting it on the wrong way. The other adult came back and Lianne showed her the creation and was complimented on having made a lovely Easter bonnet . . . to which Lianne retorted, 'It's a raining hat!'

Extract 6

Evelyn found a cardboard ring and a thin bit of cardboard tube. She brought these to me explaining her aim 'to make a magnifying glass' but said she didn't know how to stick the bits together. I suggested stickers and supported her in her efforts. On completion, Evelyn went off with it and used it in her imaginative play. As it happened, real magnifying glasses had been out for the children to use. Having been close by, Zubair went off and made a similar magnifying glass.

Throughout the majority of observations I made there were high levels of motivation. The value of motivation in learning and progression, according to Bruce (1987), is the close links made with security, self-confidence and self-esteem. The following example is illustrative of this:

Extract 7

Ishbel has recently been making hanging creations or mobiles. Initially she made a creation with bits of scrap – e.g. wire paper fasteners, and said it needed to 'hang'. The adult concerned constructed a line for it to be hung on. Ishbel made her mind up that each day she would make a new mobile, starting this moment. Her next construction was difficult to hook on the line and this was related to her. Ishbel took her construction and devised a way to hang it. The next day's construction utilised a wire paper fastener which she had pre-fashioned for the purpose of hanging it.

Here Ishbel felt fulfilled in her achievements and intrinsically motivated towards her goal. In time she filled the line.

Jameson (1974) stresses that creative activities (painting, particularly) are for the young child, a language first and only incidentally an art form. Taking this a step further, with regard to self-expression, Pile (1973) – with particular reference to painting – suggests that children express the same feelings through creative media that they express in their overt behaviour. Indeed, true feelings may be masked in overt behaviour. The following extract highlights this:

Extract 8

Johnny (one of our special children) was feeling frustrated – problems between him and his younger brother who was a newcomer to the nursery taking place at the main art activity. Since his brother was involved with an adult here, he took himself off to the DIY table, where he picked up a piece of card and used felt pens to make whirling marks, seemingly displacing his anger and frustration, (Figure 43.1) as his gaze was directed at his brother and adult (he rarely chooses to do graphic activities).

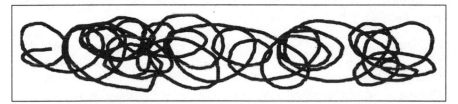

Figure 43.1 Johnny's coils of frustration

As I have stressed, the scope of the workshop table was limited. Nevertheless, a major aim was to provide opportunities for art and design and technological thought. According to Prentice:

> Using scrap materials and objects can form a basis of fruitful work in art and design. However, such activities frequently lack challenge and rigour and fail to identify technological skills and concepts. It is essential that materials are carefully selected for their intrinsic qualities and properties, and arranged and presented to the children in such a way that they learn to make informed choices.
>
> (Prentice, 1994)

Many children in my observations embraced this spirit, as in Figure 43.2. The

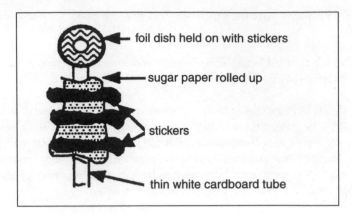

Figure 43.2 Olivia's telescopic flower

creation was made by Olivia and was a telescopic 'flower' and actually worked: the flower 'grew'!

Examples of this kind of technology are clearly in contrast to what Prentice reports as the narrow, skills-based approach to technology, associated with pre-scribed outcomes commonly in practice in many primary schools.

Many arguments for teacher-led art activities centre on the very promotion of basic skills – with particular reference here to levels of differentiation and special educational needs. Let us critically compare two observations here and draw our own conclusions:

Extract 9

Afternoon session: Norli comes in and sits down at the main art activity table, upon which is a pile of greetings cards and scissors. She sits and waits! Presumably she is waiting for the 'go ahead' of an adult to give her directions. She waits . . . The adult concerned appears. 'Do you know what to do, Norli?' No reply. 'You have to cut round the picture . . . You go snip, snip, snip and when you're finished you can put it in here.' Shows Norli an envelope she has prepared. 'Look! I can cut with scissors.' Adult proceeds to help Norli by guiding her hands around the picture.

Extract 10

Marik, Andrea, Aneesa and Justin are presently at the DIY table. Marik is cutting some card using both hands, having difficulty. I asked if he needed a little help and he did. He wanted me to hold the card while he got to grips with the scissors and the cutting. First, he made cuts all around the edge, satisfied in his ability to do so. Next he made lengthways cuts across the card to make strips, then cut the strips into smaller pieces.

In promoting basic skills, what is more important – the process or the product?

The space available for the workshop table was very limited given its popularity. However, proximity can be important in communication. Children were able to discuss their creations, draw inspiration and suggest solutions with one another. I am in agreement with Matthews (1988) here when he says: 'the interaction between children is vital'.

An important link here can be made with cooperation and gender issues. First, although it seemed more boys were interested in the workshop table than the main art activity table, girls, without doubt, made more use of the workshop table. In addition to this, girls were quite frequently observed partaking in a social interaction with peers here. Some went a step further and cooperated or collaborated on parallel or joint projects. These observations on gender and creative activity bear a close resemblance to research findings in this area – for example, that cited by Carol Ross (see Chapter 17) in her research in four nurseries where she found that 81 per cent of girls engaged in creative activities over an observation period of 3 hours, 20 minutes, as opposed to only 40 per cent of boys.

Gender issues and creative arts are clearly an area that needs illuminating, both within the nursery in question and on a wider scale.

Last, the interest and value adults placed on the children's activity were self-generating. The open-endedness of the workshop table was a marvellous vehicle for interaction with interested adults along the lines of the observe, support and extend model proposed by Bruce (1987).

Extract 11

Edgar said 'I'd like to make a card for . . .' I showed him where he could find all the paper and card, etc. (Edgar being a newcomer). 'I want a folding and opening paper.' The day before one of the adults had used pre-folded paper to do folding 'butterfly' pictures. Making this link I understood and showed him how to make such paper.

On many occasions, Bruner's notion of 'scaffolding' (Bruce, 1987) was in evidence and translated quite literally, in that I became a 'human scaffold', holding bits together while the child performed the various operations.

Language and the way in which adults related to children were particularly important:

Extract 12

Lianne comes to me at the DIY table. She has a fir cone she has found on her way to school. She chooses some card and crayons. She draws horizontals and then verticals to make a grid pattern. She then folds it over and joins the ends with a sticker, proceeding next to sealing it. 'I know what you've got inside there . . . a pen top!' I say, 'Perhaps you can put your cone in it.' She puts her cone in but I realise, 'Oh, it might fall out!' Lianne suggests, 'I could use stickers.' By this she meant to seal all round the open edges like a parcel and proceeded to cover her creation completely in stickers. I had to leave at this point. She later brought her finished product out to me in the garden. However, when the children had gone home and I was tidying the DIY table I found her fir cone. In her fervour to stick, it must have fallen out!

The most productive approach here was 'tuning in' and offering children the language for their experiences. However, even this is a simplification:

> Sometimes it is silence that is required, the teacher being as unobtrusive as possible. Even here though, he or she should still observe and record the key representational behaviours of the child, for it is this information which will guide his or her future interactions and provision. Sometimes no more than encouraging facial expressions and gestures – if they arise from a genuine appreciation of the child's efforts – are sufficient. Again, there are occasions when one would choose to immerse the child in words and ideas.
>
> (Matthews, 1988)

The above statements are readily transferable in general terms and I am in full agreement here.

The adult's approach and philosophy, based on sound practice and theories about young children are important. The types of learning discussed can be addressed by a main table activity approach provided that first-hand experiences are presented along open-ended lines and by adults who interact.

Extract 13

On the main art activity table I had presented the children with off-cuts from a bamboo blind I had put up in the holidays, together with assorted card and stickers, glue (including coloured glue for those who just wanted to spread), Plasticine, scissors and anything else that would make it completely impossible for an adult to 'direct' the children in any way, since this was not desired. Razia spent most of the morning and the whole afternoon at this table absorbed in a number of ways developing her own ideas and inspiration from other children who partook, in a process-like fashion. This included:

1   Card on to card;
2   Sticks on to card;
3   Cutting card and sticking this on to another piece of card;
4   Writing 'name' with felt pen;
5   Putting stickers onto card to form a layered coverage (finding stickers to stretch the length of the bits of card);
6   Spreading glue with spreader and subsequently hands on card;
7   Noticed Vanesha using sticks on her card to scrape a picture/pattern on card that had glue spread all over it, and pursued this idea.

All in all Razia had made twenty-six creations!

Indeed, at times a degree of flexibility in the type of provision is desirable, but why cut corners when in the main, a workshop approach is the most desirable and profitable in terms of child-centred and autonomous learning?

CONCLUDING REMARKS

The last section on the role of adults draws attention to one further issue that has to be raised. It is, in my experience, that adult-led activities, as well as being product based, are often prescriptive with regard to 'topic work'. Taking this a step further Cathy Nutbrown (1994) suggests that: 'continuity in terms of a theme lasting a number of weeks is typically imposed by nursery staff, offered to the children and is content based'.

To illustrate:

Extract 14

Meanwhile . . . on the main art activity table Melissa and Charlotte are trailing glue onto a large piece of tissue to the tune of 'Oh! That's not what you're supposed to be doing!' as the adult concerned re-enters the room. Accordingly these children were shown how to stick crunched up bits of tissue paper to real bits of branches/ twigs.

Like Christmas, Spring comes earlier and earlier! Bruce (1987) warns against this kind of 'transmission model of education'. Matthews also makes this point very clearly:

> Interaction does not consist, at nursery or any other level of education, in arbitrarily imposed projects according to some fixed paradigm or fixed end in mind. Cottage-style industries of the 'today we are doing frogs' variety, so characterised and criticised by Athey (1980 personal communication), are not what is required.
>
> (Matthews, 1988)

'Continuity constructed by children' (Nutbrown, 1994), for instance, schemas, is the basis upon which a planned environment is more likely to nurture learning. Many more issues come to mind, for example, what messages do students of early childhood education get when colleges and training institutions send them into nurseries to 'do an activity'? Unfortunately, there is no room here for fuller discussion.

With regard to the nursery in question and my own practice, it is hoped that my attempts and efforts are a stepping stone in the right direction.

REFERENCES

Athey, C. (1990) *Extending Thought in Young Children: A Parent–Teacher Partnership*, PCP.

Bennett, N., Desforges, C., Cockburn, A. and Wilkinson, B. (1984) *The Quality of Pupil Learning Experiences*, Lawrence Erlbaum.

Blenkin, G.M. and Whitehead, M. (1988) 'Creating a Context for Development', in G.M. Blenkin, and A.V. Kelly (eds) *Early Childhood Education – A Developmental Curriculum*, PCP.

Bruce, T. (1987) *Early Childhood Education*, Hodder and Stoughton.

—— (1991) *Time to Play in Early Childhood Education*, Hodder and Stoughton.

Bruner, J.S. (1980) *Under Fives in Britain* (Oxford Pre-School Research Project), Grant McIntyre.

Hurst, V. (1991) *Planning for Early Learning – Education in the First Five Years*, PCP.

Jameson, K. (1974) *Pre-School and Infant Art*, Studio Vista.

Lally, M. (1991) *The Nursery Teacher in Action*, PCP.

Matthews, J. (1988) 'The Young Child's Early Representation and Drawing', in G.M. Blenkin, and A.V. Kelly (eds) *Early Childhood Education – A Developmental Curriculum*, PCP.

Moyles, J. (1989) *Just Playing? The Role and Status of Play in Early Childhood Education*, Open University Press.

—— (ed.) (1994) *The Excellence of Play*, Open University Press.

Nutbrown, C. (1994) *Threads of Thinking – Young Children Learning and the Role of Early Education*, PCP.

Pile, N.F. (1973) *Art Experiences for Young Children*, (Threshold Early Learning Library volume 5), Macmillan.

Prentice, R. (1994) 'Experiential Learning in Play and Art', in J. Moyles (ed.) *The Excellence of Play*, Open University Press.

In this long and detailed chapter Duane pays close attention to many of the themes raised in the various parts of this book.

- By observing and analysing what the children actually do and say he shows how this focus on the process is more revealing than focusing only on the end product.

- His close observation of the children at play has led him to make informed criticisms of existing practice and bring about changes. When he studies the children at play, engaged in self-chosen activities, he shows the links they are able to make with past experience.

- He looks, too, in great detail at the role of the adult and shows how complex this is if it is to extend and support learning. Not only must the adult organise the environment and the resources in it to allow children to make proper choices, but the adult has to let go of any didactic role in favour of one which gives some control to the children. He shows how adult support can, if insensitively offered, lead to overdependence on this and offers, through some of his examples, case studies of effective scaffolding and support.

- Above all, he shows how an understanding of how young children learn and develop underpins good early-years practice.

Part VII

Partnerships with parents

Introduction to Part VII

Throughout this book there has been an assumption that what workers should be striving to achieve is what might be described as 'developmentally appropriate' provision for young children. This is understood as practice that is based on universal and predictable sequences of growth and change; on seeing each child as an individual with his or her own unique history; and on appreciating that children learn primarily through play. In this very short part we start to focus more closely on aspects of each child's unique history as we consider the importance of taking account of the beliefs and values within families, societies and groups that sometimes contradict those of the described 'developmentally appropriate provision'.

In many less highly developed societies issues of poverty dominate attitudes to children. Food is regarded as more important than anything else – and indeed no one would argue that a hungry child is not likely to learn effectively. In some cultures patterns of nurturing are not those of the developed world. Where we seek to stimulate children and encourage play, in other societies (for example, the Gusii of Kenya) the emphasis is on quiet and comfort with little attention given to talk or play. In many societies children as young as 3 are expected to contribute to the life of the family by carrying out simple tasks like gathering wood. Contrast this with children in affluent families playing with miniature versions of sanitised reality rather than contributing in any real sense. Patterns of child-rearing and nurturing vary and some way of understanding these and respecting them needs to be found.

The importance of working closely with parents is something that has been recognised for some time by all those involved in both the planning of education programmes and those working with children.

What is always necessary . . . is the establishment of partnerships between parents and other educators. For this to be effective, there must be mutual understanding and respect, a continuing dialogue and sharing of expertise and information.

(DES, 1990: 13)

Establishing some sort of working partnerhsip with parents is a key goal of many early childhood workers who have become increasingly aware of just how much parents know about their own child, how keen they are for their children to be happy and fulfilled and who are the ones who ultimately play a more important and extended role in the child's life than teachers or workers do. More work needs to be done on understanding just how different value systems and beliefs impact on children and on finding ways of holding a principled view of high-quality care and education, while not negating the rights of people to their own beliefs.

REFERENCES

DES (1990) *Starting with Quality: The Report of the Committee of Inquiry into the Quality of Educational Experiences Offered to 3- and 4-year-olds*, HMSO.

44 Parents' commitment to their children's development

Building partnerships with parents in an early childhood education centre

Margy Whalley

There is one keynote chapter in Part VII, written by Margy Whalley, an acknowledged expert in this field and well known for the innovative work she did with parents at the Pen Green Centre. Dealing with the effects of poverty, isolation and unemployment are the themes as the author describes both the setting of Pen Green and the successes achieved with some parents.

The Pen Green Centre is a multidisciplinary service for under-fives and their families where nursery education, day care, family work and community health services are all on offer. It is located in the Midlands, in Corby, a small town (population 50,000) in Northamptonshire. It was a steel town in the 1930s with a teeming population of steelworkers who had come down from Scotland and across from Central Europe to find work. By the 1980s when the Pen Green Centre opened, the steelworks had closed, the housing estates were boarded up, shops were barricaded with wire grilles and 45 per cent of the male population was unemployed. Poor nutrition, inadequate housing and high infant mortality rates were all major factors influencing the lives of young families. There were minimal statutory services for parents and young children and few traditional voluntary services for families in need of support.

A NEW KIND OF SERVICE

It was clear, even in the early 1980s that what was needed in Corby was a radically new kind of service: a service that integrated the education and care of children, the health needs of young families, adult community education for parents and community regeneration. There were four main strands to the work we undertook.

Nursery education for children from two-and-a-half to five years with:

- Part-time and full-time places;
- Extended-day, year-round provision (we only closed for three weeks);
- Home visiting – all children were visited at home to forge a close link between the children's key worker and the family;
- Parents' active involvement in observing their children and in record keeping;
- Day care for a limited number of children under 3 years;
- The full integration of children with disabilities;
- Full integration of children defined as 'at risk'; or 'in need' by the Social Services Department.

Family work which involved:

- Individual preventative support;
- Activity sessions run by and for parents;
- Support for childminders;
- An extensive Group Work Programme (twenty-three different groups running in the daytime and in the evening with crèches provided);
- A drop-in centre where parents could sit and chat and children could play for extended periods of time;
- Healthy lunches;
- An advice shop on welfare rights, run by parents;
- Holiday play schemes; a caravan at the seaside; family holidays.

A health resource with:

- A baby clinic and vaccination clinic;
- A Well-Woman and family planning clinic, pregnancy testing;
- Specialised groups for new babies; aromatherapy and massage; groups for parents with children with disabilities; miscarriage/stillbirth support group.

Adult/community education programme including:

- Courses for women returning to work;
- Courses for men as carers;
- Open University study groups;
- Writing/poetry groups;
- Adult literacy;
- Assertiveness classes;
- Courses offering qualifications, e.g. 'O' and 'A' levels and the new National Vocational Qualifications.

The nature of this new service meant that staff had to be recruited from all the academic disciplines that in the UK traditionally offer highly differentiated services to families and young children, i.e. education professionals, social work professionals and health professionals.

All these professional groups traditionally speak 'different languages', have different value bases and usually have very different priorities, so recruiting the right kind of staff was critical. Staff often reflect on the number of people they have to be in a day, to work in this new kind of service:

> friend, educator, organiser, driver, negotiator, comedienne, compromiser, manager, referee, cleaner, co-ordinator, team member, decision-maker, counsellor, advocate – as well as wife, mother, daughter.

Staff had to be able to immediately involve parents and the local community in setting up the new service. We adopted a method of working that was based on cooperation between parents and workers:

> a radical notion of self-help as personal growth and the development of a sense of community responsibility.
>
> (Hevey, 1982)

Staff had to be accountable, flexible, open-minded, able to face conflict and, above all, to see parents as equal partners. We wanted to make services relevant, responsible and acceptable to *all* parents.

THE EDUCATION AND CARE DIVIDE

This last point was particularly important to the Corby community. In the UK there has always been a damaging division between the educational needs and the day-care needs of young children, and between the very limited services offered to support parents generally and the services offered to parents who are defined as 'unable to cope'.

There is an expectation in the UK that parents should cope on their own. The state usually only gets involved when things are going wrong. Far more money is still invested in reactive services for families who are in crisis than in preventative services that offer the kinds of practical support that *most* parents need.

Parents in the housing estate in Corby where the centre is based did not want the new service we were setting up to be for 'problem families'. They wanted it to be available to *all* families. Local activists set up a parents' action group to *oppose* the new centre. Local people resented the fact that officers of the local government departments who were setting up the new services had failed to consult the local people who were supposed to be using them. This meant that, from the beginning at Pen Green, we had to work with a very vocal and fairly hostile group of people. Without exception, those angry parents who, eleven years ago were very concerned about how the new service would develop, have all been actively involved in setting it up. They have sent their children to the nursery at Pen Green; used groups; taken part in activities and helped to make the centre a comprehensive community-based resource for the whole neighbourhood.

The partnership we created with parents was *equal, active* and *responsible* (Nicholl, 1986). Parents decided how they wanted to be involved. The Parent Education programme at Pen Green has a strong and explicit value base. The assumptions we make are that:

- First, parents and children *both* have rights. We live in a society where parents get very little practical support and an increasing number of children are brought up in poverty. Too often children's rights and the rights of their parents are seen as inimical.
- Second, parenting is not just 'the mother's problem'. Fathers have rights and responsibilities and parent education programmes need to engage men.
- Third, we all experience problems while trying to become competent parents.

> Parenting is not simply an aggregate of skills, though some skills can be learnt, but it is a unique relationship between two individuals.
>
> (Puckering *et al.*, in press)

Parents are not a heterogeneous group and we all want different things for our children.

Looking at one parent's experiences of using the parent programmes at Pen Green illustrates these principles in practice.

Maria is now in her mid-twenties. She is a single parent, has two young sons and lives on state benefit. Maria started attending Pen Green Centre for Under Fives and Families some years ago as a young parent. She described herself then:

> I wasn't a member of the community. I lived there, but that was it . . . my life was in my house or I'd go to my mother's or my boyfriend's mother's . . . I was a dead person most of the time . . . My greatest achievement was staying alive. I didn't trust myself with anything. I didn't feel safe to cross the road.

Education for Maria was a 'painful memory' (Armstrong, 1986). Although a bright and able young woman she had left school at 16 with a few GCSEs, having spent her last two years at school in constant conflict with her teachers.

Maria became involved in the community education programme at Pen Green because, as she put it, 'my child deserves an educated mother'. She took up the opportunities offered to continue her own learning. At the same time she got very involved in her young children's education.

Maria came to the centre then as a mother, a single parent and unemployed. Despite opposition, she went on to become a writer, a serious student, a voluntary worker in the after-school club, a parent manager at the family centre and a school governor. She became a community activist and ran a very successful campaign at her local junior school. She also became very involved in her children's learning and closely observed her children at home, in the nursery and at school.

Maria was involved in a community development/parent education programme at Pen Green with three developmental strands which are: parents learning about their children; parents learning for themselves; and citizenship. This is the kind of parent education programme which gets community workers and teachers in touch with parents whom others may find it hard to reach. It is a programme rooted in the active life of the local community and is readily accessible to all who want it, whatever their circumstances (Venables, 1976). It is the kind of parent education programme where parents initially share their problems and perceptions (Powell, 1988) and get personal support. This is the developmental strand that addresses the adult learner's needs. Parents are then encouraged to observe and to be involved with their children (Athey, 1990). This is the second developmental strand that addresses the children's early educational needs. The third strand, 'citizenship', is an important by-product of meeting the needs of parents appropriately and I will deal with this later. What we are committed to at Pen Green is the kind of parent education programme in which parents negotiate their own curriculum and feel in control of their own lives.

Maria made her own priorities and negotiated her own learning, in her own time. She became interested in her own learning and more involved in her children initially through informal community education study groups. She then began to take action in her children's schooling. On one occasion she withdrew her child from a school where she felt his needs weren't being met. This proved to be an important step for Maria and she took on more responsibility in the community. She became a parent manager at the Pen Green Centre and later on a primary school governor. As she became more aware of her children's persistent concerns and more interested in observing the patterns in her child's play at home, she became more involved in helping in the nursery within the family centre. As she made friends and felt respected in the community she felt empowered to fight against what she saw as injustice. On one occasion she fought and won a campaign to get parent-appropriate information when the government appeared to be inappropriately encouraging schools to withdraw from local democratic forms of management.

Maria is now about to embark on a university course. She wants to be a teacher. She describes herself as she is now:

> I trust my judgement a lot more easily now. I'm proudest of doing things for myself . . . taking a risk . . . trying to live on state benefit. Bringing up two boys on my own, me with three sisters, I didn't know anything about bringing up boys . . . Last week, Daniel, my son, said 'I'll go to school and go off to college and university' . . . It's really changed the children.

The clear message from this case study of Maria is that a community development approach to working with parents and young children needs to combine action for the parent – helping parents to reclaim their own education and build up their self-esteem – and action for children – encouraging parents to 'childwatch', to be more involved and sometimes more respectful of their children's learning process.

Maria is just one of many hundreds of parents who have used the community education and family support programmes at the Pen Green Centre over the eleven years since it opened. Other parents may access the parent education programme by more circuitous routes.

A teenage mother with a new baby might start to use the baby clinic which was run very informally with big cushions, sagbags, easy chairs and toys for the children. Volunteers are on hand to make coffee; health workers are available to offer counselling and support; digital scales were provided so that parents can weigh their own babies. She might then meet some other young parents and decide to join an Open University study group during the day; or she might work with the education materials on 'Living with Babies and Toddlers' in an evening group. She might feel later that her toddler wanted company and different kinds of play provision and might join a parent and toddler session either run by nursery staff and community service volunteers or by nursery staff and parents.

Carrie was just such a seventeen-year-old when she first came to Pen Green. In the extract below she describes the choices she made about her level of involvement with the centre:

> Lizzie, my daughter, was four weeks old when I was introduced to the Pen Green Centre in 1987. I first went to the Baby Health Clinic. The day was her Weigh-In. Many mums find this an easy way into the Centre. It is also a good way for people to become a person, not just a mum. Next I joined the Mother and Baby group. This group has been one of my favourite groups as I learnt how to play with and how to enjoy my daughter. I was introduced to the Single Parents group. A very good support in my life. I have made lots of new friends and found that I am not the only one finding the ups and downs of single parenthood a strain. I then joined the Stillbirth and Neo-Natal Death Group. This group has been a very sad, happy and loving group to me. I was able to touch and release pains that had made me feel depressed. Many women come to just talk about their babies and cry or laugh about their lives. And finally, the Women's Writers Group which met in the evening. At the moment about eleven parents use this group. We either share our written work or we try to enlarge our knowledge on writers.
>
> (Whalley, 1994)

Tracey had a very different experience. Her child, Alan, developed retinopathy of prematurity at birth and was blind and physically developmentally delayed. At 14 months when he could not crawl or talk, eleven different professionals were 'involved' with the family; from health visitors to social workers, to pre-school homevisitors, doctors, paediatricians, etc., etc.

From Tracey's point of view, there were far too many professionals and not enough practical support. She was living on state benefit and was hard pressed to find the cash to pay her bus fare to the hospital. In her experience, all the professionals had their own 'agendas' and not all were listening to her or to her son. Some were very judgemental, others very prescriptive; she and Alan had rapidly to become 'clients' and were perceived by the professionals as a 'problem to be managed'.

What Tracey wanted was a local service, an *inclusive* service where a blind child could be educated and cared for alongside other local children. She wanted support from other parents in similarly stressful situations and she needed professional advocates and allies to help her establish her rights within the system and to help her with practical problems. She also needed someone she trusted to listen to her anger and grief.

Tracey used the community nursery for her son and shared in his education and care. She developed a strong relationship with her child's family worker and who often visited her at home and took her to see other schools and centres for blind children. She started using a support group where she met other parents with special-needs children. She is now contemplating embarking on the NVQ in Working with Children and Families: she can do this and be accredited for it in the same centre where her child is now a lively, intelligent and fully integrated four-year-old.

Parents who have beenn involved in this kind of a partnership become much more active as citizens. I have already demonstrated how involved Maria became in the local community. Carrie went on to become an active volunteer and then a paid worker at the family centre. She is now completing her GCSEs and wants to train as a midwife and is still heavily involved as a volunteer encouraging new parents into the centre.

The centre has been open for eleven years and, after that time, many parents are now *providing* services at the centre as well as using services. Parents run: a toy library; a home-visiting service for other parents under stress; a scrap recycling project for children; a youth club and after-school clubs; a playgroup for 60 children from 3–5 years old. Most of the groups we run *for* parents are now co-led by experienced and well trained 'parent group leaders'. Other parents are very actively involved in the community nursery or in providing play sessions for younger children and babies. With parental participation we can offer heuristic play, aromatherapy and baby massage and have a snoezelen and a bouncy softroom available for 0–3 year-olds and particular services for babies and toddlers with special educational needs.

Parents who are technically at home all day often choose to use the centre and see it as an accessible place for socialising and sharing the care and education of their children (Leach, 1994). Parents who work out of the home either part-time or full-time may also lack a social network and often need differentiated forms of parental support. Often health professionals in the community will encourage working parents to come in to the centre to make friends and use the health resource. Other working parents will be using the community nursery for childcare and their child will then have an assigned family worker who home-visits and sets up a dialogue with the family. Groups are all open access and parents who work shifts can be accommodated in the evening or during a daytime session when they are not working.

Fathers were initially harder to access in what was a very traditional community.

Despite the high levels of male unemployment there was very little shared care between partners and it was rare to see a man pushing a buggy in the centre. We became heavily involved with the European Childcare Network, Men as Carers project. By taking positive action we were able to substantially increase male involvement in the family centre, particularly in the nursery and also in the use of groups or courses that were co-led by male and female workers. The whole centre is much more men-friendly and accessible to fathers than it was in the early 1980s. We now have male nursery staff and group leaders and positive images of men on the walls. Staff have carried out research and undertaken training to help them to be more effective in this area of work.

It was vitally important that we did differentiate between men's needs and women's needs within the parent programme and developed and refined our approaches to both genders. In the early 1980s there were very few places where women could go during the day, to socialise, share the care of their children and get support as parents and this is also true today. Men, on the other hand, had a plethora of bars, working men's clubs, unemployment centres, etc., where they could spend time, but in none of these establishments was there any provision for children. Women users who had in many cases for the first time been encouraged to see the fragmentation of their lives in a positive way (Hughes and Kennedy, 1985) were reluctant to let men into the centre. Women, whose lifestyles had been challenged and thrown into disarray by early pregnancies and enormous domestic responsibility had used our community education programme and had become very effective adult learners. They had begun to have some insight into the education system that had previously failed them and were beginning to criticise the oppressive social framework which left them at home literally 'minding the baby'.

Much of the work at the Pen Green Centre involves staff and parents in resolving fundamental conflicts. Staff have to be prepared to learn, to take risks, to trust the parents, to respect them and to acknowledge the parent's role as their child's first educator and as mature, self-governing adults. Staff also have to be able to deal with parents' anger and frustration. What I have outlined in this chapter is one local response to meeting the needs of young children and their families. It is a local response based on a local diagnosis of what was needed. The UK has as yet no real commitment to offering early childhood education or parent education pro-grammes to support parents in their role.

REFERENCES

Armstrong, H. (1986) *Making the Rungs on the Ladder: Women and Community Work Training*.
Athey, C. (1990) *Extending Thought in Young Children: A Parent–Teacher Partnership*, PCP.
Hevey, D. (1982) *The Wider Issue of Support and Planning*, Parenting Papers No 3, National Children's Bureau.
Hughes, M. and Kennedy, M. (1985) *New Futures: Changing Women's Education*, Routledge and Kegan Paul.
Leach, P. (1994) *Children First*, Michael Joseph.

European Commission Network on Childcare (1993) *Men as Carers.*

Nicholl, A. (1986) *New Approaches to Build Health Care: Is There a Role for Parents?*, Parents' Partnership Papers No 8, National Children's Bureau.

Powell, D.R. (1980) in S. Kilmer (ed.) *Advances in Early Education and Day Care*, vol. 1, JAI Press.

Puckering, C. *et al.* (in press) *Mellow Mothering: Process and Evaluation of Group Intervention for Distressed Families,*

Venables, P. (1976) (chair) *Report of the Committee for Continuing Education*, Open University Press.

Whalley, M. (1994) *Learning to be Strong*, Hodder and Stoughton.

45 You and your child

Pam Stannard

This book ends with a very practical chapter by Pam Stannard who wrote a booklet for parents who use her centre. This is an extract from it.

SETTLING IN POLICY

Settling a child into a new environment should be a happy experience and to enable this we allow a period of two weeks as minimum, reviewed each week. The maximum is until the child is settled and happy to be left by parent or carer. Parents/carers are encouraged to participate within the group room and its activities, and to support the child in transition to nursery. During this settling in period the parent/carer is always expected to be available within the building.

The initial visit is usually for about an hour, where the child and parent/carer visit the group room, meet the staff and children. They are invited to visit the other rooms and meet all staff. The second and third visits are usually between one and a half and two hours, depending on the child's acceptance of the situation.

A plan is produced by staff, in consultation with parent/carer, guided by the child's acceptance of the new environment, but generally on the fourth visit we ask the parent/carer to leave the room for a brief period – about 15 minutes – during the three-hour visit. On the fifth visit, if the child is settled, we ask the parent/carer to leave the room for 30–60 minutes, with the child and parent/carer staying for lunch.

The following week the separation time and length of stay are extended. Many factors influence the length of the settling in period and each child responds differently. Therefore settling in must be flexible and child-orientated.

We hope that your child's settling in is a happy experience for us all – your child, you and the staff.

PARTNERSHIP WITH PARENTS

Time is made every day for parents and carers on arrival and departure to discuss their child's time spent in the nursery or at home. Sometimes the arrival/departure time allows us to have a long conversation, but there are other times, due to various situations – for example, shortage of staff, staff meetings, other meetings, etc. – when this is not possible. But if you feel that you need to discuss an issue with the staff of the room who are not available, other staff members will always see you.

We have a 'teatime' for parents/carers every three months where any issues can be raised – e.g. new practices in the room, other changes, any concerns. All meetings are minuted and parents/carers read and agree the minutes before they go on file.

In planning the curriculum we include cultural and homestyle activities and appreciate the participation of parents/carers. You are always welcome to join in all activities and share your skills.

RECORD KEEPING/ASSESSMENTS

WHY do we keep records?

- To see what your child CAN do.
- Records allow us to plan suitable activities and identify areas needing more experience.
- They show us your child's developmental progress.
- They give us information that we can pass on to you and to future educators.

WHEN do we keep records?

- When your child starts at the centre we fill out an index card with relevant information.
- Daily/weekly information is recorded and after each three-month period a review is held.

WHAT do we record?

- Relevant history of the child, for example, siblings, home language, special names/toys/comforters.
- Settling in information.
- Details about social, intellectual, language, emotional and physical developments.

HOW do we record?

- By observing your child in lots of different situations.
- By discussions with you and other carers and input from other staff in the centre. (If parents/carers do not read English, translations can be sought.)

WORKING WITH THE CURRICULUM

In our room we aim to provide within the curriculum an opportunity for 'holistic' development – development of the whole child. To assist us in providing artefacts, information, craft, skills, language, music, etc. we appreciate the help that parents/carers provide as we wish to extend and promote our understanding and knowledge to enable us to provide a better holistic curriculum.

In developing the curriculum we have eight headings that help us achieve the 'holistic' development. These are: social/emotional awareness, creative, imaginative, tactile, constructive, science, maths and physical. All of these activities interlink – for example, scrap modelling can be creative, imaginative and tactile and would include social skills, maths, construction and physical skills.

Equal opportunities/gender roles

All the children have equal access and opportunity and are encouraged to participate in all activities.

Language/literacy

We do not treat this as a separate subject as we feel we include this naturally throughout the day through discussion, negotiation, reading, singing and through all activities where communication skills are being used. Books are freely available to all children.

LANGUAGE . . . COMMUNICATION

We encourage the use of the children's/parent's/carer's home languages. We use various language tapes at song and storytime. Some books are in two languages and we encourage parents/carers to come into the centre to sing or read in their own language. Children are able to distinguish the sounds of each language and to recognise their own. It is important for all children's self-esteem to have their language and lifestyle recognised.

We also use Makaton sign language for the over-threes as we recognise that children and adults with hearing and speech disabilities are able to communicate in this way. The under-threes unit introduces some simple Makaton signs like 'please', 'thank you', 'toilet', 'good', and so on.

46 A last word: the search for the 'crock of gold'

Sandra Smidt

This book has been underpinned by a particular philosophy – that the early years of life are crucial and that what is learned during those years influences learning and attitudes to learning throughout life. This is certainly not a controversial view, but an understanding of how children's learning is best supported in these crucial years is, and debates continue not only in this country but throughout the world as to what constitutes a 'quality' learning environment.

This book, set in the context of a highly developed industrialised society, can afford to focus its arguments on how to support children's learning through the provision of a rich learning environment in which the adults working with children are literate, educated and aware of Western theories of child development. In this country, although we may have to contend with working in premises not specifically designed as nurseries or crèches, sometimes having to share facilities and often not being able to provide as many books or blocks or toys as we think are necessary, we don't have to contend with goats wandering through our learning sites, having no running water or toilets or having to deal with whole communities who have been traumatised by war, discrimination and acute poverty.

In the new South Africa, for instance, the majority of young children who have any sort of group provision are accommodated under trees, in backyards, in informal settlements, in mud huts. There are no books in the majority of these sites. Equipment for imaginative play has to be made from waste materials and is often gnawed by the rats who share the site. Many of the adults working with these children have minimal education and a great number are semi-literate or illiterate. Yet, in many of these sites, the children are learning because of the dedication of the practitioners and because of the tenacity of children and their intense desire to learn from everything that happens to them.

Martin Woodhead, in his booklet *In Search of the Rainbow* (published by the van Leer Foundation in 1996) discusses how important it is to remember that there is more than one way of viewing childhood and child-rearing. He argues that quality can only be defined when the views of the community – their values and beliefs – are taken into account and respected. When searching for 'universals' in discussing quality he urges that care is taken. Yet some 'universals' genuinely emerge and it is these that are addressed by many of the pieces in this book.

- That children learn through play, exploration and language.
- That the adults working with young children need to pay attention to what it is that children are doing and paying attention to.
- That young children need to be shown respect and affection and be allowed the time to explore their own concerns.
- That the learning needs of young children are different from those of older children.
- That all children are entitled to have their languages and cultures shown respect.
- That working in partnerships with parents, family members and the community will enhance children's learning.
- That children learn through their interactions with others and that the role of the adult is the most crucial factor in supporting and enhancing learning.
- That children learn from seeing models of how things can be done.
- That children learn when they are able to reflect on what they have done and achieved.

We hope that you have found the articles and extracts in this book interesting and thought-provoking and found the range of styles and voices fascinating – even if there is only one 'voice' in the book which speaks to you and affects your practice.

In your work, as you seek to improve the quality of what is on offer for the children, it is important to remember that 'quality' like the crock of gold at the end of the rainbow, is elusive, but the search for it – the journey you undertake with the children and their families – is immensely rewarding. As Woodhead puts it:

> When I was in Kenya during my fourth round of visits, I was beginning to wonder whether the word 'quality' had any substantive meaning at all. As we drove back to Nairobi, the sky was filled with a magnificent rainbow. This experience suggested a perfect metaphor to encapsulate the search for quality. English children are told the ancient Celtic legend, that if you dig at the rainbow's end, you will find a crock of gold. I later learned that African children learn a similar legend. It seems to me that trying to pin down 'quality' is a bit like trying to find the crock of gold at the end of the rainbow. We may make progress in the right direction, but we never quite get there! Children learn that the rainbow's beauty is real enough, but the 'crock of gold' exists only as a cultural myth. In the same way, I want to argue that those involved in early childhood development must recognise that many of their most cherished beliefs about what is best for children are cultural constructions. As with the rainbow, we may be able to identify invariant ingredients in the spectrum of early childhood quality, but the spectrum itself is not fixed, but emerges from a combination of particular circumstances, viewed from particular perspectives.

Index